*The search for authenticity in modern
Japanese literature*

The search for authenticity in modern Japanese literature

HISAAKI YAMANOUCHI

CAMBRIDGE UNIVERSITY PRESS

CAMBRIDGE

LONDON · NEW YORK · MELBOURNE

Published by the Syndics of the Cambridge University Press
The Pitt Building, Trumpington Street, Cambridge CB2 1RP
Bentley House, 200 Euston Road, London NW1 2DB
32 East 57th Street, New York, NY 10022, USA
296 Beaconsfield Parade, Middle Park, Melbourne 3206, Australia

First published 1978

Printed in Great Britain by
Western Printing Services Ltd, Bristol

Library of Congress Cataloguing in Publication Data

Yamanouchi, Hisaaki, 1934–
The search for authenticity in modern Japanese literature.

Bibliography: p.
Includes index.
1. Japanese literature – 1868– – History and criticism. 2. Japanese literature – European influences.
3. Japanese literature – American influences. 4. Authors, Japanese – Psychology. I. Title.
PL726.55Y32   895.6'09'004   77-84815
ISBN 0 521 21856 X

Contents

Preface

This book consists of seven introductory essays on Japanese literature since 1868 with reference to twelve representative writers. These essays are based on a series of lectures given for undergraduates in the Faculty of Oriental Studies, University of Cambridge, during the Lent and Easter Terms in 1975 and made possible by the generosity of Mitsui & Co. Ltd. I am most grateful to the Company for the grant to the Faculty of Oriental Studies which provided me with the opportunity of giving these lectures.

The book is a product of my mixed identity during the extended period of my stay in Cambridge, writing a Ph.D. dissertation on the late eighteenth-century and early nineteenth-century English poets while at the same time teaching my own language, Japanese. I wish to thank all my colleagues in the Faculty of Oriental Studies for providing such a pleasant environment in which to work. My special gratitude is due to my colleagues in Japanese who originally proposed that I give these lectures, and in particular to Dr C. E. Blacker and Dr D. E. Mills who made every effort to get them published. Without their constant encouragement this book would never have come into being.

Some of the material has appeared elsewhere in a slightly different form. Chapter 2 is partly based on a lecture given to the Japan Society of London in March 1970 and published in the *Bulletin* of the Society, number 62 (October 1970); chapter 6 is a revised version of a paper read at the Far East Centre, St Antony's College, University of Oxford in May 1971 and published in *Modern Asian Studies*, VI. 1 (January 1972); and chapter 7 is based on a paper read at the European Conference on Modern Japan held at St Antony's College in April 1973 and published in *Modern Japan: aspects of history, literature and society*, ed. W. G. Beasley (London: George Allen & Unwin, 1975). I wish to thank the editors and publishers of the above publications for permitting me to use part of the original material here.

I must once again gratefully acknowledge my debt to Mitsui & Co. Ltd, who most generously made a subvention which greatly facilitated the publication of this book by the Cambridge University Press. I should also like to record my thanks to the Publications Committee of the Faculty of Oriental Studies and in particular to Mr E. B. Ceadel, Dr D. E. Mills and Professor Denis Twitchett for their support.

The completion of the manuscript was long interrupted by my return to Tokyo in March 1976 and by the slow process of my readjustment to the hustle and bustle of the metropolis. In the last-minute rush of completing the draft, I benefited greatly from the generous help of Mr J. P. McDermott who read my manuscript and made invaluable suggestions for improvement. I wish to thank my wife Reiko who also made useful critical comments on the text as well as undertaking the laborious task of typing the manuscript.

Summer 1977   Hisaaki Yamanouchi

Note

Throughout the book all the names of Japanese writers are given with their surname first and given name second. Some of these names are pen names or pseudonyms: i.e., Tsubouchi Shōyō (Yūzo), Futabatei Shimei (Hasegawa Tatsunosuke), Kitamura Tōkoku (Montarō), Shimazaki Tōson (Haruki), Natsume Sōseki (Kinnosuke) and Mishima Yukio (Hiraoka Kimitake). It has been customary to refer to these writers by their given names, whether they are real or pseudonyms. The book adopts this custom only partially: thus, Shōyō, Tōkoku, Tōson and Sōseki are all their given names, while Shiga, Akutagawa, Tanizaki, Kawabata, Mishima, Abé and Ōe are all their surnames.

On the assumption that it would be tiresome for some readers to come across a number of Japanese titles scattered in the English text, the policy is adopted throughout the book of referring to them in English, whether in standard translation where available or in my own translation, with the original Japanese titles given only in the first reference accompanied by dates in parentheses. There are, however, a few exceptions to this policy in chapter 2, where the titles of some poetry magazines and Tōson's collections of poems are given first in Japanese, followed by the English translation which in itself would scarcely mean anything. The order is also reversed in the bibliography which exists for a purpose different from that of the text.

The dates for individual works are problematic: there are dates for (1) composition, (2) publication in periodicals, which is a uniquely Japanese phenomenon, and (3) publication in book form. They sometimes coincide with and sometimes differ from one another. The date (2), where applicable, is adopted in the text on the grounds that it indicates the time when the work concerned first became available to the public. Otherwise it could be either (1) or (3), whichever is more appropriate in individual cases.

Modern Japanese literature has been accessible to the English-speaking reader through the excellent translations done by such scholars as Professors Howard S. Hibbett, Donald Keene, Edwin McClellan, (the late) Ivan Morris, John Nathan, Edward G. Seidensticker and Kenneth Strong. Throughout this book the author has resorted extensively to these and other translations where available, and wishes to express thanks to the translators and publishers for permission. The indebtedness to these translations is acknowledged in the notes to the text, and otherwise the translation is the author's.

Introduction

It has been common practice to treat Japanese literature in accordance with the chronological divisions of political history. By modern Japanese literature is usually meant the literature of Japan since 1868, the year in which the Meiji Restoration effected great political change by abolishing the 200-year-old Tokugawa regime (1603–1867) and restoring the long-eclipsed Imperial throne to the centre of power. One may wonder, however, to what extent one can justly treat modern Japanese literature as an entity separate from Tokugawa and earlier literature of Japan. There is no doubt that the Meiji Restoration in political and social terms clearly marked a historical watershed. But how did this critical change affect the nature of Japanese literature? One cannot write literary history in socio-political terms alone. Literary climates do not change overnight like a political system caught in the turmoil of a revolution or a radical reform. The relationship between literature and society is far more complicated than this simple model would suggest. And even when socio-political changes lead to changes in literature, the link need not be immediately apparent. The work of writers can even remain unaffected by the changes in their social environment. We should always heed these cautionary tenets of literary criticism. But, as will soon become apparent, the writers treated here were all locked inextricably into the violent vortex of modern Japanese history. Right from the opening shot of the civil war that led to the Meiji Restoration, the political and social changes of this country were to find their echoes in the pages of Japanese novels. The Meiji Restoration justly serves as a critical landmark in the literary history of Japan.

The influence, oddly enough, did not appear immediately, but writers in mid-nineteenth-century Japan were very few in a literary world which was not particularly fertile. There is scarcely any great literary figure of this time who voiced in his works his views of the Restoration that was so dramatically changing the world about him. No Milton appeared to thunder into print his views on the outcome of this civil war. Some important Tokugawa writers had long been dead: for instance, Ueda Akinari (1734–1809), Santō Kyōden (1761–1816), Tamenaga Shunsui (1790–1843), Jippensha Ikku (1765–1831) and Takizawa Bakin (1767–1848). As for the noted Meiji writers, most had not yet learned to write. Tsubouchi Shōyō had been born in 1859, Mori Ōgai in 1862, Futabatei Shimei in 1864 and Natsume Sōseki in 1867. Kitamura Tōkoku was born in 1868, and a host of important writers were yet to be born in the 1870s. There were a few exceptions that only prove our rule. For instance, Kawatake Mokuami (1816–93), the Kabuki playwright, was producing his works both before and after 1868, as did Kanagaki Robun (1829–94), a novelist. However, one may say that Kabuki lies far outside the main stream of modern literature, and that Robun is of decidedly minor stature.

More important than these incidental features, however, are the qualitative distinctions between the literature before and after 1868. During the Tokugawa period different genres of literature had come to have different social functions. *Waka* poetry and *kanbun* poetry had been practised and enjoyed by a small number of people of the ruling samurai class, while prose fiction had existed for a wider audience, including merchants. After reaching its pinnacle in Ihara Saikaku's (1642–93) realism, this genre deteriorated into the frivolous prose written by the so-called *gesakusha* (frivolous writers) such as Jippensha Ikku and Tamenaga Shunsui, or a didactic prose which preached the doctrine of *kanzen chōaku* (reward virtue, punish vice), such as in *The Biographies of Eight Dogs* (*Nansō Satomi Hakkenden*, 1814–42) by Bakin. Meiji writers sought to discard this heritage. Prose fiction, they agreed, should be neither frivolous nor didactic, but should represent human affairs in realistic terms and thereby exercise a criticism of life. Emboldened with such a change in purpose, prose fiction was to shed its once inferior status to poetry and rise to a far more eminent position in literature than all other genres. There was to be nothing disgraceful about writing prose fiction. In fact, some of its early Meiji practitioners were of a samurai background, unimaginable during the Tokugawa period. Thus one may safely claim that prose fiction has dominated poetry and drama in modern Japanese literature. Or, in professional terms, the noted man of letters proved to be a novelist more often than a poet.

The changes in the Japanese literary scene after 1868 demand more concrete descriptions. The moral effect of the Restoration's socio-political changes was the collapse – at least partial – of the feudalistic morality of Tokugawa Confucianism, which was replaced by a longing for individual freedom. Literature thus became the writer's means of self-realisation. For the assertion of individual freedom the Meiji writers looked up to the philosophical heritage that can be traced back to the European Enlightenment. A number of the leading authors of Meiji Japan were expertly trained in English and other European languages as well as in classical Chinese. Western literature was popularised in Japan through endless translations and adaptations, thereby influencing Japanese literature in both content and form. The impact of the West caused some writers to feel no longer at home with their native traditions. This tension itself came to constitute one of the central themes of modern Japanese literature.

The changes in literature also involved some linguistic problems. For many centuries there had existed a chasm between the many colloquial dialects and a literary style that derived from the language written and spoken by imperial courtiers. One of the tasks of the Meiji writers was to synthesise the spoken and written languages, a challenge that led to the so-called *genbun-itchi* (agreement between the spoken and the written) movement. Another problem was how to use a compact evocative language of verse suited to a poetic sensibility for the purpose of dealing with the kind of problems which the Meiji writers faced – for example, the assertion of their individual freedom, the search for their own cultural and individual identity in their rapidly changing environments and so on. The solution to this problem entailed much linguistic borrowing from the West, imports which in turn led to major changes in the Japanese language. In this respect, too, modern Japanese literature distinguishes itself from the literature of the 'closed door' Tokugawa.

These preliminary observations may serve to prefigure some distinctive features in modern Japanese literature, which should emerge from the main body of the book but which one may still outline in anticipation. The modern Japanese writers pursued, often with great moral integrity, their serious concern with life and were under much strain in order to capture it in an authentic art form. One may find singularly relevant to these men the following words of W. B. Yeats ('The Choice'):

> The intellect of man is forced to choose
> Perfection of the life, or of the work,
> And if it take the second must refuse
> A heavenly mansion, raging in the dark.

The clash between these writers' moral vision and the actual society they inhabited tended to end in personal failure, a fate that often served as the subject matter of their work. In extreme cases, such failure in their personal life proved to be the unavoidable cost they had to pay for their artistic creativity. Alienation was thus one of the commonest traps of self-hatred these writers felt doomed to live with and write about. The writers' predicament was further aggravated by another factor, their confrontation with the West, as touched upon above. How could Western culture and their native tradition be harmoniously reconciled to one another when often it persuaded them to hate whatever of their own culture and themselves they had been reared to respect? They felt compelled to imitate and *thus* be authentic, a contradiction that obviously gnawed at their consciousness. Consequently they came to suffer from insecurity and identity crises. These circumstances are partly responsible for the many instances of mental breakdown and suicide among modern Japanese writers.

In the following seven chapters twelve modern Japanese writers will be discussed: Tsubouchi Shōyō (1859–1935), Futabatei Shimei (1864–1909), Kitamura Tōkoku (1868–94), Shimazaki Tōson (1872–1943), Natsume Sōseki (1867–1916), Shiga Naoya (1883–1971), Akutagawa Ryūnosuke (1892–1927), Tanizaki Jun'ichirō (1886–1965), Kawabata Yasunari (1899–1972), Mishima Yukio (1925–70), Abé Kōbō (1924–) and Ōe Kenzaburō (1935–). All of these writers should represent modern Japanese literature in one way or another. Missing from the list are some important names such as Mori Ōgai (1862–1922), Nagai Kafū (1879–1959) and Dazai Osamu (1909–48) whom I wish I could have included, but space would not allow.[1] In five out of seven chapters two writers are paired for comparison as their writings naturally link them closely together, showing at once similarities and differences. Once again, the general features outlined above should, I hope, prefigure the major concerns that will be pursued throughout the book: the ways in which these writers tackled difficult questions – personal, social and intellectual, including the confrontation with the West, and the ways in which they tried, with or without success, to represent their experiences in an authentic form of literary art.

1

Two precursors:
TSUBOUCHI SHŌYŌ and FUTABATEI SHIMEI

I

The early life of Tsubouchi Shōyō (1859–1935) matters only in so far as it relates to his later career as a writer. Like some other Meiji writers, Shōyō came from a lower samurai class family. Despite his role as a champion of modern Japanese literature, he too was introduced to literature, from the age of thirteen onwards, by reading extensively the works of the *gesakusha* novelists of the Tokugawa period. At the age of fourteen, as was still customary for samurai in those days, he studied the Chinese classics at a local school in his native Owari, the present Aichi prefecture. At the same time he learned English at another local institution. In 1876 he was chosen as a prefecture-sponsored scholar to study at Tokyo Kaisei Gakkō, a school which was to become the University of Tokyo in the following year. After finishing the three-year preparatory course, he moved on to the advanced course in the Faculty of Humanities.

In those days the University of Tokyo had a different system from the present one. There were four faculties, i.e. Law, Science, Humanities and Medicine, and the faculty and departmental divisions seem to have been less rigid. The Faculty of Humanities, for instance, offered courses not only in literature but also in law and economics. A list of some subjects Shōyō studied is highly instructive on the breadth of learning he was expected to master:[1]

The first year (1879) – English Literature; Logic; Psychology; History; Japanese Literature; Chinese Classics; and French.
The second year (1880) – History of Philosophy*; History; Psychology; English Literature**; Japanese Literature; Chinese Literature; and French.

The third year (1881) – Moral Philosophy***; (Greek
and Roman) History***; Politics*; Economics*;
Japanese Literature; Chinese Classics; and English
Literature.**
The third year repeated (1882) – International Law;
Economics*; Finance; Chinese Classics; Japanese
Literature; and German.
The fourth year (1883) – Administration; Economics*;
Law; Constitutional History of Japan; Chinese Classics;
and Finance.

Some of these courses were taught by foreign teachers. Notable
among them was Ernest Fenollosa (1853–1908),[2] through whose
works on Japan W. B. Yeats and Ezra Pound came to learn about
the Noh plays and Oriental culture.

While a student at the University of Tokyo, Shōyō already
exhibited his interest in literature by writing and circulating
his own literary magazines and by translating works by British
authors such as Walter Scott's *Bride of Lammermoor* and
Lady of the Lake. Prose literature was still regarded as feeble
and somewhat frivolous at a time when the ambitious and
eager students of the University of Tokyo were generally supposed to seek their fame in more practical fields. As a result of
his literary activities, Shōyō was eyed with suspicion by such
practically minded contemporaries. Shōyō had to repeat his third
year of study because, allegedly, he failed his Shakespeare examination. In fact what was directly responsible was not his
failure in the Shakespeare examination but merely his failure in
Fenollosa's course in economics. The Shakespeare course was
taught by a visiting American professor, William A. Houghton.
When the students were asked to discuss the character of
Gertrude, Shōyō criticised Gertrude in terms of Confucian
morality. He was repentant enough about his examination failure
to realise the essential difference between his native literary and
moral tradition and Western literary theories, and he felt the
need to study these theories systematically. He then read articles
in some current English and American periodicals in the University Library, such as the *Fortnightly Review, Contemporary
Review* and *Forum*. While reading these journals he carefully
took down notes, which he later used together with the materials

from other sources for his *The Essence of the Novel (Shōsetsu Shinzui*, 1885–6).

The Essence consists of two parts, each divided into several sections. In the first section, 'The Novel in General', of part 1, Shōyō defends the novel as follows:

> After all, the novel aims mainly at depicting human sentiments and the ways of the world. The novel weaves the threads of human sentiments with fancy, knits together the infinitely subtle and mysterious causes, and as infinitely multifarious results, of phenomena, describes vividly the secrets of the play of causes and effects in human life, and makes visible what is invisible. The most perfect possible novel then describes what is indescribable in paintings, expresses what is inexpressible in poetry and portrays what cannot be performed in drama. For in the novel there is no limit to the number of words used, no fetter like poetic diction; moreover, it appeals directly to the mind as drama and paintings do not. There is thus a wider scope for the author's designing. Accordingly, it finds its place among the arts and is likely to become the highest literary art, surpassing romance and drama.

Partly modelled as it is on Fenollosa's aesthetic theory,[3] this kind of sustained argument is in itself notable. It is even more remarkable for its defence of the novel, a genre long disdained as vulgar and unworthy of educated gentlemen.

In the second section, 'The Progress of the Novel', Shōyō makes a general survey of the historical development of the novel. His analysis makes three points. First, both chronicle and romance descend from myth; romance then develops into fable, allegory and melodrama. Secondly, by portraying the ways of the world, drama supersedes romance, but due to the various restrictions inherent in dramatic expression, gives way to the novel. Thirdly, poetry occupies a place prior to romance, and is bound to be superseded by the novel. For these arguments Shōyō is indebted to the article 'Romance' written by Walter Scott and Thomas Thomson and its supplement 'Modern Romance and Novel' written by George Moir and others in volume xix of the eighth edition of the *Encyclopaedia Britannica*.[4]

In the third section, 'The Purpose of the Novel', Shōyō discusses the essential characteristic of the novel: 'The essence of the novel consists of human sentiments. Subsidiary to this are the ways and manners of the world.' The novel, as Shōyō understood it, was meant to be dramatically opposite to the Tokugawa novels, such as Bakin's, that mouthed the clichés of Confucian piety. In contrast to much conventional Confucian writing, Shōyō defined human beings as creatures of passion. Man is good or evil not by nature but in accordance with the extent to which his reason controls his passions. In human behaviour there are both external and internal aspects, but it is the latter that the novelist should aim to represent. It is wrong for him to take a deterministic view of good and evil, as had some Tokugawa writers. Certainly the novel is a fiction. Yet its characters must be so presented as to embody psychological truths. Similarly society, as the environment in which these characters live out their lives, must be depicted as authentically as possible. Only by fulfilling these conditions can the novel be said to be a novel, to have exercised a criticism of life. Shōyō's argument, as scholars of the Victorian novel would readily recognise, is fortified by a reliance on John Morley's essay on George Eliot.[5]

In the fourth section, 'Kinds of the Novel', Shōyō once again models his classification of prose fiction on the ideas in the article in *Encyclopaedia Britannica*. After differentiating the novel from romance, he divides it into the didactic novel and the artistic novel, the latter sub-divided further into the social and the historical novel. The word 'artistic' used by Shōyō sounds misguiding as well as misguided. According to him, it is made equivalent to *mosha*, literally meaning copying, and one can guess from the context that it implies realism. Significantly, the Japanese word *mosha* does not imply mimesis or imitation in the Aristotelian sense, that is the representation of the ideal through the incidental and, therefore, something more than copying.

Section 5, entitled 'The Use of the Novel', advocates two moralistic purposes for the novel: it is to enhance human nature and to admonish and instruct the reader. Though these statements seem to contradict his denunciation of the didactic novels of the Tokugawa period, there may be two ways of resolving his apparent contradiction. While rejecting the didacticism of

Tokugawa literature, Shōyō still needed to posit the existence of some kind of moral purpose for literature, if literature were to be completely acceptable both as a concern and as a profession to the educated Meiji reader. Otherwise, there would be a discrepancy between his practice, which aimed at realistic representation of the world and human behaviour, and his theory which drew heavily on Western sources. Of these two possible explanations one was as likely as the other.

While part I of *The Essence* is devoted to pure theories, part II deals with the practical ways of writing a novel. One of the interesting features of Shōyō's advice is his discussion of style. According to him, the ideal prose was neither the elegant style of the court literature nor the vulgar style of the late Tokugawa period, but a synthesis of the two. This discussion is one of the clearest manifestations of Shōyō's concern for *genbun itchi*, a synthesis of the colloquial and 'literary' styles for writing modern fiction.

Shōyō originally intended to demonstrate the theories with his novel, *The Temperament of Present-Day Students* (*Tōsei Shosei Katagi*, 1885–6). However, due to external circumstances, this work was published a few months ahead of *The Essence*. In *The Temperament* Shōyō vividly depicts scenes from the life of ten university students in Tokyo. One of them, for instance, escapes from the student dormitory, and becoming short of cash in the red-light quarters has to be rescued by his friend; another borrows reference books from his friend and then turns them over to a pawnbroker. This series of episodes would be fragmentary without a plot line that threads its way through the whole works; this is provided by the story of the affair of one of these students with a courtesan, a character portrayed sympathetically despite her present profession. Interwoven with this is the story of the search by another student for his sister missing since the civil war of 1868. A cunning madame presents her daughter as the missing girl; she is able to substantiate this claim by producing a dagger which is in her possession and which bears the young student's family crest. In fact she found this dagger while fleeing from Edo (present-day Tokyo) which was being consumed by the fires of the civil war. She came across a child lying by its dead mother, and accidentally exchanged her own child for this one. Later she threw away the changeling in the suburbs of

Edo but retained the dagger which she had found with the child. Fortunately the foundling was brought up by a local farmer. In the meantime this woman's own daughter also survived the civil war and was restored to her. By the end of this convoluted tale the farmer, who has come to know the woman and her real daughter, reveals that the courtesan whom the student loves is none other than the missing sister of his friend. This plot, which relies on the impossible to the point of absurdity, is straight out of the conventional workings of Tokugawa literature and is one of the weaknesses of the work. Yet such equally impossible plots form the cornerstone of much Western literature, from the Greek and Roman dramatists through to Shakespeare.

Broadly speaking, the requirements of the nineteenth-century European novel included such elements as sufficiently persuasive pyschological characterisation, the coherent development of plot, and a realistic narrative technique. If one tries to judge *The Temperament* by these standards, its characters are not so much living individuals as social types, the plot relies far too much on the improbable, and the narrative technique on the whole is far from realistic. Furthermore, *The Temperament* deviates even from the principles laid down by Shōyō himself in *The Essence*. Owing to this defective characterisation *The Temperament* fails to express adequately 'the human sentiment' to which he had given priority over 'the ways of the world'. While there is no overt assertion in this novel of the doctrine of 'reward virtue, punish vice', there can be no doubt that *The Temperament* inherits many features from the literature of the Tokugawa period. Though depicted as Meiji intellectuals, the university students hunting pleasure in the houses of Tokyo can easily be seen as modernised versions of those stereotyped characters of earlier literature. Thus the world drawn in *The Temperament* is the old world and not the new world of Japanese fiction – the flat-featured *Ukiyoe*, the floating world of pleasure and sorrow so familiar in Tokugawa literature.

The Temperament was thus an exceptional work in which Shōyō's conceptions of the modern realistic novel were not fully realised. Surprisingly enough, Shōyō later produced a few allegorical romances which were even more akin to Edo literature. Only in *A Wife* (*Saikun*, 1889), written four years after *The Temperament*, did he achieve something close to realism, but this was practically his last novel worth mentioning. During the remaining forty years of his life Shōyō devoted himself to writing and producing plays, teaching English literature at Waseda University and completing a monumental translation of Shakespeare's entire works.

2

Ironically enough, the transition in Shōyō's career from novelist to dramatist and scholar of English literature can be partly attributed to his encounter with Futabatei Shimei (1864–1909). Coming from the same *han* (fief) of Owari and five years younger, Futabatei looked up to Shōyō as his literary mentor when they first met early in 1886. Futabatei had read both *The Essence* and *The Temperament* and raised questions about these works in his 'A Theory of the Novel' ('Shōsetsu Sōron', 1886). His first important novel, *The Drifting Clouds (Ukigumo*, 1887–9) was read by Shōyō and revised according to his advice, and the first part of it was published with Shōyō's name printed on the title page as its author. Shōyō was perceptive enough to acknowledge *The Drifting Clouds* as a more successful modern novel than *The Temperament* and his other novels. Consequently, he grew sceptical of his own ability to pursue a successful career as a novelist and hoped his younger friend would fulfil his own earlier ambition vicariously.

The importance of English studies in Shōyō's intellectual history was paralleled by that of Russian studies in Futabatei's career. Not only did he translate some contemporary Russian literature, in particular Ivan Turgenev, he also absorbed from Russian literature nourishment for his own novels and literary theories. However, prior to commencing his Russian studies, he was given a thorough education in the Chinese classics. He recalled later that the study of Confucian philosophy moulded his moral sensibility, a native heritage that linked him, like Shōyō, to the samurai past.

Even during his earlier days Futabatei held strongly patriotic feelings, which were certainly aroused by the unequal agreement between Russia and Japan to exchange Sachalin for the Kurile islands. He sensed that one of the crucial problems confronting Japan was a possible clash with Russia over these northern terri-

tories. It was out of his sense of this imminent crisis and his feeling
of loyalty to the nation imbibed from reading Tokugawa Confucianism, that he tried three times to enter the Military Academy.
His persistent failure to enter the academy is usually attributed to
his near-sightedness, but his inaptitude in mathematics is also said
to be a possible cause.[6] He entered instead the Tokyo School of
Foreign Languages (the present-day Tokyo University of Foreign
Studies) where he specialised, naturally enough, in Russian
studies. His entrance into this school is important in more ways
than one. Unlike the University of Tokyo where Shōyō studied,
the Tokyo School of Foreign Languages was not ranked as an
élitist institution. Secondly, it was only during the brief initial
period of the University of Tokyo that the major burden of teaching was undertaken by foreigners; native teachers replaced these
professors as soon as their contracts terminated. In other words
the major Japanese universities became bastions of Japanisation.
For example, the teaching of foreign languages and literature
quickly switched to a concentrated education in translating a
foreign language into Japanese – largely what it is today. In fact,
one could say that everything studied at these prestigious universities increasingly had to be translated into the Japanese context
and not studied strictly in its own terms.

The Tokyo School of Foreign Languages was notably different.
The teaching was conducted entirely in foreign languages not
only for literary subjects but even for scientific subjects. Futabatei
was taught by a Russian-born American named Nicholas Gray,
who asked his students to discuss selected literary works and write
essays in Russian. In this sense Futabatei had more complete
access to European literature than Shōyō. He never Japanised for
his foreign instructor the character of Gertrude in the light of
Confucian morality. It was rather ironical that such a chauvinist
as Futabatei studied at an institution where the method of teaching was not hidebound with nationalistic concerns. Futabatei,
however, did not take a degree. The Tokyo School of Foreign
Languages was temporarily dissolved and merged with the School
of Commerce, which was of secondary school standard. Futabatei
could not bear the indignation of degrading himself to take a
degree from a lower level school and ceased his formal education.

Soon after this withdrawal Futabatei wrote his 'A Theory of the

Novel' and showed it to Shōyō on their first encounter. It is
worth comparing Futabatei's 'A Theory of the Novel' with
Shōyō's *The Essence*:

> There are two kinds of novels, one didactic, the other
> realistic; but the latter is what the novel should
> essentially be. I fully understand the objections raised
> by one or another of recent scholars [Shōyō certainly
> was one] against the prevalence of the didactic novel.
> My aesthetic theories, applied particularly to the novel,
> are in agreement with this view. The novel perceives
> directly the ideal of Nature in the various phenomena
> of the world; what is perceived must be conveyed
> directly. Such direct communication is possible only by
> means of realism. Accordingly, realism is obviously the
> essence of the novel. What is didacticism? It is to
> slight the phenomena of the world by assuming that
> good wins over evil. . . .It is nothing but preaching
> under the guise of the novel. Can it be worthy of being
> called a novel at all? However, if one did not define
> the novel as *mosha* or copying, people would become
> sceptical of it. Generally speaking, imitation means to
> represent the ideal by means of the real. In the
> phenomenal world the idea of Nature can be embodied,
> but it is not always apparent as it is covered by the veil
> of the accidental. The phenomena copied in the novel
> are nothing but accidental, but it is possible to represent
> clearly the idea of Nature in it by means of expression
> and dramatization – this is the aim of a realistic novel.

It is said that 'A Theory of the Novel' was intended to be an
introductory essay for Futabatei's full-length criticism of Shōyō's
The Temperament. Unfortunately, the manuscripts of the longer
essay have been lost. As it stands, 'A Theory of the Novel' is too
short to reveal Futabatei's theory of the novel in its entirety.
Since he does not elaborate his points fully, one needs to speculate
on what he may have thought about the novel beyond the elliptical
remarks in his brief essay. Several points emerge from this
questioning. First, Futabatei supports Shōyō's criticism of the
doctrine of 'reward virtue, punish vice'. Secondly, however, while
Shōyō's theories indicate little more than that the 'artistic novel'

aims at copying the phenomenal world, Futabatei's theory seems to suggest a realism based on Aristotelian mimesis, which is not a mere copying of the phenomenal but a representation of the ideal by means of the incidental. From where does this difference between Shōyō and Futabatei derive? Some of the theoretical sources to which Shōyō was indebted were British, whereas some critics have proved that Futabatei was indebted to contemporary Russian literary theorists such as Belinsky, who had fully absorbed Hegelian aesthetics.[7] This accounts for the idealistic undertone in the above quotation. However, among the many British sources he consulted, Shōyō must have come across the Aristotelian conception of mimesis, which called for the synthesis of the ideal and the incidental. Aristotelian poetics had been incorporated into English literary theories of the seventeenth and eighteenth centuries. Possibly, then, the difference between the theories of Shōyō and Futabatei derives from their different literary tastes. Futabatei's theories, elliptical though they are, point more explicitly towards the realistic novel which modern Japanese authors were seeking to write.

Can we make a similar judgment of his novel, *The Drifting Clouds*? It centres round a hero, Utsumi Bunzō, who is frustrated both in his public and private life. A well-educated man of integrity, he was a promising young bureaucrat until his dismissal from office for no particular reason. While staying with his aunt-in-law, O-Masa, he fell in love with his cousin O-Sei. His calculating aunt-in-law first favoured the idea of their marriage because of his promising future, but after Bunzō's dismissal her favour shifted to Honda Noboru, a colleague of Bunzō's, who scaled with ease the office's ladder of success not through his intelligence but through his opportunistic sycophancy. In the projected ending of this unfinished novel, Futabatei seems to have intended that Honda was going to seduce O-Sei, thereby driving Bunzō insane.

Once again, one can profitably compare *The Drifting Clouds* with Shōyō's *The Temperament*. Futabatei is far more successful than Shōyō in modernising the Japanese prose style. Both put into practice their denunciation of the doctrine of 'reward virtue, punish vice': Bunzō, for instance, while embodying moral righteousness, is defeated instead of being rewarded. There are, however, two significant differences between the two novels.

While *The Temperament* is a novel without a hero, in *The Drifting Clouds* Bunzō stands out as the hero or, rather, the anti-hero. Furthermore, despite Shōyō's claim in *The Essence* that priority should be given to human sentiment rather than to the ways of the world, *The Temperament* does not probe into the depth of the characters' psychology but only depicts the surface of the varied modes of student life. Futabatei, on the other hand, traces the development of the hero's psychology and achieves what may be called a modern psychological novel even though in crude form.

One of the Russian writers with whose works Futabatei was familiar was Ivan Turgenev. Particularly relevant in this connexion are such works as *The Diary of a Superfluous Man* (1850) and *Fathers and Children* (1862).[8] The characters who crowd these novels are prototypes of Russian intelligentsia at odds with nineteenth-century bourgeois society. The society in which Futabatei's hero Utsumi Bunzō lives had just undergone the Meiji Restoration, but many of the problems that then confronted modern Japan remained unresolved. Like most Meiji intellectuals, and in fact like the author himself, Bunzō is of a samurai, though declining, provincial family. He is well-versed in European culture, but his moral integrity presumably stems from his Confucian education. His difficulty is that the traditional values he embodies do not help him to cope with the bureaucratic system and with society at large. Futabatei does not imply, however, that the traditional values clash with the West *per se*, but rather he stresses the superficial ways in which Western culture has been imported and adopted in Meiji Japan.

Futabatei's hero, of course, is not free of flaws: he lacks the willingness to assert his own righteousness and to overcome the obstacles he confronts. He seems inclined towards defeatism. There is a curious imbalance – so prophetic of the portraits of intellectuals in later Japanese novels – between his intelligence, integrity and introspection on the one hand, and his ineffectual-ness in practical matters on the other. That the hero, embodying such values, suffers defeat was an inevitable dénouement for Futabatei who had no way of writing didactic novels, even such updated versions as the political novels of early Meiji. In a way Futabatei practised in this novel his theory of realism as laid down in 'A Theory of the Novel'. The idea of good is not explicitly preached; instead, it emerges from the defeat of the character who suggests this good. Futabatei has thus created a hero who is to some extent the prototype of a character suffering from alienation and insecurity, variations of which are abundant in modern Japanese literature.[9]

Futabatei's career as a novelist ceased for the next twenty years or so. While taking up various official posts, he kept on translating Russian literature but scarcely wrote any significant works of his own. The range of jobs he held well depicts the amateurish status of many an early Meiji novelist. In 1889 he was employed by the Information Office to translate Russian newspapers. After leaving this post in 1897, he taught Russian at the Cadet School for the Imperial Army. Two years later, in 1899, he was appointed to the post of Professor of Russian at his own university, the Tokyo School of Foreign Languages, while also lecturing part-time at the Naval Academy. This arrangement did not last long, however. Resigning all public posts in March 1902, he left for Manchuria to be a counsellor at a private trading firm. In August of the same year, he gave up this post too. In October, he moved on to Peking, to become the deputy-head of an institution, which in fact was engaged in intelligence work for the Japanese government. Within a year, in July 1903, Futabatei resigned, presumably owing to a disagreement with the head of the institution, and returned to Japan. In March 1904, a month after the Russo-Japanese War had started, Futabatei was invited to join the staff of the prestigious newspaper, the *Asahi Shimbun*. At about the same time the noted novelist Natsume Sōseki also joined the *Asahi Shimbun* to serialise his masterly works and he recorded his favourable impressions of Futabatei.[10] Futabatei had hoped to make regular contributions on Russo-Japanese politics, but instead he was asked to write novels for the newspaper. Rather reluctantly, he produced two works, *In his Image* (*Sono Omokage*, 1906) and *Mediocrity* (*Heibon*, 1907). Futabatei's concern for the practical matters of politics was finally recognised when in June 1908 he was sent by the *Asahi Shimbun* to be its correspondent in Russia. However, his hopes were shattered by attacks of consumption incurred and aggravated by the cold winter of St Petersburg. With its potential still unfulfilled, his life was cut short in the middle of the Indian Ocean on a boat heading back to Japan on 10 May 1909.

What emerges from the foregoing discussion of Futabatei Shimei is the gnawing tension between his life and his literature. Even people who have never read his works have often heard of the celebrated remark attributed to him: 'Literature is not an enterprise worth pursuing throughout one's entire life.' Although nowhere in his works can one locate this exact statement, a similar mood of despair appears in a passage from his autobiographical piece 'I am a Sceptic' ('Watakushi wa Kaigi-ha da', 1908):

> I cannot be content with my act of writing. It all looks
> futile. . . .It looks similar to children fighting a mock
> battle, or a mock dinner party. This may be partly due
> to my lack of talent, but however talented I may be,
> I can never represent truth.
>   Even if I understand something intellectually,
> whenever I speak or write it out, it becomes dissevered
> from truth. The truth may be occasionally revealed
> in one's life, but it can never be represented in a fiction
> – the more aware of this I become, the more difficult
> it becomes for me to apply myself to literature.

Here Futabatei is not denigrating literature but is voicing a warning to those people who take for granted the value of living the life of a man of letters. Fiction, he warns, is a fiction, regardless of whatever realistic moral purpose you pin to it. The kind of literary work Futabatei wished to create should have achieved in print the same ideals that he pursued in his life. However, the hero's defeat in *The Drifting Clouds* suggests his own difficulty in envisaging the victory of his ideals in either life or fiction. This awareness prompted his concentration on translation alone for the next twenty years until he reluctantly consented to write two more novels. Confronted by the difficult choice between perfecting his work or his life, he opted for the latter. To achieve this ambition he went to Russia, the country he had studied for decades from afar. This pursuit of life, however, led to no achievement but death, alone on a boat sailing between the country he had sought to live for and the country he had studied all his life. Such a meaningless ending would surprise no reader of *The Drifting Clouds*. And so, in a sense, Futabatei's life and his artistic concerns were not really so much at odds with one another. It was simply that the Japanese novel as he and his predecessors had shaped it was not yet a suitable vessel to contain adequately those tensions of Japan's 'modernity' that many Meiji intellectuals knew and felt all too well.

2

From romanticism to naturalism:
KITAMURA TŌKOKU and SHIMAZAKI TŌSON

I

While Tsubouchi Shōyō and Futabatei Shimei played the role of precursors creating modern fiction along the lines of Western models, two other literary movements attracted attention. Some writers continued to write novels in the tradition of Tokugawa literature. Ozaki Kōyō's (1867–1903) *Mammon (Konjiki Yasha,* 1897–1903) stands out as a successful continuation of this genre. But a far more historically important literary movement of the 1890s and 1900s was Japanese romanticism, which will be studied in this chapter through two of the most prominent features. A study of romanticism in Japan calls for a discussion of poetry as well as prose. We shall see how Japanese romantic poets were bound to become naturalistic novelists due partly to the inherent qualities of Japanese romanticism and partly to the nature of the Japanese poetic language. Secondly, it is necessary to indicate the relationship of Japanese romanticism with European romanticism, to note the kinds of direct influence from, or parallel with, European romanticism, and to analyse the peculiarly Japanese features of this romanticism that show no parallel with or influence from the European counterpart.

For the sake of comparison it seems appropriate to make a brief reference to some features of European romanticism. Until a revaluation took place a couple of decades ago,[1] the word romanticism had become one of disgrace and remained so for nearly half a century thanks to a host of anti-romantics, such as Irving Babbitt, T. T. Hulme and T. S. Eliot. According to these detractors of romanticism, Rousseauistic belief in human perfectibility on which romanticism was founded was completely illusory. The anti-romantics disparaged all the main features of romantic literature such as passionate aspiration, pride in one's individual ego, release of feelings, licentiousness and the cult of Nature worship and called for the need for restraint to be obtained through the classical tradition and established institutions. The anti-romantics, however, rather over-reacted in their sweeping generalisations.

Romanticism is one of those highly elusive literary concepts. For instance, in his 1924 essay entitled 'On the Discrimination of Romanticisms' Professor Arthur O. Lovejoy, that famous founder of the history of ideas school, extracted as many facets of romanticism as possible. But, dissecting the common concepts of romanticism into mutually contradictory notions, his rather blunt conclusion was that 'the word "romanticism" has come to mean so many things that, by itself, it means nothing'.[2]

In fact romanticism has mixed features, some of which contradict one another. Instances of contradiction are legion. Romanticism originated partly in the eighteenth-century Enlightenment and yet it eventually came into conflict with it. As typically exemplified by Wordsworth and Coleridge, romantics were revolutionaries in their youth but often ended up as reactionary conservatives. Bold self-assertions were made by the romantics, while the 'negative capability' was as highly valued by John Keats. Byron on the other hand created his diabolical heroes who speak in classical diction and style. In spite of these apparent contradictions, however, the romantics share some notable common characteristics. They are the espousal of (1) the organic concept of the universe as opposed to the mechanical; (2) imagination as the supreme faculty of perception and poetic creation; and (3) as a corollary of this, the use of symbolic language.[3] Furthermore, the latter two features are inherited by the symbolists, of whom even the anti-romantic Eliot is himself a descendant. This paradoxical situation is explained no better than by the following remark by Northrop Frye: 'Anti-Romanticism, in short, had no resources for becoming anything more than a post-Romantic movement.'[4]

2

That romanticism in modern Japanese literature first flourished from approximately 1890 to 1910 may be explained partly in historical terms. The first twenty years after the Meiji Restoration was the period of the Japanese Enlightenment, which was characterised by the espousal of individual freedom, belief in progress, and an empirical, utilitarian and pragmatic tendency. Like its European model, Japanese romanticism originally derived from the Enlightenment, yet later came to oppose it. First, it inherited from the earlier movement the idea of individual freedom and liberation of the ego. Secondly, it inherited the idea of progress and applied it not only to the material but also to the spiritual realm, developing infinite aspirations to transcendental reality. Thirdly, romanticism came ultimately to contradict and repudiate the utilitarian tendency of the Enlightenment. Naturally, the social conditions of Japan in the middle of the Meiji era differed from those in any of the European countries of the romantic period. The individual freedom realisable was largely limited and consequently Japanese romantics were forced to look more and more towards the inner life for the realm of their quest.

Naturally enough, poetry was one of the important means of expression for Meiji romanticism. Its keynote may best be represented by the words of the manifesto of a group of poets: 'We aim at expressing ourselves.'[5] It implied a drive to liberate the poets' ego from the restraint of the *ancien régime* and to express their ideas outside the limit of the traditional poetic forms. The poetic themes varied from straightforward social criticism to the assertion of free love. The result was not always successful: sometimes the poets found the poetic vehicle inadequate for their purposes and only managed to express the narrow sphere of their isolated sensibility. It was characteristic of the Meiji poets to belong to certain groups that published poetry magazines for example, the *Bungakukai* (The Literary World), the *Subaru* (The Pleiades) and the *Myōjō* (The Morning Star). The genres of their poetry were quite varied: dramatic poems, lyrics and innovated traditional *tanka* poems. Shimazaki Tōson (1872–1943), for example, attempted narrative poems, one of which was an adaptation of Shakespeare's *Venus and Adonis* into a traditional Japanese style. But his genius was not in that line: it was exhibited in his lyrics published in the late 1890s and early 1900s: *Wakanashū* (A Collection of Young Greens, 1897), *Ichiyōshū* (A Collection of Single Leaves, 1898), *Natsukusa* (Summer Grass, 1898) and *Rakubaishū* (A collection of Fallen

Plum Blossoms, 1901), all collected later in *Tōson Shishū* (The Collected Poems of Tōson, 1904). It is a well-known fact that 'An Ode to the Autumn Wind' was written under the influence of Shelley's 'An Ode to the West Wind'. Tōson succeeded in expressing his true emotional voice in his sometimes passionate and sometimes melancholic poems. His lyrics were exceedingly musical, contained within a regularly organised quatrain, each line consisting of traditional syllables of five and seven or seven and five. His were the lyrics in which the traditional Japanese sentiment and Western ideas were happily unified.

Tōson as well as his friend Kitamura Tōkoku (1868–94), who will be discussed in some detail later in this chapter, wrote their poems in the so-called new style first devised by the authors of the *Shintaishi-shō* (Selected New Style Poems, 1882). In the meantime the traditional *tanka* poetry still existed. But a great innovation was brought about by Yosano Tekkan (1873–1935) and his wife Akiko (1878–1942), representatives of the romantic movement in *tanka*. Tekkan observes: 'I do not find it necessary at all to draw a distinction between *tanka* poets and authors of new style poems. Both can co-exist together.' Thus *tanka* poems came to express non-traditional sensibilities and themes, including that of the liberation of individuals.

Apart from Tōson who made himself as prominent in prose as in poetry, a host of other romantic writers specialised in prose: for instance Izumi Kyōka (1873–1939), Tayama Katai (1871–1930), Tokutomi Roka (1868–1927) and Kunikida Doppo (1871–1908). Of these well-known writers Izumi Kyōka was unique due to his transition from a writer of realistic fiction to an expert on creating an artificial world of unreality or the supernatural. In contrast to Kyōka, other writers' attention was directed towards Nature. One of Tokutomi Roka's earliest works is *Nature and Life* (*Shizen to Jinsei*, 1900), in which he displays an organic and pantheistic view of Nature quite in harmony with its European counterpart. This is also true of Kunikida Doppo whose indebtedness to Wordsworth is worthy of special note. His descriptive sketch in prose of Musashino or the western outskirts of Tokyo (*Musashino*, 1901), the natural beauty of which was then still intact from the ravages of urbanisation, is reminiscent not so much of Wordsworth's poetry as of his sister Dorothy's journals. For Wordsworth's treatment of Nature veers between the poles of an exalted transcendental vision and a concrete earthiness, whereas Dorothy's journals, like Doppo's prose, are rich in vivid, sensory descriptions of Nature. Doppo's more direct indebtedness to Wordsworth can be illustrated by his short story 'A Bird in Spring' 'Haru no Tori', 1904). The hero is an idiot boy, who aspired to become a bird and died as a result of jumping from the ruins of a castle. Apparently the author had in mind Wordsworth's fragment on the boy of Winander later incorporated into *The Prelude* and also 'The Idiot Boy' (though the latter ends as a happy story of 'a little boy lost and found'). The interesting thing about these writers is that except for Izumi Kyōka they all started as romantic poets and ended as naturalistic or realistic novelists. The implications of this metamorphosis will be considered later.

3

Instead of a long list of writers and their works, one author, Kitamura Tōkoku, may serve to illustrate in more concrete terms some aspects of Meiji romanticism. Among his fellow poets he cannot be as important as Tōson for instance. His poetic product is meagre in quantity as well as in quality. Nevertheless he made up for this defect with his prose works which reveal an unusually wide scope of interest in multifarious subjects, literary, philosophical and social, and a mind genuinely confronting European romanticism. Unfortunately he was not able to establish a consistent system. His life was cut short by his suicide which was preceded by mental breakdowns – reminiscent of the lives of some English pre-romantic poets.

His first poetic work was a long poem, *A Prisoner* (*Soshū no Shi*, 1889) modelled on Byron's 'The Prisoner of Chillon'. The narrator is the first person 'I', who is now imprisoned as a political criminal. Tōkoku's own concern for politics is reflected in the narrator, although he himself was never imprisoned. As early as 1881, at the age of twelve, Tōkoku came to know about the Democratic Rights Movement and in 1883 he became acquainted with members of that Movement. His political enthusiasm increased, but he did not take part in the uprising of activists in 1885. They were arrested and imprisoned. Tōkoku no doubt had this incident in mind when he wrote and published *A Prisoner* four years later. The poem as it stands, however, is not so much a record of an external incident as the description of the inner state of a prisoner's mind. It is nothing but Tōkoku's own mental state as it could have been if he had taken part in the ill-fated uprising and had been imprisoned.

The poem is thus concerned with imprisonment both in the literal and metaphorical sense. The prisoner's state of mind is 'sunken, withered, dwindled and depressed'. His present state contrasts with his life in the past which is compared to that of 'an eagle on the mountain/Flying over trees in freedom'. Also imprisoned in a separate cell is his beloved, for whom he expresses his yearning in paragraphs four to ten. The protagonist is so preoccupied with her that he absurdly identifies a bat, which has strayed into his cell, with her spirit. More naturally he identifies a nightingale singing outside the prison with her incarnation (paragraph 15):

> The nightingale has resumed her song
> Which brings a message to my heart.
> It is filled with consoling words of love.
> Is she of this world or of Heaven?
> To me she seems like a divine messenger.
> Oh, my beloved! or the nightingale!
> Oh, she flies away!
> Is she after all a mere bird?
> Were she my beloved, why should she leave me
> In this miserable grave dark and void?
> The air is murky, the floor musty and cold –
> This is my grave: for I am buried alive.

The poem ends with an abrupt dénouement, in which both the prisoner and his beloved are released on special parole. The poem is defective both in style and ideas. For instance, the prisoner's political concern and his yearning for his beloved do not merge together in the context of the poem. This defect derives partly from the author's own personal background. When Tōkoku wrote this poem, he had just dissociated himself from the Democratic Rights Movement although he still retained his radicalist position. At the same time he was in love with the sister of one of his political associates, whom he was later to marry. Thus different concerns were fermenting in Tōkoku's mind without reaching an ultimate solution.

While *A Prisoner* concerns the imprisoned state of a political criminal, Tōkoku's second long poem *Mt Hōrai* (*Hōrai Kyoku*, 1891) presents the hero as a prisoner of his own mind and of life in general. As the author notes in a prefatory apologia, he has deliberately written a dramatic poem far removed from traditional Japanese drama. He claims he has no intention of seeing it performed on the stage and has inserted into the play supernatural elements. These introductory remarks remind us of those dramas of the English romantic period so divorced from theatrical tradition as to be almost unstageable. In fact the analogy with the English romantic plays is more than incidental. As his models Tōkoku had in mind Goethe's *Faust* and Byron's *Manfred*.

The hero of the play is an aristocrat like Manfred and Byron himself. The setting, Mt Fuji, for which the ancient name Hōrai is used, corresponds with Mont Blanc, the setting for *Manfred*. Both represent the sublimity of Nature. Both heroes are described as a 'son of clay' or 'dust' and yet they are full of pride. Both heroes suffer from mental agonies. Manfred is anguished by his past sin of illicit love with Astarte, which is based on Byron's own relation with his half-sister Augusta Leigh. The hero of *Mt Hōrai* has not committed any specific sin but is tortured by the internal conflicts within his own mind. In both cases their minds are preoccupied with their love and the heroes are confronted by demons, which in turn are counterbalanced by devout characters – the Abbot in *Manfred* and the Monk in Tōkoku's play.

As mentioned earlier, Manfred suffers from feelings of guilt for a sin committed through his incestuous love and is consequently alienated from the world. The hero of *Mt Hōrai*, on the other hand, is not a sinner in the same way, but he shares with Manfred a sense of alienation. For him too 'the world is not his friend, nor the world's law'. In this respect he is a fine example of the solitary wanderer whose innumerable specimens are scattered throughout European romantic poetry. As a Japanese romantic, he is a poet, carrying a lyre in his hand, and a lover, aspiring to the ideal beauty incarnate in his beloved. His character as a romantic hero is nowhere better revealed than in his self-portrait (Act II, scene ii): 'I always look into myself and never outwardly; I search into the curious facts of my mind and never leave them unexplored'. The description reminds one of Coleridge's romanticised picture of Hamlet 'as for ever occupied with the world within him, and abstracted from external things'.[6] The alienation of the hero of *Mt Hōrai* from the world originates in his own 'mind's abyss' or his capacity for introspection, which can both aspire to celestial heights and descend to the demonic underworld. As a setting for this play Mt Hōrai is at once sublime and ominous, divine and demonic. Thus, in the last Act, after rejecting the Monk's admonition that he should resort to religion, the hero proceeds to a cave where the phantom of his beloved resides. It is actually the entrance to the demonic underworld. Here he comes face to face with the Devil, saying, 'I have within myself two opposed natures warring with each other: the one divine, the other human.' He defies the Devil and dies a tragic death, the only fate appropriate for the proud mind which commits itself neither to the divine nor to the demonic.

Tōkoku's political and social concerns, which he expressed in prose as well as in such a poem as *A Prisoner*, gradually underwent a shift of emphasis. Already in 1887, soon after the failure of the Democratic Rights Movement, he had become a Christian. His association with Christian missionaries increased year after year. In 1892 he became the editor of the periodical *Heiwa* (Peace). In his foreword to its first number Tōkoku declared his manifesto: 'Peace is my ultimate ideal....If the stronger victimises the weaker, how could mankind claim its supremacy? That is prohibited equally by Christ, Buddha and Confucius.' He concludes the foreword as follows: 'Wars from now on will become that of one race against another. Once a war starts, it will not stop until it turns all cities into waste lands. In view of this fact we have a proper cause for publishing the *Peace*.' Tōkoku's pacifism isolated him from the trend of a Japan strengthening herself under the centralised government of Meiji and moving towards the Sino-Japanese War of 1894-5.

Perhaps it was not simply his pacifism but his way of thinking as a whole that alienated him from the current trend. A distinct contrast may be drawn between Tōkoku and Fukuzawa Yukichi (1835-1901) who laid the foundation of the Meiji Enlightenment. In an essay on Meiji literature Tōkuko says: 'Certainly he [Fukuzawa] was a great performer. But his was an external reform and was not adequate as an ideal to lead the nation.'[7]

Elsewhere he complains that 'the present age is one of material revolution and is deprived of spirit'.[8] The argument is developed to the distinction between what he calls the 'horizontal thinker' and what he calls the 'vertical thinker'.[9] According to this distinction the former 'pays his attention to what happens, talks of social reform and engages in various activities'. A nation needs this type of thinker, without whom there will be no progress in society. 'But remember', Tōkoku goes on to say, 'that he alone is not sufficient: for the sake of culture there should exist another type of thinker', who is called the 'vertical thinker'. The distinction here is between the practical and theoretical, utilitarian and non-utilitarian, and roughly corresponds to the distinction made by J. S. Mill between the Benthamite and Coleridgean.[10] Earlier Tōkoku's romantic aspiration had found its outlet in the Democratic Rights Movement as the product of the essentially utilitarian Meiji Enlightenment, but now it came to dissociate itself from the utilitarian bent of society. Tōkoku as a romantic thinker was thus destined to become increasingly alienated from society as were many of the major European romantics.

Just as complex as Tōkoku's social viewpoint is his attitude to the problem of how Japan should assimilate European culture. His view can be called dialectic. There is, for instance, his essay entitled 'My Chauvinism' ('Isshu no Jōishisō', 1892), which he contributed to the third issue of *Peace*. The title is misleading if it gives the impression that the author is a nationalist opposed to the tide of Western civilisation flowing into the country. In his opening statement at least he certainly sounds nationalistic or slightly chauvinistic: 'I am not devoted to the cult of Westernisation. I believe no less firmly than the so-called nationalists in our own cultural tradition that has lasted for three thousand years'; 'I am proud of the continuity of our imperial family.' Yet these statements are followed, and counterbalanced, by the following:

> But I cannot sympathise with those who try to reject everything that is imported from abroad. Nor can I ever side myself with narrow-minded chauvinism.
>   I have no mind at all to resist the importation of democratic ideas and try to stick to the old tradition. The current of world-wide progress is inevitable and

cannot be resisted by human powers. I am ready to
follow the trend of the world as far as ideas and thought
are concerned.

Tōkoku thus ambivalently acknowledges the value of the native
cultural tradition and the inevitability of importing Western
culture.

Tōkoku's views about this matter change from time to time.
Sometimes he is explicitly critical of the traditional culture of Japan.
In his review of a nationalistic article which extols the genuine-
ness of the Japanese language when compared with English as a
mixed language, he harshly criticises the article by praising the
richness of English because of its impurity and pointing out its
superiority to Japanese.[11] It is not only of the language but also of
the traditional Japanese literature that Tōkoku is critical. He is
especially dissatisfied with certain aspects of Tokugawa literature.
According to Tōkoku, the Tokugawa novelists and the contemporary inheritors of their tradition tended to be realistic or
naturalistic in a superficial sense. They were skilful only in
describing the trivial daily life of common people. He is also
greatly dissatisfied with the traditional concept of love, which in
his view is merely limited to the mundane. 'Sometimes', Tōkoku
says, 'love is even heightened to that pure love which leads us
above to Heaven.'[12] He further develops his argument in relation
to literature: 'The lack of sublime love in our literature is due to
our lack of the concept of the world beyond. . . .Ideas which are
limited to this world do not beget aspirations.'[13] The question
then turns to the supernatural in literature. 'Some say that we
have our own ancient myths which are suitable for poetic subjects.
In my view they may be suitable for vulgar curiosity but not for
the mysterious world of poetry.'[14] Tōkoku's worries ultimately
amount to a sense of the inferiority of Japanese literature at large.
As he says: 'Where is true literature? I do not expect a *Les
Misérables*, a *Divina Commedia*, not to speak of a *Paradise Lost*,
to be written in this country. But why is there not one novelist
who really sheds tears for the sake of the nation?'[15] And he says
elsewhere: 'I must admit with regret that we are inferior to the
West in politics, thought and learning. Nobody knows the future
of the nation, but if things go as they now stand, ultimately God
will not favour us.'[16]

Concerning the alternative between the native tradition and

Westernisation, Tōkoku offers a parable.[17] A family maintained
its respectable history for three thousand years thanks to the
isolation of its small village. The family declined immediately
after the village opened communication with the outside world
some thirty years ago. There were two daughters in this family.
The elder one was adopted and brought up by a family in the
adjoining village. She came home for the first time after she had
grown up. The two sisters looked different: the elder one well-
nourished and full of vitality; the younger one, though preserving
her inborn nobility, looked meagre and unhealthy. The one
boasted of her looks and the other of her devotion to the family
tradition. Tōkoku associates the one with democracy, individualism, power and a bright future, and the other with an impoverished tradition and pessimism. Tōkoku asks the reader
which of the two sisters he would like to marry? Tōkoku answers
the question with a consistent metaphor, giving immoral advice
for bigamy. As he says elsewhere conclusively:

> Mine is not chauvinism in the ordinary sense. What I
> hate and oppose is the cult of pseudo-civilisation, or the
> attitude to try to import indiscriminately everything of
> Western origin.
>
> However, I am most willing to abolish the distinction
> between us and the West in respect of really valuable
> things. I despise those chauvinists who insist that living
> in a corner of the East we do not have to pay any
> attention to the West.
>
> It is most regrettable if the East and the West alienate
> each other. . . .At such a time is it not encouraging that,
> like our society of Peace, both Western and Eastern
> thinkers collaborate with a devout, sincere objective in
> common?[18]

Tōkoku died too early to build his philosophical and aesthetic
views into a system. They are not free from defects and are sometimes immature, but they are full of perceptive insights. The
quintessence of his philosophy is epitomised in the title of one of
his best essays, 'On the Inner Life' ('Naibu Seimei Ron', 1893),
in which he says: 'Today there is no such thing as the conflict
between Christianity and Buddhism. The real conflict is between
the philosophy of life and that of death. . . .What I am trying to

do is to use the former to refute the latter.' Elsewhere he also
says: 'There are two ways of looking at the universe: one is to
regard it as a dead body and the other as a living organism.'[19]
The distinction may be paraphrased as the one between the
philosophy of mechanism and that of organism. The former was
dominant throughout the seventeenth and eighteenth centuries
and it was in reaction to it that the English romantic poets
advocated the philosophy of organism such as is found in both the
poetry and prose of Wordsworth and Coleridge. In promoting
the same cause Tōkoku was a true romantic.

Tōkoku's world view is founded on his belief that latent in the
universe is an organic life with which the human mind is in
communion. This belief is expressed by means of the metaphor
of 'a great harp...hung in the centre of the universe'. Of this
harp he says: 'There is no heart, no mind that does not touch this
great harp and produce sound on it. All hearts and minds are
different, but they are so just as the sounds produced by the harp
are different only in tone; once they are reproduced on the harp,
they are all equal.'[20] It is most likely that for the metaphor of the
harp Tōkoku is indebted to R. W. Emerson, who uses it as one
of the central images in his prose as well as poetry.[21] It is as likely
that Emerson's use of this poetic symbol in turn is modelled on
English romantic poetry. For example one of its prototypes is
available in Coleridge's poem 'The Eolian Harp' (lines 44–8):

> And what if all of animated nature
> Be but organic Harps diversely fram'd,
> That tremble into thought, as o'er them sweeps
> Plastic and vast, one intellectual Breeze,
> At once the Soul of each, and God of all.

In Coleridge's poem the harp serves as a felicitous symbol of
harmony pervading the whole universe. This image is supplemented by another key concept (lines 26–9):

> O! the one Life within us and abroad,
> Which meets all motion and becomes its soul,
> A light in sound, a sound-like power in light,
> Rhythm in all thought, and joyance everywhere

The same concept is also found in a letter in which Coleridge
compares the Greek and Hebrew modes of perception: 'In the

Hebrew poets each Thing has a Life of its own, and yet they are all one Life.'[22] Conversely, Wordsworth attaches importance to the vital particularity of individual objects as well as their oneness (*The Prelude* (1805), II, 317–21):

> gentle agitations of the mind
> From manifold distinctions, difference
> Perceived in things, where to the common eye,
> No difference is: and hence, from the same source
> Sublimer joy;

All these central ideas of romantic epistemology find their echoes in Tōkoku: 'It is the poet who is aware of the oneness and at the same time differences of all. . . .No one can understand that the universe is one great poem who is not capable of becoming aware of oneness by observing closely the minute differences between different objects.'[23] Tōkoku's essay 'The Inner Life' thus proves to be one of the most interesting and important Japanese attempts to formulate a romantic view of the universe.

From the foregoing discussion emerge some general features of Meiji romanticism. First of all, most of the writers discussed had yearnings for individual freedom and social reform, which they sought to express in literature. In its initial stage these writers' literary and imaginative aspirations coincided with the external realities. The Enlightenment of the early Meiji era was at once the cause and effect of their literary activities. The Democratic Rights Movement, in which Tōkoku took part, however, met with suppression by the government. Furthermore, as illustrated by Tōkoku's thought the utilitarian aspect of the Enlightenment proved inadequate for the literary imagination which envisaged the transcendental above the mundane. Thus, truly serious writers came to find themselves at odds with and alienated from contemporary society.

This feature of Meiji romanticism must also be considered in terms of literary expressions. Initially the poets' aspiration for a release of their romantic egos was possible through their poetic vehicles, whether it be *tanka* poems, traditional or reformed, or the new-style poems. But these poetic forms proved far from adequate for the purpose of confronting the overwhelming social realities. There were limitations inherent in the language of

Japanese poetry: its short form and rigid metric scheme made it
not particularly suitable for discursive reasoning and argument.
The various new poetic styles attempted by the Meiji romantic
poets were not sufficient to overcome these limitations. Consequently some of them turned to prose as a means of expressing
their ideas.

4

That the romantic poets of Meiji came to play a major role in
the development of realistic or, more precisely speaking, naturalistic novels is a peculiarly Japanese phenomenon. The major
English romantics, for instance, were all poets. Perhaps one may
mention the case of Walter Scott, but his prose works were mostly
romantic chronicles which differ in quality from the realistic
novels of the nineteenth century. Some of the continental
romantics, such as Novalis, Victor Hugo, Gérard de Nerval,
were at once poets and novelists; but, again, their novels were
written in the romantic key just as their poems were.

The history of the nineteenth-century novel, particularly when
seen from the late Meiji and Victorian perspectives, may be
described as an evolution towards realism. It depicts with realistic
touches the mechanisms of bourgeois society and the psychology
of the people living in it. Meiji Japanese novelists learned about
realism mainly through French and Russian models as well as
English ones. Since their knowledge of French and Russian was
not always sufficient, they often read French and Russian literature in English translation; though Futabatei Shimei is a notable
exception to this rule. Among Meiji Japanese writers there was at
one time a vogue for the French naturalists, Maupassant, Zola
and the Goncourts. Under the influence of these writers the
modern Japanese novel developed further, for better or for worse.
And it was no other than Shimazaki Tōson who participated in
this development.

With its tight organisation, authentic characterisation and
fully developed modern prose, Tōson's first long novel, *The
Broken Commandment* (*Hakai*, 1906) stands out today as a
relatively successful Meiji novel. In this work Tōson chose a
subject no novelist had dealt with and, surprisingly enough, no
other novelist has dealt with ever since. The hero of *The Broken
Commandment*, Segawa Ushimatsu, is a young schoolmaster,

who comes from a family of the *buraku-min*, a discriminated minority group in traditional and modern Japanese society.[24]

One can easily imagine what courage it took for Tōson to handle such a delicate subject in his first novel. The word *hakai* of the title is used in a slightly anomalous way. Normally it means the violation of a religious commandment. Here what is violated is the commandment given to the hero by his dying father that if he wants to succeed in the world, he must keep forever secret the sordid facts of his social background.

Tōson has created a situation in which the hero feels obliged to confess this secret. It is quite natural that Ushimatsu admires Inoko Rentarō, himself a *buraku-min* and a fellow campaigner for the emancipation of the *buraku-min*. Inoko's political rival, Takayanagi, happens to discover Ushimatsu's background and threatens to disclose the secret unless he stops helping Inoko's election campaign. With rumours spread at his school that there is a *buraku-min* among the teachers, Ushimatsu finds it an unbearable torture to keep the secret any longer. He finally reveals it in front of his pupils who all admire him. At the end of the novel, Ushimatsu emigrates to Texas to find a place far better than any he has known before. The Hollywood-style ending betrays the author's lamentable naïveté and ignorance.

Tōson's choice of the subject, however, was certainly admirable. His objective was not to promote the emancipation of the *buraku-min* but to draw a realistic picture of the hero's inner conflicts. As a *buraku-min* Ushimatsu is destined to be the invisible man to himself and others. He may survive by wearing a social mask that conceals his true identity. This deceit means, however, that he is alienated not just from society but also from himself and so must eventually become schizoid. Thus to conceal his true identity from himself he creates within himself a garrison of psychological guilt that imprisons him in the society's own illusions. He is not authentic as an existentialist would say. To confess his true identity would destroy his career, but that honesty would be necessary to restore his integral self and authenticity. Viewed in this way, the novel shows how Tōson was concerned with his own longing for a fully integral self, represented in the perfectly fictitious character of Ushimatsu. In the details of its structure *The Broken Commandment* is not free from defects, but in this novel Tōson achieved something close to the ideal of the modern realist novel.

In 1907, a year after the publication of *The Broken Commandment*, Tayama Katai published *The Quilt* (*Futon*), a novel important in its own way in the history of the modern Japanese novel. The story is simple enough. The hero is a middle-aged novelist bored with his wife and life in general. A would-be blue-stocking writer comes to live in his house as a kind of disciple. They come to feel master-disciple attachment of a platonic kind, but love develops in more concrete terms between the girl and a university student. Her parents disapprove of this relationship and the girl is forced to go home to live with them in the country.

The story follows exactly what happened in the author's own life. The audacity with which the author disclosed his own personal suffering in this triangular relationship made a tremendous impact on the contemporary audience. Critics often mention the last scene of the story, in which the day after the girl's departure the hero (that is, the author) lies down on her bed and buries his face in tears under her quilt. Today there is perhaps nothing extraordinary about this self-flagellation in public, but in terms of the stiff-collared decorum of Meiji it was very shocking. It also represented a 'naturalistic' attitude with which the author depicted life as it really was – in this case, his own life. Perhaps, this 'misunderstanding' of European naturalism could have given a fresh impetus to the development of naturalism in Japan. But, if one is to judge the results of this Japanese movement even in its own 'naturalistic' terms, this 'misunderstanding' amounts to a very superficial, naïve and misguided naturalism that culminated in the so-called 'I-novel' (*watakushi shōsetsu* or *shi-shōsetsu*).

The I-novel is a peculiarly Japanese phenomenon with the following features. First, it is a straightforward autobiographical confession by the hero who is none other than the author himself. Secondly, the hero is in search of a peculiarly personal ideal or moral vision, which is at odds with the bourgeois standard of life. Thirdly, as a result the hero inevitably becomes alienated from and eventually defeated by society. Fourthly, the hero sometimes revenges himself on society with deliberate immorality, embodying the paradox that the initial moral vision assumes Satanic immorality. These features may not look particularly Japanese: they simply indicate that the I-novel is concerned with the realisation of the modern ego. Unfortunately, however, the I-novelists were never successful in fulfilling what their egos so earnestly desired. Consequently they simply depicted the misery of their life with a monotonous touch. Failing to be masters either of art or of life, they allowed art to serve life instead of securing its autonomy. This was in fact derived partly from the anomalous origin of the I-novel. It originated in the pseudo-naturalistic novels of Tayama Katai (1871–1930), who had earlier begun his career as a romantic writer. In a sense the history of modern Japanese literature may be summed up as the process by which the initial romantic aspiration towards the fulfilment of the ego came to be suppressed under the heavy burden of society. According to the late Itoh Sei (1905–69), modern Japanese writers were forced to become either 'masked gentlemen' pretending to conform to society, or 'runaway slaves' living as social outcasts.[25] The latter was exactly the fate of the I-novelists. The alternatives for them were madness or suicide.

Tōson's *The Broken Commandment* and Katai's *The Quilt* thus contrast in a significant way. Tōson's concern for the fulfilment of his integral self is represented in a reasonably objective form, while the trivial details of Katai's own private life are presented as if on a tray for all to stare at. The author, then, does not create a work of art but, as it were, becomes the work of art himself, a spectacle fit for public consumption like an animal in a zoo. It would have been much better if naturalism in modern Japanese literature had developed along the lines of *The Broken Commandment* rather than along those of *The Quilt*. Ironically, however, Tōson himself followed in the wake of Katai and wrote novels in which the material is taken more overtly from his own life.

Tōson's *Spring* (*Haru*, 1908) is based on real events that had taken place in his life. The central figure Kishimoto Sutekichi is none other than Tōson himself. Tōson's title is a parody of Botticelli's celebrated *Primavera*. Like the personification of spring by three ladies in this painting, Tōson presents three metaphorical aspects of spring in this novel. First, an aspiration to the spring of idealism and its failure is embodied by Kishimoto's friend Aoki, who is accurately modelled on Kitamura Tōkoku. Secondly, the spring of art is embodied in the other characters who are all modelled on Tōson's literary friends of the *Bungakukai* magazine. Thirdly, the spring of life is embodied in the hero himself. The last aspect centres round Kishimoto's (hence Tōson's) affair with a pupil of his at a girls' school, which affair forced Tōson to resign his post and leave Tokyo to lead the life of a recluse in Sendai, a provincial city in northern Japan. *Spring* gives an account of Tōson's state of mind subsequent to this affair. As is usual after such an experience, Tōson suffered from guilt feelings which led to mental depression, uncertainty and anxiety. One may fruitfully compare this dilemma with Ushimatsu's situation in *The Broken Commandment*. Ushimatsu suffers from alienation, a split personality and insecurity due to external circumstances. In *Spring*, in contrast, Kishimoto's guilt feeling arises from a sin he himself committed. The novels, however, share a curious resemblance. In *The Broken Commandment* Ushimatsu's confession or disclosure of his hidden identity against his father's commandment serves as a kind of absolution, a means of escaping from his psychological impasse. In *Spring*, since Kishimoto is identical with Tōson himself, Tōson's account of Kishimoto's guilt serves as a literary (and, thus, psychological) means of absolution from his own guilt. When Tōson wrote *The Broken Commandment* he had already been suffering from guilt, but he dealt with it in a rather objective form of fiction. In *Spring*, however, he dealt with a similar anxiety in a less disguised, less objective form of confession – his variation of the I-novel.

Already in *Spring* his account of the bankruptcy of Kishimoto's elder brother had shown Tōson's interest in the theme of the decline of a once distinguished family. This theme is expanded and elaborated in *The House* (*Ie*, 1910–11), a novel concerned with the decline of two distinguished families in the Shinshū area, the Koizumis and the Hashimotos, related to each other through marriage. The hero of the novel, Koizumi Sankichi, modelled on Kishimoto Sutekichi of *Spring*, and needless to say, on Tōson himself, airs a central theme of this novel: 'Wherever we go, whatever we do, we seem always to be haunted by our father. . . . Wherever we go, aren't we all living under the burden of our ancient houses? . . .I wish I could exterminate them' (part II, chapter 8). The meaning of this burden of the past is further developed in Tōson's later masterpiece, *Before the Dawn* (*Yoake Mae*, 1929–35).

The title of *A New Life* (*Shinsei*, 1918–19) is of course a parody of Dante's *La Vita Nuova*. The novel deals with a subject far more shocking and sensational than Tōson's repressed love for his pupil in *Spring* or Katai's unfulfilled love for his disciple in *The Quilt* – namely his incestuous relationship with his niece, an affair that forced him to live three years of self-exile in Paris. Once again he disguises himself as Kishimoto Sutekichi and traces the events as they really happened to himself. The first half of the novel describes the development of the hero's illicit relationship and his life of self-exile in Paris. The second half is concerned with how Kishimoto, a novelist like Tōson himself, came to disclose his own scandal in the form of a novel just as Tōson himself did by writing *A New Life*. It is thus a typical example of a Japanese naturalist novel. The author is more audacious in his public self-exposure than in his imagination. He discloses his immorality, his obsession with guilt feelings stemming from the hero's (or the author's) sin, the hero's (or the author's) insecurity, and subsequent longing for confession as a means of wished-for absolution. By this means Tōson certainly communicates his sincere preoccupations, but the simplistic confusion of the author's life with that of the 'created' character deprives the work of the kind of autonomy inherent in European naturalist fiction. The favourable reception to this novel from literary circles tolled the death-knell for any native Japanese naturalism akin to its European parentage. What did remain, however, was that peculiarly Japanese I-novel.

Earlier, this discussion of Tōson as a novelist tried to compare his *The Broken Commandment* and Katai's *The Quilt*. I mentioned that instead of developing the possibilities for naturalistic fiction shown in *The Broken Commandment*, Tōson ironically followed in the wake of Katai's realism, although his novels have a much wider scope than Katai's. Up to this point he had been concerned with his own problems. Towards the end of his career, however, he attempted a search for his identity not by looking into himself but by seeking it in the past – not the very distant past but just two generations before his – in his voluminous

Before the Dawn. It is modelled on his own family history during the Meiji Restoration.

Tōson's family had been for centuries the *nanushi* and *shōya*, that is, village headmen, in the Shinshū district. In the novel Kichizaemon is based on Tōson's grandfather, and Hanzō his father. Kichizaemon is a conservative and faithful adherent of the Tokugawa regime. But Hanzō, believing in the *kokugaku* or national learning of Hirata Atsutane, is critical of the feudalistic oppression of the peasants, and hopes for reform through a return to Nature along lines recommended by the Hirata school. Naturally, he is also in favour of the restoration of Imperial power. In brief, Hanzō can be judged a radical thinker within the context of Japanese politics on the eve of the Meiji Restoration. However, history never lacks irony, especially at a time of drastic and rapid change. The radicalism of one moment soon becomes anachronistic. For peasants the improvement in their material conditions takes precedence over ideological purity. The Meiji Restoration brings temporary alleviation of their problems, but the new administration soon starts to impoverish them. Hanzō as an idealistic royalist becomes alienated from both the peasants and the new bureaucracy bent on utilitarian efficiency and progress. Here, in the defeat inflicted by history, lies the origin of Hanzō's tragedy. The central government judges him to be the ringleader of a peasant uprising and deprives him of his post as village headman. The rest of the novel portrays Hanzō's further decline and fall in public life, his isolation from his family and, finally, his confinement in a lunatic's cell. Tōson depicts the increasing miseries of Hanzō's life as realistically as he did in earlier novels like *The House*. He draws on a grand scale a picture of the personal tragedy of Hanzō and the decline of his family against the background of historical change during the Meiji Restoration. This last work of Tōson's no doubt stands as an important specimen of the historical novel in modern Japanese literature, but by the time he wrote it, Japanese naturalist novels had reached a dead end as a result of the writers' exclusive preoccupation with the narrowly limited range of their own life and their drab presentation of its contents.

3

The agonies of individualism:
NATSUME SŌSEKI

I

Natsume Sōseki (1867–1916) stood apart from the naturalist-I-novelist tradition. It was Sōseki who really enhanced the artistic quality of modern Japanese novels to a point approaching the quality of those Western models which they had been struggling to emulate. In this his educational background as a university student and teacher of English literature helped him a great deal. Scarcely any Japanese writer has been more proficient in his knowledge and understanding of Western literature than Sōseki. Yet nobody was more critical of the superficial worship of Western culture in Meiji Japan than Sōseki was. He was as well-versed in traditional Japanese literature and Chinese classics. Like Kitamura Tōkoku, Sōseki was neither a jingoist nor a blind follower of Western culture. He was, in the simplest possible terms, a highly serious writer for whom personal and cultural confrontation with the West was a matter of life and death.

His attitude to the study of Western literature had some paradoxical features. As a lecturer in English literature at the University of Tokyo, he could have become a leading Japanese scholar in the field. Despite his devotion to the subject, profound scholarship and, eventually, deeply appreciated teaching, he gave up his scholarly career to become a professional novelist. This decision proved to be at once a loss to English studies in Japan and a gain to Japanese literature. He gave up his career as a scholar of English literature partly as a result of the too rigorous standard he imposed on himself and partly as a result of his dislike of the university (government) bureaucracy which he felt turned scholars into petty bureaucrats. For the same reason he declined a D.Lit. offered by the Ministry of Education. As a novelist, he began writing rather late in life, but his major achievement comprises more than a dozen novels which were all squeezed into the final decade of his life.

As is often the case with a literary virtuoso, the inner state of his mind was far from happy. From the beginning to the end of his life, he suffered loneliness and alienation except for his association with some distinguished friends and disciples. As is well known, he was a *de facto* neurotic if not psychotic case. The following is an attempt to examine these features of Sōseki's life and works.

2

The assumption that literary works have their own inherent values independent of their authors should be true of Sōseki, who dissociated himself from the I-novelist tradition of confusing the writer's life and works. Yet there are some biographical factors that seem to have bearing on the important features of his literature. For instance, his childhood environment was peculiar. He was born in Edo just one year before the Meiji Restoration, into a family of two sisters, two brothers, a father of fifty-three and a mother of forty-one. His father served as a *nanushi*, or ward head, a civil post as highly regarded as and more financially remunerative than a samurai's. What is striking is the shame his mother felt at his birth, since contemporary standards judged her unreasonably old for bearing another child. Either for this or some hidden reason, his parents decided to cast him off as a reject to foster-parents, an impoverished and socially inferior antique dealer and his wife who had no child of their own. Sōseki grew up in their home under the illusion that this couple were actually his parents and that his real parents were his grandparents. The emotional shock he experienced when the truth was unveiled is vividly revealed in his own later recollection (*Inside the Glass Door* [*Garasudo no Naka*, 1915], section 29):

> I was born to my parents in their evening years. I was
> their youngest child. The story that my mother was
> ashamed of having a baby at her age, I hear even
> now. . . .At any rate, I was sent soon afterwards to a
> certain couple as their adopted son. . . .I was with them
> until the age of eight or nine, when one begins to
> understand things. There was some trouble between

them, so it was arranged that I should be returned to my
parents. . . .I did not know that I had come back to
my own home and I kept on thinking as I did before
that my parents were my grandparents. Unsuspectingly,
I continued to call them 'grandma' and 'grandpa'.
They on their part, thinking perhaps that it would be
strange to change things suddenly, said nothing when
I called them this. They did not pet me as parents do
their youngest children. . . .I remember particularly that
my father treated me rather harshly. . . .One night,
the following incident took place. I was sleeping alone
in a room when I was awakened by someone calling
my name in a quiet voice. Frightened, I looked at the
figure crouching by my bedside. It was dark, so I could
not tell who it was. Being a child, I lay still and listened
to what the person had to say. Then I realised that the
voice belonged to our maid. In the darkness, the maid
whispered into my ear: 'These people that you think
are your grandfather and grandmother are really your
father and mother. I am telling you this because recently
I heard them saying that you must in some way have
sensed that they were your parents, since you seemed to
prefer this house to the other one. They were saying
how strange it was. You mustn't tell anybody that I
told you this. Understand?' All I said at the time was
'All right', but in my heart I was happy. I was happy
not because I had been told the truth, but because the
maid had been so kind to me.[1]

A variation of this revelation is found in Sōseki's only explicitly
autobiographical novel, *Grass on the Wayside* (*Michikusa*, 1915).
Here, of course, the characters bear fictitious names, though it is
clear that Kenzō stands for Sōseki (section 91):

To his father he was simply a nuisance. He would look
sometimes at the boy as though he could not quite
understand how such a mistake had been made. Kenzō
was hardly a child to him; rather, he was some
animate object that had wandered uninvited into his
household. And the love that was in Kenzō's expectant
heart was brutally pulled out by the roots and left to

wither in the cold. . . .

With too many children to take care of already, Kenzō's father was very reluctant to assume any responsibility for him. He had taken the boy back only because he was his son; he would feed him, but he was not going to spend a penny on him if he could help it. After all, he had thought that the boy was off his hands for good.

Besides, Shimada saw to it that Kenzō remained legally his adopted son. From his father's point of view, then, Kenzō was a bad risk; for what is the point of spending money on the lad when Shimada could come and take him away any time he wished? I'll feed him if I must, was his attitude, but let Shimada take care of the rest – it's his business.

Shimada was no less selfish. He was content to stand by and allow the situation to continue as long as it suited him. They won't let him starve, he assured himself; when he is old enough to earn some money, I'll get him back, even if it means going to court.

Kenzō had no home, either in the sea or the hills. A wandering creature that belonged nowhere, he found his food sometimes in the water and sometimes on land.

To his father and to Shimada both, he was not a person. To the former he was no more than an unwanted piece of furniture; to the latter, he was some kind of investment that might prove profitable at a later date.[2]

What both these accounts indicate is almost self-evident. First, we note his early deprivation of parental affection, which, according to Freudian psychology and common sense, can lead to immediate or later neurosis. In a sense, he was brought up as a spiritual orphan. Secondly, he could not feel that he belonged to either of these two families, and this insecurity may well have caused in him a split personality, a schizoid temperament if not genuine schizophrenia. Thirdly, the lack of parental affection must have fostered in him potential hatred towards his parents, which in turn may have aroused his own feelings of guilt. Fourthly, there is another fact that needs to be introduced. Sōseki's foster-father divorced his wife to marry his mistress.

The event together with the tensions that must have long existed between his foster-parents, no doubt implanted in the young Sōseki a potential incapacity to handle mature love relationships as well as a mistrust of marriage. That one or more of these affected Sōseki's psychological history goes without saying.

3

Sōseki was born just in time to receive primary school education under the system established in 1872. In 1879 he entered the first municipal secondary school of Tokyo, one of the major schools attended by a number of students who later became eminent in various fields including literature. In those days there were two kinds of secondary schools, *seisoku* (regular) and *hensoku* (irregular). It was only in the latter that English was taught. As the first municipal school was one of the former, Sōseki did not learn English, which was a prerequisite for entering university. For some unknown reason, he withdrew from the school in 1881, and then entered a private school, which, surprisingly enough, specialised in Chinese studies. His knowledge of Chinese, as shown in his composition of Chinese poems, was obtained in this period. He stayed only a year, however, and there is a gap of two years before he entered in 1883 another private institution which specialised in the teaching of English. In 1884 he was admitted to the preparatory course which automatically guaranteed admission to the University of Tokyo. In Tsubouchi Shōyō's time English literature was a part of the curriculum but there was no independent department of English at the University. By the time Sōseki entered the University in 1890, the Department of English had been established for some three years. Those who taught English literature to Shōyō had already left, but it was still taught by James Main Dixon (1856–1933), an Englishman who later became naturalised as an American, known as the author of such books as *Dictionary of Idiomatic English Phrases, Specially Designed for the Use of Japanese Students* and *English Letter-Writing*.

Apparently Sōseki was not very much inspired by Professor Dixon. As he later recalled ('My Individualism' ['Watakushi no Kojinshugi']):

> I had to read English, both verse and prose, in
> front of him [Dixon]. My composition was criticised

for its omission of articles where they should be.
My mispronunciation was severely corrected. In
examinations there were such questions as: When was
Wordsworth born and when did he die? How many
folio editions of Shakespeare's works are there? Write
the titles of all the works of Walter Scott in chronological
order. . . .How could one attain true understanding of
literature by answering these questions?. . .After three
years of study I could never understand literature.

Dixon, on the other hand, seems to have acknowledged Sōseki's
capability. In December 1892 he asked Sōseki to translate into
English Kamo no Chōmei's (1155–1216) *An Account of my Hut*
(*Hōjōki*, 1212) and later drew on this translation to deliver a
lecture entitled 'Chōmei and Wordsworth: A Literary Parallel'.
Dixon published this translation not under Sōseki's but his own
name. The celebrated opening paragraph reveals how skilled a
literary craftsman Sōseki already was in a foreign language he
had been studying for only about ten years:

Incessant is the change of water where the stream glides
on calmly: the spray appears over a cataract, yet
vanishes without a moment's delay. Such is the fate of
men in the world and of the houses in which they live.
Walls standing side by side, tilings vying with one
another in loftiness, these are from generations past the
abodes of high and low in a mighty town. But none of
them has resisted the destructive work of time. Some
stand in ruins: others are replaced by new structures.
Their possessors too share the same fate with them.
Let the place be the same, the people as numerous as
before, yet we can scarcely meet one out of every ten,
with whom we had long ago a chance of coming across.
We see our first light in the morning and return to our
long home next evening. Our destiny is like bubbles of
water. Whence do we come? Whither do we tend?
What ails us, what delights us in this unreal world?
It is impossible to say. A house with its master, which
passes away in a state of perpetual change, may well be
compared to a morning-glory with a dew drop upon it.
Sometimes the dew falls and the flower remains but

only to die in the first sunshine: sometimes the dew
survives the drooping flower, yet cannot live till the
evening.

Sōseki's capability is further attested to by two articles he wrote
while still a student: 'On the Poetry of Walt Whitman the
Egalitarian' ('Bundan ni okeru Byōdōshugi no Daihyōsha Walt
Whitman no Shi ni tsuite', 1892)[3] and 'The Concept of Nature
in English Poetry' ('Eikoku Shijin no Tenchisansen ni taisuru
Kan'nen', 1893).[4] Both of these were favourably received inside
and outside the university.

He stayed on at the university for half a year or so as a post-
graduate student after his graduation in 1893. Then he started
his career as a teacher of English at Tokyo Normal College, one
of the national institutions for training teachers at the secondary
school level. After teaching there for eighteen months, he resigned for some obscure reason, probably personal, and took up
a humble post as an English teacher at a provincial secondary
school in Matsuyama, Shikoku, for one year.[5] Naturally he found
nobody there with a comparable educational background, and his
stay proved unhappy. His experience, however, was later to provide him with the materials for his novel *Little Master* (*Botchan*,
1906). Next, he assumed the post of professor of English at the
Fifth National College in Kumamoto in Kyūshū. He had been
engaged to the daughter of the Chief Secretary of the House of
Peers and now their arranged marriage took place in Kumamoto.
Sōseki's blunt remarks to his bride – 'As I am a scholar, I must
study. I have no time to pay attention to you. I hope you will
understand this.'[6] – seem today like parodies of male chauvinism.
But their married life in those days was comparatively happy, and
apparently he did not exhibit towards her any sign of the repulsion, loneliness and alienation which were later to vitiate all his
human relationships and to constitute one of the major themes of
his novels.

As is still the case today with those teaching at national universities, Sōseki was awarded a grant by the Ministry of Education
to go to England for two years of study. These two years spent in
England proved significant in various ways. First, he was to
realise the inherent difficulties for any Japanese struggling to

study English literature. Secondly, the mental ailments, of which he had already suffered occasional fits, were to become more apparent during this period. Thirdly, two years' separation from his family was to change irretrievably his relationship with his wife.

He arrived in London in October 1900 after a long journey by sea and by land. At his temporary lodging, 76 Gower Street, London, he received from a Mrs Knot, mother of a missionary whom he had met in Kumamoto, a letter of introduction addressed to Charles Frere Andrews, Dean of Pembroke College, Cambridge.[7] On 1 November 1900 he went to Cambridge and stayed overnight to meet the Reverend Andrews on the following day. Here is his own account of the occasion (Preface to a *A Theory of Literature* [*Bungakuron*]):

> The first thing I had to do after landing was to decide where I should study. I was inclined to go to either Oxford or Cambridge, since they were centres of learning well-known even to us. Fortunately, I had a friend at Cambridge who invited me to visit him. And so I took the opportunity of going there to see what sort of place it was. Besides my friend, I met two or three Japanese there. They were all sons and younger brothers of wealthy merchants, who were prepared to spend thousands of yen per year in order to become 'gentlemen'. My allowance from the government was 1800 yen a year. In a place where money controlled everything, I could hardly hope to compete with these people. . . .I thought: my purpose in coming to England is different from that of these easygoing people; I do not know if the gentlemen of England are so impressive as to make it worth my while to imitate them; besides, having already spent my youth in the Orient, why should I now start learning how to conduct myself from these English gentlemen who are younger than I am?[8]

Thus he decided to go neither to Oxford nor to Cambridge. Nor did he choose Edinburgh as he thought that the English spoken there was equivalent to the northern Japanese dialect. In a way it suited Sōseki as a native of Edo to live in London. He found a lodging house at 85 Priory Road, West Hampstead.

In the meantime he contacted Professor W. P. Ker of University College. However, two months of attending Professor Ker's lectures bored him. Instead, he began to receive private lessons from Professor W. J. Craig, the famous editor of the older version of the Arden Shakespeare.

As time went on Sōseki came to feel more and more frustrated both academically and personally. As he later recalls (*ibid.*):

> On reflection, my knowledge of Chinese classics is not outstanding, yet I can fully appreciate them. My knowledge of English is not very deep, but it is not inferior to that of Chinese classics. If the same amount of knowledge produces such different results in each subject, it is owing simply to the different natures of each subject. In other words, Chinese literature and English literature are entirely different from each other and cannot be treated as of the same species.

This is just one example of Sōseki's many confessions of his declining confidence in his ability to study English. Furthermore, he even nurtured doubts of the sense of such an enterprise, even if it could be successful (letter to Terada Torahiko, 12 September 1901): 'If you want to be a scholar, you should choose a universal subject. English literature will be a thankless task: in Japan or in England, you'll never be able to hold up your head. It's a good lesson for a presumptuous man like me. Study physics.'[9] Coupled with this declining confidence in his study of English literature was his growing sense of inferiority about his identity as a Japanese. Nowhere do people become more conscious of their national identity than in a foreign country. As Sōseki says:

> The two years I spent in London were the most unpleasant two years of my life. Among English gentlemen, I lived miserably like a lost dog in a pack of wolves.
>
> (Preface to *A Theory of Literature*)

> Everyone I see in the street is tall and good-looking. That, first of all, intimidates me, embarrasses me. Sometimes I see an unusually short man, but he is still two inches taller than I am, as I compare his height with mine when we pass each other. Then I see a

dwarf coming, a man with an unpleasant complexion –
and he happens to be my own reflection in the shop
window. I don't know how many times I have laughed
at my own ugly appearance right in front of myself.
Sometimes, I even watched my reflection that laughed
as I laughed. And every time that happened, I was
impressed by the appropriateness of the term 'yellow
race'.

I was looking in a shop-window the other day when
a couple of women passed by, commenting on the 'least
poor Chinese' [Sōseki's phrase]. I was more amused
than angered by these expressions. . . .A few days ago
I went out in a frock coat with top-hat, and a couple
of working men sneered at me, saying 'a handsome
Jap'.

('A Letter from London' ['London Shōsoku']).

Here Sōseki is relieved by his detached sense of humour as self-
deprecating as it was accurate. But sometimes, his experiences
and reflections led him to far more morbid deprecation.

Talked with Brett. He said that the Japanese race needs
improvement, and that intermarriage with Westerners
should be encouraged for that purpose.

(*Diary*, 24 February 1901)

We are country bumpkins, nincompoop monkeys,
good-for-nothing ashen-coloured impenetrable people.
So it's natural the Westerners should despise us. Besides,
they don't know Japan, nor are they interested in Japan.
So even if we deserved their knowledge and respect,
there would be no respect or love, as long as they have
no time to know us and no eyes to see us.

(*Diary*, about April 1901)

Ironically enough, the period of Sōseki's stay in England coincided with the signing of the Anglo-Japanese Alliance of 1902.
But he could only have been aware of the chasm between the
military expediency of this Alliance and the cultural ignorance
and differences that separated the two countries.

Presumably, he must have realised the contradictions inherent
in his own career. Had he been a scholar of Japanese literature, he

might have felt more at ease, for there would have been no contradiction between the subject of his academic pursuit and his own national identity. In fact the problem was not so simple as that. It was his professional duty to improve his understanding of English literature, while such efforts at improvement made him increasingly aware of its difficulty and of the insecurity of his own cultural identity. Thus he experienced a split in his personality, or a cultural schizophrenia. More than a few modern Japanese intellectuals have found themselves in similar straits. But cursed with a particularly sensitive and perceptive mind, Sōseki must have been aware of his dilemmas more keenly than most other Japanese victims. Moreover, in his particular case his schizoid temperament was aggravated by the tensions in the cultural milieu in which he was enmeshed.

There is some evidence of the appearance of his psychic abnormalities during his London days. In August 1902, when one of his Japanese friends called on him at his lodgings,[10] Sōseki looked extremely melancholic and scarcely spoke a word to him. In fact, Sōseki himself spoke of his state as 'neurotic' in a letter to his wife dated 12 September. Another friend of his, the poet Tsuchii Bansui, discovered from Sōseki's landlady that 'he had been confining himself to his room for days on end and desperately crying in the dark'. Another friend, Okakura Yoshisaburō, the younger brother of the famous Okakura Kakuzō or Tenshin, sent a telegram to the Ministry of Education, saying 'Sōseki has gone mad.'[11] Sōseki's own words reveal his abnormality further: 'My landlady and her sister are very kind to me. But behind my back they speak ill of me. . . .Like detectives they are always spying on me.'[12] This abuse is nothing but a symptom of paranoia. Later, his kind landlady advised him to learn to ride a bicycle for physical exercise. Clumsy Sōseki had 'five major falls and innumerable minor falls',[13] only proving again to himself how ill-fitted he was for anything but being a Japanese scholar. He considered bicycle riding not a means of recreation but a torture maliciously invented by his landlady. His entire London stay amounted to a prolonged trauma that haunted his thoughts even years later. One day, while sitting face to face with his eldest daughter beside a charcoal brazier in his Tokyo home, he suddenly hit the girl in a fit of fury on finding a coin on the edge of the brazier. One may wonder at the irrationality of his impulsive behaviour. But, within the context of the late Victorian London he had suffered and remembered, his slap was capable of rational explanation. For, during his London years, he had once given a penny to a beggar. On returning to his lodging house, he found a penny on the window sill in the bathroom. Immediately he imagined that the landlady had espied his act of generosity and laid the same kind of coin in the bathroom to ridicule him. He recalled this string of events when he saw a coin on the edge of the brazier, and in his phantasy he identified his poor little girl with his English landlady as a persecutor. London was a mental prison he could never fully escape, even in Tokyo.

On his return to Japan he did not go back to the Fifth National College in Kumamoto but took up a post of teaching English at the First National College and concurrently a lectureship in the English Department at the University of Tokyo. The latter appointment involved a complicated situation. His predecessor was the celebrated Lafcadio Hearn, then a naturalised Japanese citizen under the name of Koizumi Yagumo. For no stated reason he was dismissed by the Ministry of Education, which by now was implementing its policy of purifying the faculties of Japanese national universities by closing doors to all non-native academics. Sōseki himself had a very high opinion of Lafcadio Hearn and indeed had a guilty conscience about replacing him. Besides, the students were hostile to Sōseki, at least initially. Thus, the circumstances in which he began teaching at the University of Tokyo were far from pleasant. However, he soon proved himself to be an excellent lecturer and attracted responsive audiences, much larger than those of Ueda Bin, the famous translator of French symbolist poetry, who at that time was also lecturing at the University of Tokyo. Out of Sōseki's lectures, on a variety of authors from Shakespeare to George Eliot, grew two substantial critical works, *A Theory of Literature* (*Bungakuron*, 1907) and *Literary Criticism* (*Bungaku Hyōron*, 1909).

Of these two critical works the former is a product of the painstaking effort that he made in London in the midst of his neurosis. As touched upon above, Sōseki was seriously worried about the difficulties that confronted him and Japanese students of English literature in general. The cultural barrier that existed between England and Japan undeniably prevented Japanese students from understanding English literature with the same ease and sensitiveness as English scholars did. Japanese students might follow in the wake of English scholars and study English literature, adopting their methods of approach to it, but so long as they did this, they would never overtake English scholars. The alternatives, then, would be either to express a uniquely personal view or to establish some objective standard similar to that of science. In conceiving of a plan to systematise literature in analogy to science, Sōseki was probably inspired by the frequent dialogues he had with Dr Ikeda Kikunae, a Japanese chemist, who was also studying in London at the time. In *A Theory of Literature* Sōseki thus tried hard to lay down a scientific theory of literature. The product that he made available to us is not very successful, but still his intention should be appreciated. In *Literary Criticism*, too, Sōseki is as keenly aware of the difficulties confronting Japanese students of English literature. However, while *A Theory of Literature* consists of a theoretical system, *Literary Criticism* is a survey of eighteenth-century English literature, dealing with individual authors such as Addison and Steele, Jonathan Swift, Alexander Pope and Daniel Defoe. Of these writers especially important to Sōseki is Swift, with whom he shares a deep-seated misanthropism and pungent satire. *Literary Criticism* differs from *A Theory of Literature* in another respect. In *A Theory of Literature* Sōseki aims at scientific objectivity, while in *Literary Criticism* he boldly expresses his personal and Japanese views although he incorporates, where relevant, English scholarship with exemplary exactitude. In brief, he demonstrated here an attitude which he was later to call 'inner-directed'.[14]

In the meantime Sōseki was publishing a few novels and stories of varying lengths, some of which will be discussed shortly. Throughout this period his neurosis harassed him continuously. Apart from the discord with his wife, he was plagued by his incurable scepticism about the significance of his English studies. Although this anxiety from his London days was never to be resolved once and for all, a solution, at least partial, came from outside the university. The *Asahi Shimbun* offered to serialise one novel a year in its daily paper. No longer did he have to worry about the many limitations to which he and other Japanese scholars of English literature were subject. Now he could create literature in his own language and thus directly partake of the creative literary life of his capital. Besides, his knowledge of English literature would prove highly beneficial for his new trade.

4

During the last ten years of his life, from about the age of forty, Sōseki produced more than a dozen long novels and some shorter works of varying content and form. Some results of his experiences in Britain and his knowledge of English literature are projected into the earlier works written before he resigned from the university. 'The Tower of London' ('Rondon-tō', 1905) and 'The Carlyle House' ('Kārairu Hakubutsukan', 1905), for instance, are the by-products of his stay in London. 'The Tower of London' is a short piece narrated with historical and topographical accuracy. For the pathetic episode of the little princes murdered by order of Richard III Sōseki is indebted to Shakespeare's play and for the figure of an executioner to W. H. Ainsworth's *The Tower of London*. Even more interesting than these historical details, however, is the way in which Sōseki fuses the past and the present. Such an ingenious overlapping of a real character with a historical figure in the story effects the willing suspension of disbelief in the reader's mind. In the same year Sōseki wrote two stories with their settings in the times of King Arthur, 'A Shield of Phantom' ('Gen'ei no Tate') and 'An Elegy' ('Kairo-kō'). The latter is indebted to Malory's *Morte Darthur* and Tennyson's *Idylls of the King*. Sōseki's tale, however, differs from these sources in stressing the sinfulness of Lancelot's and Guinevere's illicit love and their consequent deaths. It seems possible that under the guise of medieval romance Sōseki represented the theme of tangled love relations and associated states which he was to elaborate in his later realistic novels.[15]

The striking feature of *I am a Cat* (*Wagahai wa Neko de Aru*, 1905-6) is that the whole novel is narrated by a cat. Consequently, Sōseki very amusingly tricks, or forces, us to look at the world through the eyes of this cat. The model for this omniscient creature was his own cat, which had strayed into his house and became the family pet. Likewise, the cat's master named Kushami-sensei or Professor Sneeze is a self-caricature of Sōseki, whom the cat wryly observes in a self-detached tone rare in modern Japanese novels. The following, for instance, is the cat's account of Professor Sneeze (chapter 1):

> My master seldom comes face to face with me. I hear
> he is a schoolteacher. As soon as he comes home from
> school, he shuts himself up in the study for the rest of
> the day; and he seldom emerges. The others in the
> house think that he is terribly hardworking. He himself
> pretends to be hardworking. But actually he works
> less than any of them think. Sometimes I tiptoe to his
> study for a peep and find him taking a snooze.
> Occasionally his mouth is drooping onto some book
> he has begun to read. He has a weak stomach and his
> skin is of a pale yellowish colour, inelastic and lacking
> in vitality. Nevertheless he is an enormous gormandiser.
> After eating a great meal, he takes some takadiastase
> for his stomach and, after that, he opens a book. When
> he has read a few pages, he becomes sleepy. He drools
> onto the book. This is the routine religiously observed
> each evening. There are times when even I, a mere cat,
> can put two thoughts together. 'Teachers have it easy.
> If you are a human, it's the best to become a teacher.
> For if it's possible to sleep this much and still to be a
> teacher, why, even a cat could teach.' However,
> according to the master, there's nothing harder than a
> teacher's life and every time his friends come round
> to see him, he grumbles on and on.[16]

Other characters are the professor's friend Meitei (or a cottage for the lost or stray), and the professor's ex-pupil Kangetsu (the winter moon). These ineffectual intellectuals and dilettantes contrast with an upstart millionaire named Kaneda (money field). Kaneda's daughter is courted by Kangetsu. Kaneda would not approve of the courtship unless Kangetsu obtained his Ph.D. for his research on how to grind a glass ball to the right degree of convexity. The courtship, as might have been predicted, falls through because there is little room for reconciliation between the ineffectual sophistication of dilettante intellectuals and the acquisitive utilitarianism of the Kaneda coinage. Apart from this interplay there is very little development of the plot, and the whole novel consists of a series of episodes combined by free association

as in Laurence Sterne's *Tristram Shandy*.[17] Sōseki's indebtedness
to this novel is also illustrated by his reference to the discussion of
'nose' (*Tristram Shandy*, Book iv, chapters 31 and 32), which is
likely to have incited a satire on Mrs Kaneda's big nose (chapter
4). Similar allusions to English literature are innumerable all
through *I am a Cat*. A striking feature of this novel is the fact
that the hostility between the professor's circle and the surround-
ing world, which otherwise could be depressing, is enveloped by
the sense of humour permeating the rest of the novel. While
writing this novel, Sōseki suffered from persistent neurotic melancholy. Obviously repression is a conscious method of containing
melancholy. But humour, as Freud noted, is a less conscious and
more automatic mechanism of defence against depression.[18] This
literary and psychological device is exactly what Sōseki exercises
in *I am a Cat*, a novel which, by virtue of its narrative technique,
has no distinguished equivalent in modern Japanese literature.

Humour is also the keynote of *Little Master* (*Botchan*, 1906).
The hero is a teacher of mathematics arriving from Tokyo at a
school in Matsuyama where Sōseki once taught English. But, unlike Sōseki and Professor Sneeze, the main characteristic of the
protagonist of *Little Master* is not intellectual sophistication but
a straightforward, and even reckless, bravado with which he
fights for justice and against hypocrisy. Perhaps Quixotic is a
suitable epithet for his character and behaviour. In this novel
Sōseki is very skilled at vividly depicting the crudity, vulgarity,
absurdity and boredom of life at a local school, from which the
hero becomes more and more alienated. At the end of the novel
the hero confronts his enemy, the deputy headmaster nicknamed
Akashatsu (red shirt), coming out of a brothel, and thus exposes
his hypocrisy. Instead of berating this pedant, the hero gives
'red shirt' a gratifying thrashing. Consequently, the little master
resigns his post and goes back to Tokyo. Despite their obvious
differences in other respects, the hero shares with Sōseki at least
a deep sense of justice and outrage against hypocrisy. If Professor
Sneeze is a caricature of Sōseki the introverted scholar, the hero of
Little Master is perhaps a projection of the other side of Sōseki's
character, a moral integrity, striking furiously against bureaucrats
and other meddling fools.

Pillow of Grass (*Kusamakura*, 1906) is a novel entirely different in kind from the two playful works just discussed. Sōseki calls

it 'a novel in the manner of a *haiku*',[19] or in more general terms one may call it 'a poem in prose'. The narrator is a painter, who leaves Tokyo for a remote mountain village to paint its scenery. The novel consists of the painter's reflections on art, scenic descriptions, encounters with people such as a Zen priest, and Nami, the daughter at the inn where he stays. The whole work is pervaded by some kind of ethereal other-worldliness stemming partly from the inherent qualities of the objects described and partly from the artistic detachment with which the painter eyes his subjects including Nami. While preoccupied with memories of his past, the narrator is pleased to be awakened from his reverie by the arrival of an unexpected visitor when in his bath (chapter 7):

> The dark shape descended to the next step without a
> sound, making it seem that the stone underfoot was as
> soft as velvet. Indeed, anyone judging from the
> sound would have been excused for thinking that there
> had been no movement at all. The shimmering outline
> had now become a little more clearly discernible. Being
> an artist, I have an unusually good sense of perception
> concerning the structure of the human body, and no
> sooner had this unknown person moved down a step
> than I realised that I was alone in the bathroom with a
> woman.
>
> I was still floating there, trying to decide whether
> or not to give any indication of having seen her,
> when quite suddenly and without any reserve
> she appeared directly before me. She stood there
> surrounded by swirling eddies of mist into which
> the gentle light suffused a rose-tinted warmth,
> and the sight of her lithe and upright figure, crowned
> with billowing clouds of jet-black hair, drove all
> thoughts of good manners, civility and propriety out
> of my head. My whole being was filled with the
> realisation that I had discovered a beautiful artistic
> subject.[20]

In common with some poems by the English pre-romantic and romantic poets, this episode creates in its description of a woman something at once tangible and intangible:

Just then, however, her thick blue-black hair streamed around her with a swish like the tail of some gigantic legendary turtle cleaving through the waves. Next moment her white figure was flying up the steps tearing through the veils of mist. A clear peal of feminine laughter rang out in the corridor and gradually echoed away into the distance, leaving the bathroom quiet again. The water washed over my face, so I stood up. As I did so, startled waves lapped against my chest, and splashed noisily over the sides of the tank.

The name Nami, written in Chinese characters, can signify beauty. The painter's relationship to Nami as portrayed so far suggests that beauty is an elusive entity which becomes intangible at the very moment when it looks tangible. Nami is thus presented in a heightened tension between the tangible and intangible, concrete and abstract, real and unreal, and image and idea. Word is going about that she is a divorcée and insane. She is fused with her ancestor who drowned herself in the 'mirror pond' as well as the legendary 'maid of Nagara' who also drowned herself after having been loved by two men. The female figure that emerges from these amalgamated characters shares with Shakespeare's Ophelia the fate of broken love, madness and death by water. So in creating Nami, Sōseki probably had in mind the picture of drowned Ophelia painted by J. E. Millais. There are other sources which might also have influenced Sōseki. The phantom-like song, probably sung by Nami, which the painter hears half awake and half dreaming (chapter 3), is reminiscent of that sung by Winnifred on Mt Snowdon in Watts-Dunton's *Aylwin* (chapter 3, section 4) as well as that sung by Sandra in Meredith's *Sandra Belloni* (chapter 2). Another reference to Meredith is found in chapter 9, where the painter reads to Nami a passage from *Beauchamp's Career*, chapter 8, in which against the background of Venice at dusk Renée and Nevil spend their last evening together before parting company. The pathos evoked by these young lovers not only corresponds to the elusive sentiment enveloping Nami and the painter but also foreshadows the compassion that Nami later feels towards her cousin and her divorced husband, both departing for Manchuria. Towards the end of the novel, a way is prepared for the painter to be brought back to mundane reality. While contemplating the village landscape from a hill, he happens to witness Nami handing over a purse to a shabbily dressed stranger. Nami and the stranger part company. The painter pretends not to have noticed them. But then (chapter 12):

'Sensei. Sensei,' she called.

O Lord, that's done it, I thought, and wondered when she first realised that I was there.

'Yes, what do you want?' I asked, raising my head above the quince and losing my hat in the process.

'What on earth are you doing there?'

'I was lying down composing poetry.'

'Don't tell fibs. You were watching what happened just now, weren't you?'

'Just now? Just now, over there, you mean? Well, yes. I did just have a peep.'

'Ha, ha, ha, ha. You should have had a long look.'

'Well, to tell you the truth – I did.'

. . . . . .

'You should be happy-go-lucky wherever you are. If you're not, life isn't worth living. Take me for instance: I'm not at all ashamed that you were watching me just now.'

'You have no reason to be, have you?'

'Perhaps not. What do you think of that man I was with?'

'Well now, let me see. I'd say that whoever he was, he wasn't very rich.'

'Ha, ha, ha. You've hit the nail right on the head. You must be psychic. He came to get some money from me, because he says that he's so poor he cannot remain in Japan any longer'.

'Really? Where had he come from?'

'From down in the castle-town.'

'That's quite a way. And where is he off to?'

'It seems that he is set on going to Manchuria.'

'What for?'

'Who knows. To get some money maybe, or perhaps to die.'

As she said this, I raised my eyes and glanced at her
face. Her mouth was set in a thin line, and the faint
smile which usually hovered there was, for some
unknown reason, beginning to fade.
'He is my husband.'

In the last scene of the novel people go to the station to see
Nami's cousin off, a conscript about to be sent off to Manchuria
to fight in the Russo-Japanese War. When the departing train
passes alongside the platform, Nami notices her husband is also
on the train. They gaze upon each other for an instant; an instant
which becomes an epiphany when 'compassion' betrays itself on
her face. And the painter cries out, 'That's it! That's it! That
makes a picture!' His journey to the village has been a conscious
escape from the real to the ethereal. The whole process is now
reversed, as, through this 'picture', he is made ready to return to
the reality of Tokyo. Similarly Sōseki returned by leaving behind
the quasi-romantic world of *Pillow of Grass* and moving to the
more realistic one of *Autumn Wind* (*Nowaki*, 1907).

In *Autumn Wind* Sōseki contrasts Nakano who represents the
social establishment, with two poor and socially alienated outsiders, Shirai and Takayanagi. Shirai devoutly believes in the
cause of social reform, whereas Takayanagi, tubercular and depressed, is merely bitter about his own unhappiness. At the close
of the novel Nakano offers Takayanagi a hundred yen so that
he may leave Tokyo for a change of air. After persistently declining the offer, Takayanagi eventually takes it on the condition
that Nakano will accept the novel he will write during his
absence. Takayanagi then visits Shirai to say farewell. He finds
Shirai pestered by a money lender, presents Shirai with the
hundred yen, and in return takes with him the unpublished
manuscript of Shirai's novel. The ending thus suggests Takayanagi's imminent death and his inability to fulfil his literary
ambition vicariously through his friend's work. A further explanation of a psychological nature is possible. Both Shirai and
Takayanagi are alienated from society; but for Shirai the existing
world is unreal or 'derealised' while he preserves his integral self.
In Takayanagi's case, it is not only the external world but his
self that is unreal. In other words, Takayanagi suffers a dissolu-
tion of his self, a loss Shirai has never experienced. This pair of

characters may tell us of the conflict in Sōseki's own mind. Takayanagi may partly be a product of Sōseki's own sense of alienation and insecurity, which, however, he had to surmount like Shirai; such was the task Sōseki imposed on himself by choosing the career of a professional writer.

Wild Poppy (*Gubijinsō*, 1907), Sōseki's first novel serialised in the *Asahi Shimbun*, draws heavily on English literature for the characterisation and plot convention. Fujio, the arrogant and self-centred heroine who is proud of her own beauty and eventually commits suicide, is modelled on Cleopatra, the philosopher Kōno, her half-brother, on Hamlet and his friend Munechika on Horatio. The echoes of Meredith are also obvious. The fate of Ono, who nearly forsakes his fiancée Sayoko for Fujio the enchantress, resembles Sir Willoughby Patterne in Meredith's *The Egoist*; Patterne forsakes Letitia Dale for Constantia Durham, then asks for Clara Middleton's hand and having been rejected he finally returns to Letitia. And the abortive plan for Ono and Fujio to meet at a railway station has a parallel in *Diana of the Crossways* when relations are disrupted between Percy Dacier and Diana Warwick as a result of Diana having kept Percy waiting in vain (chapter 26). Far from enriching the novel these echoes from English literature are responsible for the stereotyped characterisation.

Sanshirō (1908), *And Then. . .* (*Sorekara*, 1909) and *The Gate* (*Mon*, 1910) are regarded as Sōseki's trilogy. *Sanshirō* may be compared with Tsubouchi Shōyō's *The Temperament of Present-Day Students*, for both deal with the life of university students. However, the comparison is not very fruitful, as Sōseki's novel is in every respect by far the superior one. The plot is more authentic, characterisation more realistic, and the underlying philosophy more profound. Some of the characters in *Sanshirō* are modelled partly on the people who gathered round Sōseki as his disciples from 1905 onwards. The scientist Nonomiya is based on Terada Torahiko, who later became a professor of physics at the University of Tokyo as well as a talented essayist. Sanshirō himself derives from Morita Sōhei, a novelist, whose affair with Hiratsuka Raichō, the original Japanese blue-stocking, caused a big sensation. Mineko, a beautiful and sophisticated girl, who thwarts Sanshirō's innocent love, may owe something to the image of Miss Hiratsuka. Professor Hirota, nicknamed 'Great Darkness', is the guardian figure just as Sōseki himself was the mentor to about a dozen protégés. The novel centres round Sanshirō's innocent but unrequited love for Mineko. In some respects the novel is like a comedy of manners, but its ultimate theme proves to be a tragic one. There is nothing intentional about Mineko's thwarting of Sanshirō's naïve affection, nor is there any bitterness in the latter's reaction to his lost love. Yet Mineko herself refers to her act as a kind of guilt (chapter 12), quoting a line from the Book of Psalms: 'For I acknowledge my transgressions: and my sin *is* ever before me' (Psalm 51, 3). Mineko's sense of guilt about jilting Sanshirō complements what lies behind Professor Hirota's celibacy. Towards the end of the novel Hirota tells Sanshirō about the difficulty for some people to marry (chapter 11):

> 'What kind of men?'
> 'Well, for example – ', he began to say, then became silent. He continued to puff at his cigarette. 'Here's a man, a certain fellow I know. His father died early, and he grew up relying on his mother. Then she became ill. Just before she died, she called him to her bedside and told him to go to Mr. X for help after her death. The boy had never heard of this man. He asked her why he should go to him rather than someone else. She said nothing. He asked again. Finally, in a faint voice she said that Mr. X was his real father. – It's only a story, of course, but let's assume that such a man exists. Wouldn't you say that he would quite naturally have little faith in marriage?'
> 'I doubt that there are many such men.'
> 'No, there aren't many, but they do exist.'
> 'But sir, you are not one of them?'
> He laughed.[21]

Thus from *Sanshirō* emerges the theme of man's vulnerability in love relationships, which is reiterated in the other two works of the trilogy.

In the second of the trilogy, *And Then. . .*, the tragedy originates from two men loving one woman, just as in a later work, *Kokoro*. In the earlier novel Daisuke renounces love for the sake of his friend Hiraoka, but within a few years all three find themselves unhappy. Daisuke, noticing that there no longer exists any love between his friend and his wife, asks his friend to give her away. Daisuke's conduct angers his father whose dependant he has been right up to the age of thirty. At the end of the novel, Daisuke's life has come adrift. Disowned now by his father and looking for a job, he is still seeking to obtain his friend's wife. Daisuke is thus a rebel against the social code of the late Meiji period in two respects, first in his determination to marry the wife of his friend and secondly in his unwillingness to put his talents to the use of society. Though immoral from the point of view of society, he is nevertheless true to his heart's desires and embodies some kind of moral integrity. He is in this sense a descendant of those apparently superfluous characters whose prototype is Utsumi Bunzō in Futabatei Shimei's *The Drifting Clouds*.[22] Daisuke represents Sōseki's awareness of a tragic situation in late Meiji Japan, where the chasm between the moral vision of the ineffectual intellectuals and the rapidly 'modernised' society was becoming ever greater.

What would have happened to Daisuke and Michiyo later? This question is dealt with in the third of the trilogy, *The Gate*, in which the protagonist Sōsuke has betrayed his friend Yasui by snatching away his wife O-Yone. Sōseki begins the story in *medias res* and only halfway through gives a minimal and retrospective account of how Sōsuke betrayed Yasui. As a consequence of his act of betrayal Sōsuke suffers from insecurity, both social and psychological. With only limited prospects in his career as a low-rank bureaucrat he is another example of a character who feels himself redundant. His psychological insecurity is apparent from various symptoms such as his Freudian slip of memory in his failure to recall a certain ideogram (chapter 1) and his feeling of unreality (chapter 2):

> Daily he rode on the streetcar to and from work,
> passing morning and evening through the bustling
> streets. But he was always so fatigued in mind and body
> that he travelled in a daze, completely unaware of his
> surroundings. Recently he had even lost consciousness
> of the fact that he was living in the midst of so much
> activity. He was so busy usually that he did not have

time to think about it, but when the seventh day of the
week came round, the day of holiday, and he had a
chance to rest and compose himself, he would suddenly
become aware of the nervous tension of his daily life.
When he reflected that though he lived in the heart
of Tokyo, he had never really taken a good look at
the city, a strange melancholy would come over him.[23]

That Sōsuke and O-Yone are doomed by their guilt is suggested
by a fortune-teller's prediction about O-Yone's sterility due to
'a terrible deed' done to another (chapter 14). Curiously ironical
is the fact that they become tied to each other even more firmly by
their guilt, while they are inevitably alienated from society
(chapter 14):

It was natural that their lives could not escape monotony.
They were not prey to the disasters that fall upon those
who live in a complicated society, but by the same token
they denied themselves the opportunity to experience
directly the variety that life in normal society offers.
While living in the city, it was as if they had turned their
backs on the privileges accorded to cultural city people.
Occasionally they were keenly aware of the lack of
variety in their daily lives. They never experienced the
slightest feeling of boredom with one another or desire
for more than they possessed, and yet each had a clear
realization that the rhythm of their lives was too jejune
and lacking in stimulation. That they had spent these
long years in daily repetition of the same routine,
however, was not because they had from the first lost
all interest in the outside world, but rather because this
world had placed them in isolation, then turned its
cold back upon them. They were not left the space to
turn outwards and grow, and so they faced inwards and
sank their roots ever deeper and deeper. What their
life lost in breadth it thereby gained in depth. For these
six years they had not sought to establish and maintain
a relationship with the world about them, but had
explored instead each other's hearts. In the course of
time they had succeeded in penetrating deeply into each
other's inner being. To outsiders, they were as ever,

separate; but to themselves, they had become one,
completely indivisible in mind and heart. They were
like two drops of oil that have dripped on to the surface
of a large basin of water. The drops do not come
together to repel the water; it is more accurate to say
that the pressure of the water forces them to adhere to
each other, making it impossible for either to get away.

The bond between Sōsuke and O-Yone is jeopardised in isolation from society. Having little contact with the external world, Sōsuke is bound to lose enthusiasm for life. Of the two characters O-Yone looks more sympathetic in her solicitude for Sōsuke and in her willingness to cheer him up. But her life, too, is darkened by her declining health – an apparent consequence of their guilt.

The insecurity of Sōsuke's life can also be attributed to another factor beyond his control. He lost his father while still a child, and then his uncle's mismanagement dissipated the legacy to which he and his younger brother Koroku were entitled. The theme of betrayal converges in Sōsuke, who is at once the betrayed and the betrayer. His inability to cope adequately with the financial plight caused by the mismanaged legacy contributes to a tense relationship between him and his brother Koroku. Sōsuke's insecurity is aggravated by the news of Yasui's return from Manchuria where he has been in self-imposed exile. He seeks in vain to attain enlightenment by means of Zen practice (chapter 2):

He had come here to have the gate opened to him, but its
warden had remained obstinately within, and had not
so much as shown his face, however long he knocked.
The only greeting he had received was, 'It's no use
knocking. Open the gate yourself and enter.' He had
thought how he might unbolt the gate, and he had
formulated a clear plan in his head. But he had been
incapable finally of developing in himself the power to
achieve his purpose. He was standing now in exactly
the same spot in which he had stood before he had
even begun to search for a solution. He was left
standing before the closed door, ignorant and impotent.
Through the years he had relied solely upon his own
powers of discretion. It was cruelly ironic that it should

be this very self-reliant discretion that had proved to
be a curse to him now. In his present mood he envied
the unsubtle simplicity of the fool, who follows a course
of action without having to weigh the possibilities or
puzzle over the means; and he looked with near
reverence upon the dedication of the simple good men
and women who were firmly anchored in their beliefs
and undisturbed by intellectual doubts. It seemed to
him that he had been fated from birth to stand forever
outside the gate, unable to pass through. There was
nothing he could do about it. But if the gate were
really impassable, then it had been a contradiction to
come here in the first place. He looked behind him and
he lacked the courage to retrace his steps along the
road he had come. He looked ahead at the firmly-bolted
door that would never open to reveal the view beyond.
He was not a man, then, to pass through, nor was he
yet one who could be content to remain on the outside.
In short, he was a poor unfortunate doomed to squat
before the gate waiting for night to fall.

Sōseki so constructs this novel that the passage of time from
autumn to winter coincides with the aggravation of Sōsuke's
insecurity and O-Yone's declining health. At the end of the novel
O-Yone celebrates with a touch of hope the coming of spring, to
which Sōsuke responds only with anticipation of another winter:
'Yes, but it will be winter again.'

Sōseki's concern with the theme of the difficulty of communication between individuals reappears in the novels he wrote in his
last years. In *The Wayfarer* (*Kōjin*, 1912–13), for instance, the
protagonist Ichirō is tantalised by his wish and inability to love
and to be loved heart and soul by his wife Nao. He represents the
type of unhappy intellectual whose abstract attitude to life lacks
emotional suppleness. Alienating and alienated from Nao, Ichirō
even becomes susceptible to a paranoiac phantasy that Nao bears
illicit love desires towards his younger brother Jirō. When Ichirō
asks Jirō to test her by giving her an opportunity to let her heart
out, Jirō declines his brother's request, but at least agrees to talk
to Nao so that her relationship with Ichirō could be improved.

To this end Jirō and Nao spend a day at a seaside resort. The action of the novel is imbued with a dramatic intensity when an unexpected storm forces them to stay overnight together at an inn. This unexpected storm serves effectively as an objective correlative to a potential upsurge of emotion. Left to themselves Jirō and Nao could, if they wished, allow Ichirō's paranoiac phantasy about their illicit love to materialise. This novel then could be linked with the earlier works in which Sōseki dealt with triangular love relationships. *The Wayfarer*, however, clearly differs from the earlier works. In *The Gate*, for instance, the protagonists become alienated from society through their guilt but the emotional ties between them are strengthened as a result. By contrast, in *The Wayfarer* Jiro's virtuousness prevents him from committing a sin with Nao but this does not facilitate communication between them, nor does it improve the relationship of Nao with her husband.

In *The Wayfarer* Sōseki provides an interesting psychological study. That Ichirō is suffering from acute neurosis is obvious from part II, 'Brother'. This is further confirmed in part III, 'After the Return' and part IV, 'Anguish'. In part III, section 22, Jirō declares decisively: 'My report will never provide substance for the phantasy that you entertain. It is a phantasy created in your mind with no objective existence.' There is also the students' report conveyed to Mr H about Ichirō's peculiarity in the lecture hall, which suggests his neurosis (part III, section 30). Part IV, which consists in the main of Mr H's letter, ultimately reveals and confirms Ichirō's abnormal state of mind (section 31):

> Your brother is frustrated, for he thinks whatever he does, no matter how, becomes neither his end nor his means. He is completely insecure; as a result he cannot stay still. He gets up because he cannot sleep in peace, so he contends. Once he gets up, he cannot stand being merely awake, so he walks. Once he walks he cannot just keep walking, so he runs. And once he starts running he cannot stop no matter where he may run. Not only must he not stop anywhere, but he cannot help accelerating his speed every moment. And he says it frightens him to imagine what it will ultimately

lead to; he says it is so frightening that he breaks into a cold sweat. Yes, he says it is unbearably frightening.[24]

And Ichirō's own words as quoted in Mr H's letter (section 12):

Man's insecurity stems from the advance of science. Never once has science, which never ceases to move forward, allowed us to pause. From walking to ricksha, from ricksha to carriage, from carriage to train, from train to automobile, from there on to the dirigible, further on to the aeroplane, and further on and on – no matter how far we may go, it won't let us take a breath. How far it will sweep us along, nobody knows for sure. It is really frightening.

It emerges from these passages that by the word 'wayfarer' is meant a person who is eternally harassed by the lack of purpose in life, by perpetual insecurity and by estrangement from external reality. According to Mr H's account, Ichirō seems to want desperately both to maintain his individuality and to unite with other individuals (part 4, section 36): 'How far do your mind and mine meet together and from where do they part?' A struggle is going on within Ichirō's own mind (section 39): 'But it is his mind which interrupts, as well as his mind which is interrupted; in the last analysis he is controlled by these two minds which accuse each other from morning till night just as a wife and her mother-in-law might. As a consequence he cannot have even momentary peace.' Mr H's account in the last quotation suggests that Ichirō's state is almost schizophrenic.

Part 1 of *The Wayfarer* consists of episodes which at first sight seem irrelevant to the main action of the novel: the reunion in Osaka of Jirō and his parents with their former maid servant now married to their former houseboy; Jirō's arrangement to meet his friend Misawa; and Misawa's hospitalisation due to a stomach ulcer. These episodes, however, justify their inclusion by intricately linking up to the central theme of the novel. Take, for instance, Misawa's infatuation with a geisha girl (also hospitalised for stomach trouble) solely because she resembles an insane relative of his who was under his parents' guardianship after her marriage broke up. Every morning this insane woman used to see Misawa off on his way to work with a most touching farewell.

There was no knowing whether she really cared for him or in her derangement took Misawa for her divorced husband and so expressed her ungratified love. The subject in fact is discussed by the brothers in part II (section 12):

'In a word, whether that woman really cared for Misawa as he seems to have thought she did, or whether in her insanity she had merely begun voicing all that she had tried in vain to convey to her husband – which do you think was the case?'

'There are a lot of things people ordinarily just can't speak their mind about – for the sake of decency or obligation, much as they may like to.'

'Now, let's suppose that the woman is a victim of this type of insanity. Then all that ordinary sense of propriety would completely vanish. And if so, she could then speak her mind freely, regardless of the consequences. Looked at this way what she said to Misawa ought to be far more sincere and genuine than the usual empty civilities.'

'Ah, then can we never find out what a woman really is like, unless we make her insane?' sighed my brother painfully.

Later, in part III, while reflecting on the episode of the mad woman, Jirō hits upon an idea (section 31):

I began to see that it was possible that my brother might wish his wife to suffer from such insanity so that she might also lay bare her inmost thoughts which perplexed him. But to outsiders, he himself might rather seem to be becoming insane. Indeed, with his mind deranged as a result of his nervous breakdown, he might go wild and rave through the house shouting all kinds of terrifying things.

Indeed, Ichirō himself is aware that madness would be one of the ultimate solutions for his predicament (part IV, section 39):

'To die, to go mad, or to enter religion – these are the only three courses left open for me.'

'And yet I do not think I can possibly enter religion;

nor can I take my life, being too much attached to it.
That leaves me only one way out – madness.'

There thus coexist at once a similarity and a difference between
Ichirō and the mad woman. The latter, suffering from a pathological case of insanity, is not subject to suppression imposed
either by herself or by the society. Ichirō, who suffers from
neurosis, is subject to every possible kind of repression and is
therefore in a much more unbearable state of mind. Released
from reason as a moral censor, insanity could liberate the mind
as well as embody potential immorality. Reason, on the other
hand, should be the core of the integrated personality of a free
individual and yet when exercised too rigorously as in someone
like Ichirō, it can no longer be adequate.

The contents of *The Wayfarer* cannot be discussed separately
from the novel's structure. It centres round the psychology of
alienation in neurotic Ichirō. Sōseki has so deftly constructed the
novel that it contains multiple points of view, even though
throughout the novel Jirō serves as the narrator. The episode of
the mad woman in part I, for instance, is meant to parallel and
contrast with Ichirō's state of mind. Part II leads up to the
dramatic situation in which Jirō as the narrative point of view
becomes fully involved in the task of investigating unsuccessfully
what Nao really feels towards Ichirō. Jirō continues to function as
the point of view in part III. The last twenty-five chapters in
part IV consist of the letters written by Mr H, who accompanies
Ichirō on his trip. While revealing the symptoms of Ichirō's acute
neurosis, they also show the limits of Jirō's knowledge and understanding. There is therefore every reason for Mr H to supplement
what has been narrated by Jirō. Because of the complexities of
Ichirō's psychological state, it is natural for the author to adopt
these multiple points of view without imposing an interpretation
of his own. Looked at in this way *The Wayfarer* is an example
of Sōseki's experiment with the psychological novel, a form which
he developed in *Kokoro* and finally in *Light and Darkness*.

In *Kokoro* (*Kokoro*, 1914) Sōseki abandons the position of
an omniscient author and has the first two parts narrated by a
first person. The third part consists of the suicide note of Sensei,
the mentor of the narrator for the first two parts. Sōseki constructs the novel so that the conflicts of value in the narrator's

mind coincide with the bifocal structure of the novel. The narrator is attracted to Sensei because of his intelligence and sage-like detachment from the world. In Sensei Sōseki has created another of those characters who is intellectually powerful but socially ineffectual. The narrator's parents are a kind of landed gentry of the provincial countryside who can conceive of his future career in nothing but pragmatic terms. Just when his own father is lying on his death-bed, the narrator receives by post a thick envelope containing Sensei's suicide note. He rushes to Tokyo without even saying goodbye to his dying father. Sensei's suicide note discloses two main causes for his misanthropism and eventual suicide. First, as a young man he was cheated of part of his legacy after his parents' death. Secondly, and more important, his marriage to a woman with whom both he and his best friend were in love drove the latter to suicide. Because of his feelings of guilt he could never again establish perfect rapport with his wife. Having been the victim of evil, Sensei in turn inflicted it upon another. Sōseki is thus concerned with moral evil stemming from egotism.

The narrator loses both his actual and his spiritual fathers. Their deaths further overlap with the decease of the Emperor Meiji and General Nogi. In comparing his own suicide with that of General Nogi, Sensei says that he is going to kill himself because of the spirit of Meiji. What is implied by this testament? The assertion of ego was one of the major concerns in Japan's modernisation along Western lines. The failure of personal egotism in his own case makes Sensei look back with mixed feelings upon the ideals of the early Meiji, when forward-looking modernisation and right spiritual values appeared inseparable, indeed identical. By the end of the Meiji this coherence was breaking apart, with the spiritual ideals increasingly overshadowed and atomised by the material progress of an impersonal industrialisation. Sensei's suicide then represents one answer to the predicament of perceptive intellectuals in a post-Meiji Japan. *Kokoro* thus depicts the seamy side of the same 'self-reliance' which Sōseki extols in 'The Enlightenment of Modern Japan' and 'My Individualism';[25] it shows both how difficult it is to achieve such independence in Japan and how it could even entail moral evil.

Among Sōseki's works *Grass on the Wayside* (*Michikusa*, 1915) is unique as an explicitly autobiographical novel, although it differs from the works of the I-novelists. Kenzō, the main character, is pestered by his foster-parents and their relatives for the money to which they claim to be entitled. He has thus to deal once again in flesh and blood with people who have been continually present in his subconscious as ghosts from the past. His childhood experience of the pettiness of his foster-parents, of their discord leading to separation and of his being sent back and forth between three households are factors that later cause his psychological insecurity. All these correspond more or less to what happened to Sōseki himself. Another theme of the novel centres round the tense relationship between Kenzō and his wife, the causes for which are various. The reminders of the past when he was pestered by his foster-parents cannot exert anything but a baleful influence upon Kenzō and his wife. The straitened financial state of her parents' family helps to engender further tension. These external circumstances might have had little adverse effect but for Kenzō's character which only serves to complicate the relations between him and his wife. His attitude to women inherited from Meiji Japan does not allow him to acknowledge his wife as an independent person. Besides, his tendency to intellectual abstraction serves as an obstacle to establishing a rapport not only with his wife but with the world at large. Failing to attain authenticity in his mode of life, he is insecure.

All these themes are recurrent in other works of Sōseki's later period. *Grass on the Wayside*, however, is quite distinct. Kenzō's afflictions in his present life are tightly bound up with those in the past. He is aware of the continuity in time when he refers, rather like Sōsuke does in *The Gate*, to the lasting quality of human sufferings (section 102): ' "Hardly anything in this life is settled. Things that happen once will go on happening. But they come back in different guises, and that's what fools us." He spoke bitterly, almost with venom.'[26] In writing *Grass on the Wayside*, Sōseki projected a great deal of his own life history not only by dealing with his present sufferings but also by tracing their origins in his childhood. It is an autobiographical novel unique in modern Japanese literature. Unlike many of the I-novelists Sōseki is free from self-pity or masochistic probing into his own malady; he penetrates into the depths of his subconscious, observes what he sees with objective detachment and represents it in an artistic form.

In Sōseki's last and unfinished work, *Light and Darkness*

(*Meian*, 1916), the action develops slowly and uneventfully round the protagonist Tsuda and his wife O-Nobu. As the major characters in the novel they have nothing very distinctive about them. Their married life is peaceful on the surface, but there exists a barrier beyond which they cannot get through to one another. Instead of O-Nobu, Tsuda might have married Kiyoko, who suddenly left him to marry another man without giving any explanation. This may be partly responsible for Tsuda's inability to love O-Nobu totally. Other characters intrude to complicate their relations. O-Hide, Tsuda's younger sister, for instance, meddles with the arrangement for Tsuda to receive financial assistance from his father. Kobayashi pesters Tsuda with requests for alms. Mrs Yoshikawa, the wife of Tsuda's superior, arranges things so that, under the pretext of convalescence from an operation on a fistula, Tsuda goes to a hot spring where Kiyoko is staying on her own. Left unfinished owing to Sōseki's untimely death, *Light and Darkness* allows little room for conjecturing how it might have developed further.

It emerges from the plot summary so far traced that Sōseki was trying to project all his major concerns into this novel. Estrangement or lack of communication between individuals is the central theme as in *And Then...*, *The Gate*, *The Wayfarer*, *Kokoro* and *Grass on the Wayside*. It also shares with these works the theme of tangled love relations although there is no shadow of guilt in this work. There is also the problem of money which alienates relatives and friends as in *Kokoro* and *Grass on the Wayside*.

In *The Gate* and *Kokoro* the alienation of an individual from others is closely linked with guilt feelings. In *The Wayfarer* alienation derives not from guilt but from excessive reasoning which leads to repression. There is no such objective background, whether guilt or repression, in the mutual alienation between the characters concerned. Paradoxically enough, *Light and Darkness* shows that the world would be just as much or even more infernal if individuals were alienated from one another in apparently normal circumstances rather than as a result of guilt feelings. The alienation of the main characters in *Light and Darkness* arises not so much from any particular external circumstances but from their personalities. Tsuda fails to show willingness to consolidate his affection for O-Nobu in the way that she does.

Her love, however, is inseparable from her wish to hold him under sway. She is also motivated by her wish to win over Okamoto, her uncle, who was against her marriage with Tsuda. She thus makes an effort to love her husband for the sake of self-satisfaction. There is no genuine love lost between Tsuda and O-Hide, let alone O-Nobu and O-Hide. O-Hide is prettier than and therefore feels superior to O-Nobu. Yet she is jealous of the financial extravagance which Tsuda grants O-Nobu. She consequently dissuades Tsuda's parents from helping him, but in order to disguise her real motive she ingratiatingly offers some money to her brother. Tsuda is torn between the horns of dilemma: he yearns for the money, yet he dislikes his sister's ingratiating activities. Nor does O-Nobu like it. All of these characters are thus driven by egocentric feelings such as envy, pride, selfishness and vanity. Kiyoko, in contrast, seems to lack positive self-assertion and to be subject to external circumstances. This may explain why, without really intending it, she deserted Tsuda. To wage psychological warfare with Tsuda is beyond her and in this respect she contrasts with O-Nobu.

In *Light and Darkness* everybody is shut up within his or her own cell partitioned off from one another by impenetrable walls. In presenting this theme Sōseki expanded more than ever the range of the psychological novel with which he had experimented in *The Wayfarer* and *Kokoro*. That the psychological analysis of the characters is much more detailed is evinced by the short period of time. All the events take place in one week, which, if not comparable with the one day of James Joyce's *Ulysses*, is nevertheless a short time for a novel of several hundred pages. The novel achieves high drama in the scene in which O-Nobu confronts O-Hide in Tsuda's ward room and all three characters wage a subtle psychological warfare. Having successfully persuaded Tsuda's parents to discontinue financial assistance to him, O-Hide now offers to help him not out of genuine magnanimity but out of her wish to inveigle herself into his favour. Tsuda in turn is confronted by the choice of alternatives, one as unpleasant as the other, of telling O-Nobu about the financial arrangement so far kept secret from her, or of receiving money from O-Hide. Sōseki ends Book 1, section 102, with a dramatic situation in which O-Hide threatens Tsuda with the taunt that he is afraid of O-Nobu because of 'someone else you're concerned about', imply-

ing Kiyoko, and this is heard by O-Nobu who has been eavesdropping all this while outside the room. What passes through
O-Nobu's mind, in turn, is as follows (section 103):

> She thought she might continue to stand there perfectly
> still until she had made out the nature of the dispute.
> But at that moment the sentence 'While you're caring
> so much for O-Nobu there's still someone else you're
> concerned about,' burst forth from O-Hide like a final
> barrage of gunfire and suddenly shook O-Nobu to
> her very heart. Nothing in the world was more
> important to her than this one sentence which she had
> heard exceptionally clearly; but at the same time,
> nothing was more unclear to her. If she did not hear
> what followed, that one independent sentence would be
> of no use to her whatsoever. She felt that no matter
> what the cost she would not be satisfied unless she
> heard what followed. And yet, on the other hand, she
> was utterly unable to hear what followed, for she was
> made to realize that the exchange between the two,
> which for some time with every word had been
> heightening in intensity, had then reached its peak.
> It had arrived at the extreme point where it could not
> advance one step further. If either did try to push it
> further, he would have to use physical force. Thus, to
> prevent such a possibility, she absolutely had to enter
> the sick room.
>   She knew very well how things stood
> between brother and sister. She also had always
> known that the cause of their discord lay with her.
> Thus, to make her appearance there at that time
> required considerable dexterity. But she was
> completely confident that she possessed it. She
> decided on her move in a split second, and
> then she purposely opened the sliding door to the
> sick room quietly.[27]

In the sections that follow, the three characters resume the discussion about the money problem, which, however, ends in an
unexpected way for Tsuda and O-Hide (section 108):

As she [O-Nobu] passed the cheque to Tsuda, at the
same time pointedly showing it to O-Hide, her manner
indicated a kind of command towards her husband.
Indeed it was a distinct command emerging both from
the course of the conversation and from her natural
disposition. She prayed Tsuda would attune himself with
her feelings and accept the cheque willingly. Whether
he would smile genially, nod, and cast it gently near his
pillow, or whether he would say just one word to her
expressive of extreme gratitude, and then return it to her
– in either event, if by the effect of this cheque O-Hide
could only be shown that a strong bond of conjugal
affection existed between them, she would be satisfied.

Unfortunately, both O-Nobu's action and the
emergence of the cheque were too sudden for Tsuda.
Furthermore, the dramatic sense he derived from such
a situation differed somewhat from O-Nobu's. He
looked at the cheque strangely, and then asked quietly:

'What in the world did you do to get this?'

Already, at the outset, this cold tone and the equally
cold question itself sadly dampened her enthusiasm.
Her expectations were betrayed.

'I didn't do anything. It's just that you needed it, so
I managed to get it.'

Even though she spoke lightly, inwardly she trembled.
She was afraid that he would continue to ask prying
questions, which would be tantamount to revealing to
O-Hide that there did not exist any perfect accord
between them.

'You needn't ask for any explanation while you're ill.
You'll find out all about it afterwards anyway.'

Even after she had said this she was still extremely
uncomfortable, and before Tsuda could say anything in
response, she immediately proceeded:

'It certainly doesn't matter if you don't understand
now, does it? After all, it isn't such a great amount.
When we really need money, I can always get it from
somewhere.'

Tsuda finally threw down by his pillow the cheque he
had been holding in his hand. He was a man who liked

money; yet he was not one who worshipped it. Though he felt more keenly than others its necessity for having things one wants, with regard to despising money itself he was of a disposition that accorded completely with O-Nobu's words. He therefore made no comment, and for the same reason uttered no word of thanks to his wife.

She was dissatisfied, thinking that even if he said nothing to her, he should at least have said something to his sister to satisfy his grudge against her.

On her part, O-Hide, who had been observing the behaviour of the two during their conversation, suddenly addressed her brother. She then took out from her kimono a handsome woman's purse.

'Yoshio, I'm going to leave here what I brought.'

She took something wrapped in white paper out of her purse, and placed it near the cheque.

'It's all right if I leave it here in this way, isn't it?'

Although there is a comic relief in the scene in which Tsuda is unexpectedly presented with two cheques, there yet remains the dismal chasm, the lack of genuine understanding between the three characters. Throughout this scene, which is limited to a mere hour or two, a heightened dramatic intensity is sustained. These characters are so much divorced from one another that the author is not in a position to provide a unified, omniscient point of view in which every character is grasped as part of a totality. In conceiving such a structure for the novel, Sōseki to some extent transcended nineteenth-century realism and came a step closer to the psychological novels of Henry James and after.

5

In August 1911 Sōseki gave a talk in Wakayama entitled 'The Enlightenment of Modern Japan' ('Gendai Nihon no Kaika'), which, together with another of his talks given three years later, 'My Individualism' ('Watakushi no Kojinshugi'), evinces his insight into the cultural milieu of modern Japan. The gist of his talk is that the Enlightenment in the West was a process of self-awakening, whereas in Japan it was brought about by external forces. For this growth and reaction Sōseki coined, respectively, the words *naihatsu-teki* (inner-directed) and *gaihatsu-teki* (outer-directed).

> In brief, the enlightenment in the West (that is, the enlightenment in the ordinary sense) is inner-directed, while the enlightenment in modern Japan is outer-directed. By the phrase 'inner-directed' I mean spontaneous growth like the process by which a flower blossoms with its bud opening and petals growing outward. By 'outer-directed' I mean the moulding of a shape by means of external forces imposed from outside. To add an explanation, the enlightenment in the West is comparable to drifting clouds and running water; this is not the case with the enlightenment in Japan.

Sōseki had no illusion about the fact that under the overwhelming influence of the West modern Japanese culture was inevitably bound to be derivative or parasitic:

> The currents that control the enlightenment of Japan are those of the West, and since those of us who cross these currents are not Westerners, we tend to feel diffident as if we were hangers-on whenever a new current arises.

Out of this derived Sōseki's ultimate criticism of the Enlightenment of modern Japan: that it is superficial. Anybody with as sensitive a perception as Sōseki's must have found himself under heavy strain:

> If for ten years we try our best as university lecturers, most of us ought to have nervous breakdowns. I cannot say that those who do not are all fakes. It is more natural, however, that we should have breakdowns.

'My Individualism', given at the Peers' School on 25 November 1914, can be read as a supplement to 'The Enlightenment of Modern Japan'. Sōseki elaborates his argument by referring to his own experiences of studying English literature. In his account he introduces the word *tanin-hon'i* (reliance on other people). What he means by this word is that as a Japanese student of English literature, he had for a long time no choice but to rely on the achievements of English scholars and critics. Reliance on Western scholars and critics was part of the phenomenon which Sōseki previously described as 'outer-directed'. As he says:

> Bergson and Eucken have been popular in Japan recently, but we are merely following the fashions of the West. It is no wonder that in those days we imitated indiscriminately and spoke proudly of whatever the Westerners taught us.

Sōseki's dilemma was greater because of his conscientious attitude towards the study of English literature:

> Suppose a Westerner says it is a good poem or it has an excellent tone. It is, however, a Westerner's point of view. It is certainly not useless to me, but unless I am really convinced by it, I cannot accept or convey it to others as if it were my own opinion. . . .
>
> Yet I am a student of English literature. I should feel uneasy if there were discrepancies between the English critics' views and my own. I therefore have to consider whence these discrepancies derive. . . .
>
> I then began reading books that had nothing to do with literature in order to consolidate the basis on which my views of literature should be founded. Briefly, I hit upon the idea of self-reliance (*jiko-hon'i*) and to prove it I began to apply myself to scientific studies and philosophical reflections.

The 'self-reliance' Sōseki thus attained is a variation of what he described in the previous talk as 'inner-directed'. After explaining the process by which he attained this notion, Sōseki discusses it in a general, social context. He extends the notion of 'self-reliance' to the fulfilment of individual potential in society. This concept is what he means by 'individualism' in the title of his talk. There are additional noteworthy features of Sōseki's individualism. First, it must be distinguished from mere selfishness.

> It would be a life-long misfortune if you did not fight through until you discover an occupation perfectly suited to you so that you can settle down where you can develop your individuality. However, if society allows

your individuality to be esteemed, it is reasonable that
you should recognise other individuals and esteem their
inclinations.

To sum up what I have said so far: first, if you want
to develop your own individuality, you must also esteem
other individuals; second, if you wish to use your power,
you must always be prepared to perform the obligation
that accompanies it; third, if you want to show your
financial power, you must esteem the responsibility that
accompanies it.

In other words, Sōseki's individualism is a 'moralistic individualism', something similar to Kantian 'autonomy'. Secondly, it
stands out distinctly against the factionalism or group behaviour
characteristic of Japanese society.

To put it in simplified terms, it [individualism] is the
principle which eliminates partisanship and bases itself
solely on right or wrong. It repudiates partisan or
factional activity for the sake of political or financial
power.

Sōseki illustrates his argument with reference to his own experience of having once been criticised by a jingoist group 'Japan and
the Japanese' led under the banner of Miyake Setsurei (1860–
1945). Hence Sōseki goes on to delineate the third and final trait
of his concept of individualism – its priority to nationalism
although the two need not conflict with each other:

the word individualism is often taken to be the antithesis
of and to be inimical to nationalism.
It is not such an irrational and ambiguous thing. . . .
Some people not only assert but also are fully convinced
that Japan will not be able to survive without resorting
to nationalism. Moreover, a considerable number of
people even assert that the country will vanish unless
individualism is trampled down. However, such
nonsense cannot be true. In fact, we are nationalists,
internationalists and individualists at one and the same
time.

It emerges from the foregoing discussion that one of the major themes of Sōseki's work is his concern for individual freedom and the difficulty of its realisation in modern Japanese society. Instead of attaining fully integrated personalities, many of his characters often suffer from alienation, insecurity and other abnormal states of mind. Individual freedom is the basis on which interpersonal communication should be established, and yet in actual fact it is bound to bring about the conflict of interest and to lapse into selfish egotism. Everybody is then estranged from everybody else and all become enemies of one another. Sōseki was especially aware of two cases in which egotism entails moral evil: tangled love relations and man's acquisitive desire for properties. His preoccupation with complex love relations may have originated in his aspiration to the eternal female figure, either real or imaginary. His concern for the money problem derived from his involvement with his foster-parents and other relatives. Notably enough, it is not only that the characters he created to represent these themes often undergo the disintegration of personality, but also that the way in which he was preoccupied with these themes is obsessively neurotic.

Inseparable from his personal suffering was Sōseki's cultural confrontation with the Western world. The anxieties and worries he endured as a scholar of English literature might never have disturbed a less scrupulous and less perceptive person. To overcome the difficulties of English literature he proposed two solutions for Japanese scholars: to aspire to scientific objectivity and to cultivate one's personal taste in literary studies. Neither, in fact, proved entirely successful. Sōseki's attempt to base literary criticism on his personal taste was a declaration of independence from English scholarship, and yet, ironically enough, it was a Japanisation of an essentially English attitude. In this instance as well as in his defence of individualism he showed that Japanese culture should be an 'inner-directed' synthesis, for which neither jingoism nor superficial imitation of the West would do.

Sōseki demonstrated all this in the process by which he became a professional writer during the last decade of his life. His earlier works echo to the sounds of English literature in such forms as allusions, character types and plot conventions. These ostensible echoes became less apparent as he matured into a realistic novelist. This does not mean, however, that he discarded English literature. On the contrary it had been assimilated and had become part and parcel of his writing in a most fruitful way. His expert knowledge of the English novel as well as his psychological studies enabled him to achieve the kind of realism which distinguishes itself from that of the Japanese naturalist I-novelists. While the latter were concerned with self-exposure in their naïvely auto-biographical novels and stories, Sōseki rendered his experiences into an authentic form of literary art.

4

The rivals:

SHIGA NAOYA and AKUTAGAWA RYŪNOSUKE

Japanese literature during the period immediately after the death of Sōseki may be represented by Shiga Naoya and Akutagawa Ryūnosuke, two writers who can be profitably compared in many respects. Shiga Naoya (1883–1971) was a member of a congenial group of writers called Shirakaba-ha (White Birch School), named after the magazine they published. Apart from Shiga Naoya, the group included such writers as Mushanokōji Saneatsu (1885–1976), Arishima Takeo (1878–1923), and his two younger brothers, Arishima Ikuma (1882–1974) and Satomi Ton (1888–). As his family name indicates, Mushanokōji was of aristocratic origin. The Arishimas and Shiga Naoya himself were born into samurai class families. All of them represented the firmly established *haute* bourgeoisie of the late Meiji and Taishō periods. Many of them received their early education at the Peers' School. But it was only while they were students at the University of Tokyo that they launched their magazine *Shirakaba* (April 1910 to August 1923), in which they published not only their literary works but also highly sophisticated articles on visual art, both European and Oriental. Another feature of this group of writers was that through the writings of Tolstoy they became champions of idealistic humanitarianism. Their ideals were not restricted to theory alone; with his friends' aid, Mushanokōji practised it in his 'New Village' (Atarashiki Mura) Movement. Buying some land in Kyūshū, he created and maintained for several years an ideal communistic village. Their idealism exhibited even a socialistic tinge: for instance, Arishima Takeo gave away his extensive farm land in Hokkaido to his tenants before he participated in a sensational double suicide. Thus not only were they able to cultivate their literary and aesthetic tastes at their leisure but also their affluence allowed them to have a more progressive and even radical view of society than many less well-to-do.

The initial objective of the Shirakaba-ha group may be summed up as a conscious reaction against the Japanese naturalists who had become a major force in the preceding period. The Japanese naturalists had formed an exclusive clique called *bundan* (literary circle). These writers had to belong to this narrow circle, partly because the act of writing was necessary for their livelihood. The subjects of their writings were limited to the narrow sphere of their own lives, which were in most cases poor and miserable. Very often they dramatised their misery and poverty with more than a little masochism, and some even deliberately led a life of misery so that they could render it in their work. From this derived, as I mentioned in the previous chapters, the peculiarly Japanese literary institution of the I-novel, or *watakushi-shōsetsu*.

The Shirakaba-ha group shared this reliance on the personal life for writing fiction, as the autobiographical works of Mushano-kōji and Shiga show. However, there were far more differences than similarities between these two literary factions and their contrasting life styles. First, the writers of the Shirakaba-ha group could remain detached from the *bundan*. Secondly, they had no need to write for money. Thirdly, due to their bourgeois and even aristocratic backgrounds, the writers of the Shirakaba-ha group cultivated a wider scope of aesthetic sensibility than that of the poverty-stricken naturalists. Fourthly, unlike the frustrated naturalists, they espoused a positive, optimistic attitude to life or at least retained some resilience with which to surmount their predicament.

Shiga Naoya is often regarded as a virtuoso of the short story form, since throughout his career he produced innumerable masterpieces in this genre. His short stories are either fictional tales or brief accounts of episodes taken from his own life, written with a compact organisation, delicate sensibility and lucid prose style. For instance, 'At Kinosaki', which is one of the most popular anthology pieces for Japanese school texts, depicts the psychological process by which the author, while convalescing from an accident that could have cost him his life, awakens to the mysteries of life and death. The fact that in twenty-five years he produced only one lengthy novel, *A Dark Night's Passing (Anya*

Kōro, 1921–37), suggests various possibilities: that he had a certain preoccupation which he needed to express in his work; that the subject was extremely difficult to handle; and that he persistently kept on tackling it despite difficulties. What then was Shiga Naoya's preoccupation with which he dealt in *A Dark Night's Passing* as well as in his shorter works? In brief it was the conflict with his father and his need to be reconciled.

Shiga's conflict with his father originated in his abortive love for one of the maid servants, an affair not approved of by his bourgeois family. The underlying cause of the conflict, however, was something deeper. Shiga's birth was preceded by the untimely death of his elder brother, a great loss to such a patriarchal family as Shiga's where the family tradition would be transmitted through the eldest son. Ascribing the death of this eldest son to his parents and placing Naoya in the position of a substitute for the deceased, his grandparents severed Naoya from his parents, brought him up under their care and thereby alienated the son from his father.[1] Naoya's own mother died when he was thirteen. His stepmother, whom his father married soon afterwards, did not widen this divide, but rather served to close the gap between Naoya and his father.[2]

'Ōtsu Junkichi' (1912) reflects to a great extent these aspects of Shiga Naoya's own life, in the way the protagonist's forbidden love for one of the maid servants leads him into conflict with his father and causes his estrangement from the family. This subject matter is coupled with another of Shiga's major concerns. Although he was never baptised into Christianity, in 1900, at the age of eighteen, he became and remained until 1907 a follower of Uchimura Kanzō's reformist Christian sect, the *mukyōkai-ha* or 'non-church' movement against the established church. Under Uchimura's influence the protagonist of the story (like Shiga Naoya himself) is obsessed with the fear of committing adultery. So far he has suffered from the split between his spiritual faith and his frustrated physical desires. Now, unless he consummates his love in the form of marriage, his relationship with his maid servant is strained by the stigma of adultery. There is, then, the urgent need for him to marry her, an act which is inevitably bound to bring about a clash with his father.

While 'Ōtsu Junkichi' is thoroughly autobiographical, 'The Diary of Claudius' ('Kurōdiasu no Nikki', 1912), written about the same time, has a fictional structure. As the title suggests, it deals with the relationship between Hamlet and Claudius, looked at not from the prince's but from his uncle's point of view. While drawing on the framework of the well-known play, the author deliberately distorts Shakespeare's text. First, Claudius pleads not guilty to the alleged crime of fratricide. Secondly, he shows utmost sympathy with Hamlet's self-imposed suffererings. Thirdly, however, in Claudius' view Hamlet's suspicion of him is nothing but a morbid phantasy. And, finally, despite Claudius' solicitude for his nephew, Hamlet turns out to be intrinsically self-centred and not sympathetic at all. What could these features of the story imply? First, by siding with Claudius and belittling Hamlet, the author seems implicitly to give warning of the danger of Hamlet's Oedipus complex, and his hatred of Claudius as a usurper of his mother. Furthermore one may hazard a guess that the author is critically judging his own hatred towards his father. Secondly, Claudius' solicitude for Hamlet may be interpreted as the author's hopeful desire for his father to soften his attitude. These implications suggest that the author was searching for a reconciliation.

In the same year that he wrote 'Ōtsu Junkichi' and 'The Diary of Claudius' Shiga Naoya launched another autobiographical project, *Tokitō Kensaku*, which was later to become *A Dark Night's Passing*. It was an attempt to elaborate in extended form his personal conflicts. Natsume Sōseki had noticed Shiga Naoya's talent in his earlier work and in 1914 invited him to contribute a serial novel to the *Asahi Shimbun*. But, because of delays in the progress of *Tokitō Kensaku*, Shiga withdrew from the project. In fact, during the three years after his marriage to a cousin of Mushanokōji Saneatsu in 1914 he hardly produced any work. It was not until 1920 that he resumed writing *Tokitō Kensaku*. In the meantime, after a few more years of strain, Shiga's conflict with his father suddenly came to an end. How this happened is told in another autobiographical story, 'Reconciliation' ('Wakai', 1917). The abruptness with which the reconciliation took place during an illness of the protagonist's (or the author's) grandmother is comparable to that of a religious conversion. The author does not try to consider why the reconciliation became possible but concentrates on depicting its cathartic effect. This reconciliation thus deprived Shiga of a possible subject for *Tokitō*

Kensaku. If the conflict with his father had continued, Shiga would have dealt with it in his autobiographical novel. As it was, he inevitably had to modify the subject of his novel. Consequently, *Tokitō Kensaku* was to be transformed into *A Dark Night's Passing* which is still mainly an autobiographical work but contains a more objectively fictional structure.

A Dark Night's Passing distinguishes itself from such works as 'Ōtsu Junkichi' and 'Reconciliation' in the degree to which the author transforms the facts of his own life. The prologue, Kensaku's recollection of his childhood, presents the key factors of the whole novel. First, Kensaku's estrangement from his father is suggested by the *sumō* wrestling episode. The father throws his unyielding child again and again until he ties up the child with his belt. The child eventually bursts into tears.[3] Secondly, his close links with his grandfather is shown: he is brought up in his grandparents' household and remains there, looked after by the grandfather's widowed mistress. Here, however, one notices a modification from the author's own life. While his own grandfather was a man of integrity and intelligence, who had a profound influence on him, Kensaku's grandfather is portrayed as somewhat repellent. Each of the four organically constructed chapters of *A Dark Night's Passing* represents a different phase of Kensaku's life, in which he suffers a different kind of ordeal and attains maturity by surmounting it.

Chapter 1 is concerned with Kensaku's unrequited love for a girl he has known since childhood. When he asks for her hand in marriage, he is rejected for a reason not revealed until the next chapter. In chapter 2 Kensaku becomes aware of his growing sympathy for the grandfather's widowed mistress and asks her to marry him. Again rejected, he is informed by his elder brother of the shocking and terrifying fact that he was an illicit son born between his mother and grandfather while his father was studying abroad. His marriage with his grandfather's mistress would be nothing but incestuous. The reason for the rejection of his proposal in chapter 1 was that the girl's parents abhorred the sordid secret of Kensaku's family. The first half of chapter 3 deals with Kensaku's happy married life but ends with the pathetic death of a new-born baby. In chapter 4 his wife is seduced, as it happens, by her cousin, a double torture to Kensaku, for it reminds him of his own mother's mistake in the past. This seduction is of course another fictional element that did not take place in the author's own life. Kensaku is willing to forgive his wife's inadvertent moral slip. However, to attain true peace of mind, he decides to lead a solitary life secluded on a high mountain in the western part of Japan. At the end of the novel he has fallen ill and is suffering from fever and exhaustion, thus leaving the reader uncertain whether he will survive or not.

Despite this ambivalent ending, there emerges from *A Dark Night's Passing* a sense of catharsis, reminiscent of the Shirakaba-ha's forward-looking attitude. The works of the naturalistic I-novelists were often replicas of the petty reality in which they dragged out their lives. There was scarcely any way out of this morass for either the created characters or the author himself. The protagonist of *A Dark Night's Passing*, based on the author's own self and yet adequately equipped with the autonomy of a fictional character, is sufficient evidence that the author has survived his own predicament.

2

Akutagawa Ryūnosuke (1892–1927) committed suicide on 24 July 1927 at the age of thirty-five. His death was premature, especially in comparison with that of Shiga Naoya, who was nine years older and yet survived him for another forty-four years. Akutagawa always respected and envied Shiga for the stoic equilibrium which the latter maintained in his way of life and writing. Shiga, in turn, regarded Akutagawa as more talented than himself. They both distinguished themselves as virtuosi of the short story form written in a faultless style, although the most important of Shiga's works is undoubtedly *A Dark Night's Passing*. They began their careers in a literary age infatuated with naturalism. For all his efforts to resist it, Shiga's autobiographical works promoted in a sense the naturalist tradition. As the legitimate heir of Sōseki's (and Ōgai's) fictional tradition, Akutagawa all along opposed the naturalists, but his effort to work outside their domain was approaching a dead end by the time of his death.

Akutagawa's life appears to have been doomed from the very beginning. Since he was born in both his parents' climacteric year, he was at first legally disowned only to be re-adopted later. Nine months after his birth, his mother went insane and accordingly he was adopted by her family. She died when he was eleven years old. All these events left an indelible mark on his mind, with his mother's insanity sparking off the fear of his own potential insanity. In his autobiographical 'In Memoriam' ('Tenkibo', 1926), the image of his mother overlaps with that of his sister whom in fact he had never seen as she died before his birth. In this phantasy his mother is thus idealised as the eternal female figure for whom he longs.[4] One may well imagine that the early loss of his mother contributed to his psychological insecurity. His adoption by his mother's family, on the other hand, seems to have fractured the relationship with his father.[5] Furthermore, it could have adversely affected his sense of rightfully belonging to a real family, as we have seen in the case of Sōseki.

Akutagawa equalled Ōgai and Sōseki in his knowledge of European, Chinese and classical Japanese literature. He read English literature at the University of Tokyo two decades after Sōseki, where he excelled academically, ranking second in his graduating class. Yet, like Sōseki, Akutagawa was doubtful about whether literature could be a subject of academic study at university. As he puts it in his reminiscence ('My Life in Those Days' ['Anokoro no Jibun no Koto', 1919]):

> The academic study of literature is something of
> extremely dubious value. What are they doing in the
> departments of Japanese, Chinese, English, French and
> German literature?. . .Can the study of literature be
> called a science?. . .In my opinion, the departments of
> literature can well be abolished. Theories of literature
> can be taught in the department of aesthetics, the history
> of literature in the department of history. All the rest
> are sheer nonsense and can be expelled from the
> University. . . .Otherwise people may be misled to
> consider university lectures superior to newspaper and
> magazine articles, which may perhaps be as nonsensical.
> In fact, newspaper and magazine articles have the whole
> wide world as their audience; since university lectures
> exist only for students, their defects are less likely to be

exposed. It is unfair that under such sham security
academic nonsense should attain more respectability.

There was, then, more reason for him to choose a career of
professional writer than that of an academic despite the certain
success he would have enjoyed as a university lecturer in literature.

While still a student at the University of Tokyo Akutagawa
published 'Rashōmon' in the *Teikoku Bungaku* (Imperial Literature, November 1915). In his renowned film 'Rashōmon' the
director Kurosawa rightly amalgamated this story with another
Akutagawa story 'In a Grove' ('Yabu no Naka', 1922), for
Akutagawa's 'Rashōmon' serves to underline the sense of desola-
tion which permeates the other story. For the main plot of
'Rashōmon' Akutagawa repeatedly resorted to the Heian folktale
collection, the *Konjaku Monogatari* (Tales of Ages Ago; early
twelfth century; Book 29, number 18). The episode of a woman
who used to 'cut snakes up into four-inch lengths and sold them
for dried fish in the military camps' is taken from another
Konjaku story (Book 31, number 1). For the reference to the
famine the author apparently drew upon a similar description in
An Account of my Hut. The description of dead bodies, realistic
and powerful, is said to be based on his personal observations at
the Medical School of the University of Tokyo.[6] The protagonist
is a social outcast, a 'servant recently dismissed by his master'.
The ending of the story varies in different versions. In the original
version as published in the *Teikoku Bungaku* and subsequently
in Akutagawa's first collection of short stories, *Rashōmon* (1917),
the protagonist 'hurried away into the street of Kyoto to rob',
while the version revised for the collection *The Nose* (*Hana*, 1918)
closes with 'beyond this was only darkness. . .unknowing and
unknown'. The ambiguity at the end of the final version, as in
'In a Grove', leaves room for the reader to conjecture about the
fate of the protagonist and creates a deeper impression of the
irrationality of the world. There is an irony in the way in which
the protagonist, first repelled by the old woman or by 'all evil'
embodied in her, commits an act of evil in robbing her. She in
turn excuses her cruelty in pulling hair from a dead woman by
claiming that this woman too was a fraud. The story, then, brings
home the truism that a life-or-death struggle for survival between
individuals could lead to extreme forms of moral evil.

'The Nose' ('Hana'), published a few months after 'Rash-ōmon', is also based on a *Konjaku* story. Akutagawa, however, modified the original story by furnishing the characters with patterns of behaviour and psychology more appropriate to our own time. The protagonist finds himself in an absurd situation in being at once a social superior as a high-rank priest and ridiculed by his inferiors because of his abnormally long nose – much longer than that of Cyrano de Bergerac. The process by which he shifts from one mood to another, such as anxiety about his abnormality, his pretended indifference to it, his satisfaction when cured of it after absurd therapies, and even greater misery in noticing others ridiculing his hard-won 'normality', is as plausible as the psycho-logy of the people who mock him. Akutagawa comments on the irony of the situation with a didactic intervention:

> In the human heart there are two feelings mutually contradictory. Of course there is no one who does not sympathize at the misfortune of another. But if that other somehow manages to escape from that misfortune, then he who has sympathized somehow feels unsatisfied. To exaggerate a little, he is even disposed to cast the sufferer back into the same misfortune once more. And before he is aware of it, he unconsciously comes to harbour a certain hostility towards him. What somehow displeased the Naigu, though he did not know the reason, was nothing other than the egoism he indefinably perceived in the attitude of those onlookers, both priests and laymen, at Ike-no-O.[7]

When by chance his nose regains its abnormal length the Naigu cannot but accept his fate with the consoling thought that now he would at least be free of ridicule.

When 'The Nose' was published in February 1916 in the *Shinshichō* (New Current of Thought), it earned unreserved praise from Sōseki. As he puts it in his letter to Akutagawa:

> I think your piece is very interesting. It is assured, and it is serious, not merely frivolous. I think its particular merit is that the absurdity is not forced, but is perfectly natural and is allowed to emerge of itself. . . . The style is concise and controlled. I admired it. Try

and write another twenty or thirty pieces like it. You could carve your own special niche in the world of letters.[8]

Apparently Sōseki seems to have been impressed by the humorous effect of the story and also by the fictional ingenuity so obviously lacking in the confessional novels of the naturalists. When Akutagawa wrote these stories, he was suffering from the pains of an abortive courtship, opposed and obstructed by his relatives. In order to relieve his pains, Akutagawa claimed he wanted to write 'fiction as hilarious and as much removed from the present state of things as possible'.[9] His explanation, however, needs some qualification. First, no description is more alien to 'Rashōmon' than 'hilarious'. 'The Nose' does have a humorous effect, as Sōseki pointed out, yet can this tale be called 'hilarious'? Certainly, readers may laugh at the ridiculous efforts the disciples take to cure the abnormality of their master's nose. Yet the laughter with which they ridicule their master is full of cruel malice. 'The Nose' therefore is not really 'hilarious' but only invokes our laughter at an absurd situation. Secondly, are both 'The Nose' and 'Rashōmon' far removed from 'the present state of things'? Again, the proper answer is not entirely affirmative. Despite the dissimilarity in subject and presentation, both stories are concerned with conflicts arising from the egotism of each individual, a problem this author certainly was suffering from in his own life. 'Removed from the present state of things', then, means that in these stories Akutagawa dealt indirectly rather than directly with aspects of his own life.

These observations on 'Rashōmon' and 'The Nose' may be supplemented by reference to 'Yam Gruel' ('Imogayu', 1916), another story based on a *Konjaku* tale (Book 26, number 17) and *Uji Shūi Monogatari* (A Collection of Tales from Uji; late eleventh century, Book 1, number 18), another Heian folktale miscellany. It centres round the irony that man is happier to remain deprived and to aspire to a goal than he is in a state of satisfaction. The protagonist, a low-rank samurai, is mocked by his contemporaries and even children for his ungainly appearance and ineffectualness. By making use of a historical setting and siding with neither the ridiculed nor the ridiculing, Akutagawa depicts the insecurity of a man alienated from a society in which individuals confront one another out of their egotistic motives.

These observations on Akutagawa's earliest stories indicate that a characteristic feature of his fiction is his deliberate restraint in drawing directly from his own experience. Akutagawa consciously strove to transcend the naturalist tradition by liberating prose from the limited essay-like function of straightforwardly projecting the author's own experience on to the 'fictional page'. One may infer that he was less at ease when dealing with the immediate experiences of his life, and that his approach to life and fiction was too abstract. Consequently, the material for most of his works comes from the literature of the past. According to their widely varying subjects his stories are classified into such types as: *ōchō-mono* (stories dealing with the pre-feudal period of Imperial rule) to which belong the three stories discussed above; *kirishitan-mono* (those that carry Christian themes especially related to the Jesuit missionaries in seventeenth-century Japan); those dealing with the Tokugawa period; and *kaika-mono* (those dealing with the early Meiji period of Enlightenment). In addition to these historical tales, Akutagawa wrote stories set in modern times as well as accounts of his own life. Interestingly enough, his 'historical' tales were written mainly between 1915 and 1922, and his 'contemporary' and 'autobiographical' fiction, with a few exceptions, during about the last five years of his life. This fairly clear pattern in his writing career serves as a useful guide to the essential characteristics of his life and work and their bearing upon one another.

In 'Rashōmon' there begins what may be called Akutagawa's obsession with the infernal, a theme which certainly permeates every feature of 'The Hell Screen' ('Jigokuhen', 1918), another of his *ōchō-mono* stories. The painter Yoshihide, while engaged in painting the 'hell screen' commissioned by Lord Horikawa, has difficulty in finishing the central scene of a woman enveloped by flames in a carriage. The model for the picture in an actually burning carriage provided by Lord Horikawa on Yoshihide's request turns out to be none other than the painter's own daughter, who is one of the lord's attendants. A talented artist, Yoshihide is also notorious for his eccentricity, and is nicknamed Saru-hide (*Saru* meaning a monkey) owing to his monkey-like visage. An ironic effect is intensified by an intentional analogy between his dotage on his daughter and the pet monkey's attachment to her. In Yoshihide the demonic passion grotesquely predominates over the human: to achieve his artistic purposes he has no scruples in chaining his disciples, or letting them be attacked by the snake and bat he keeps as paradigms of his hellish setting. He exists solely as an artist and has no attachment to the life of others except for his beloved daughter, who is taken away to serve, and nearly falls victim to the lord and his carnal desires. Her ultimate sacrifice is in a sense the lord's sadistic recompense for his baffled desires. The tragedy Yoshihide confronts is that he has sacrificed all his human values and attachments, including his own daughter, to art. And yet, the completion of his work of art brings no salvation, but is a damnation that ultimately leads to his suicide. Yoshihide's fate gruesomely anticipates many of the hellish aspects of Akutagawa's own life.

'In a Grove' is another variation of Akutagawa's infernal vision of life. In this story the author, characteristically abandoning the pose of the omniscient narrator, lets many characters each present their different points of view – a technique Akutagawa learned from Robert Browning's *The Ring and the Book*. The action of the story seems to consist of a few obvious and objective facts: the brigand Tajōmaru's rape of the wife of a warrior, who is found dead. Yet ambiguity surrounds the warrior's death and the motives and behaviour of the characters directly involved in the incident. The major accounts are given by the brigand, the wife who has come to Kiyomizu Temple to seek peace of mind, and the spirit of the murdered warrior speaking through the mouth of a medium. Yet their accounts contradict one another on crucial matters. The brigand tries to justify his rape by saying that he did it not out of carnal desire but out of real affection. As to his slaying her husband, he alleges that he was forced to do so to oblige the woman's request for a duel. The warrior's wife, on the other hand, resents her husband's contempt for her after the rape. She explains away his death by saying that he consented to her proposal of a double suicide. The warrior, in turn, accuses his wife of willingly submitting to the brigand's proposal to go away with him once she is raped. In his version of the story he also saves face through his apparently warrior-like suicide. All that is common to these mutually contradictory accounts is each character's self-centred wish to justify himself or herself. There is no way for us to know which version is true or even closest to the truth, since as far as we can know one version may claim as much authenticity as another. By deliberately refraining from committing himself to any definitive point of view, Akutagawa implies that the meaning of life is too complex to be subjected to one single interpretation and that truth is hard to obtain.

Akutagawa's *kirishitan-mono* vary in tone and scope. 'Tobacco and the Devil' ('Tabako to Akuma', 1916), for instance, is a humorous allegory, in which as in some of the *ochō-mono* the serious and the absurd are mingled. The disguised Devil who came to Japan together with St Francis Xavier proposes to give his plantation of tobacco to a cow-dealer if he accurately identifies the plant previously unknown in Japan. If he fails, however, the cow-dealer is doomed to damnation. By eavesdropping on the Devil's conversation, he obtains the necessary knowledge and thus is released from his fate, but instead the country itself is doomed to the vice of smoking. 'Therefore, as the luck of the man was coupled with his fall, was not the failure of the Devil accompanied by success?'[10] With such humorous irony the author tells us that the Portuguese missionaries brought into Japan evil in the form of tobacco as well as Christianity. Other tales, however, treat Christian themes in their own right. For instance, 'The Life of St Christopher' ('Kirishitohoro-shōnin Den', 1919) is a straight narrative of the saint's life. More interesting is 'Ogata Ryōsai's Memorandum' ('Ogata Ryōsai Oboegaki', 1917), a tale which deals with the mysterious resurrection of a dead girl through the powers of Christian faith. With superb psychological insight Akutagawa depicts the conflict within a frenzied woman caught up in the dilemma of either abandoning her faith or having her daughter treated by a doctor. 'The Martyr' ('Hōkyōnin no Shi', 1918) is concerned with the martyrdom of Lorenzo, a novice expelled from the monastery because of the allegation that he was responsible for the pregnancy of a girl who had taken a fancy to him. Later, in trying to rescue her baby from a fire, Lorenzo is burnt to death. The girl then confesses that her allegation was false, and Lorenzo in fact turns out to be a woman disguised as a man. These stories aim at neither the confirmation nor the rejection of Christian belief. Just as with the Japanese historical sources he used in other stories, Christianity merely provided Akutagawa with a narrative framework within which he spun out some interesting stories.

One Akutagawa tale dealing with the Tokugawa period, 'Absorbed in Letters' ('Gesaku Zanmai', 1917), vividly depicts scenes from the daily life of the writer Takizawa Bakin. However, Akutagawa presents Bakin not only in his own right but as the idealised prototype of the writer. The choice of Bakin is not accidental, since Akutagawa admires him for cultivating an interest in the supernatural. Bakin as depicted by Akutagawa is worried about his literary reputation, jealous of other writers, repelled by the commercialism of a vulgar publisher and nagged by his own dissatisfaction with the manuscript form of his novel, *Hakkenden*. These mental states of Bakin's indicate something of the anxieties of the author himself. At the end of the story, encouraged by his grandson's witty joke about Kan'non's advice to Bakin to 'work hard, refrain from losing his temper and persevere', Bakin immerses himself completely in writing *Hakkenden* – a writer's ecstasy which Akutagawa wishfully aspires to attain.

Although 'Withered Fields' ('Kareno Shō', 1918)[11] deals explicitly with the reactions of Bashō's disciples to their master's death, the origins of this story may be traced to Sōseki's death. The disciples' reactions are shown to represent a far wider emotional range than grief alone. Kikaku is physically repelled by the ugliness of the dying master's face. Otokuni is displeased by a fellow disciple who cries excessively, yet he himself cannot stop crying. Shikō's controlled reflectiveness may represent Akutagawa's own reaction to Sōseki's death:

> Predominant in his mind at attending the master's death, therefore, are such matters as what the other schools [of *haiku* poetry] would hear about the occasion, the conflict of interests among Bashō's own disciples, and his own interest and calculation. All these have nothing to do with the master's death itself. The master therefore can be said to have been exposed in the withered fields of life as he predicted in his poem. We disciples are not so much mourning the master's death as our loss of the master. We are mourning not the master who died in

withered fields but ourselves who in the dusk have lost
the master.

Priest Inen is suddenly struck by the fear of his own death which
could come immediately after the master's. Only the Zen priest
Jōsō experiences a feeling in which grief and calmness are harmoniously joined.

One of the distinctive features of Akutagawa's tales is thus his
ruthless investigation into the workings of the human mind.
Further evidence of this central concern in his fiction is offered
by 'One Day in the Life of Ōishi Kuranosuke' ('Aruhi no Ōishi
Kuranosuke', 1917). Despite his successful revenge of his late
lord, Ōishi Kuranosuke, the leader of the famous forty-seven
rōnin, undergoes fits of depression, annoyed by the news that the
practice of revenge has become fashionable in Edo. He is also
disturbed by the reflection that while he was playing the role of
a merry-maker to deceive his enemies, there were moments when
he really enjoyed the wine and the women. Akutagawa thus per-
forms a kind of cultural iconoclasm pulling down from his
pedestal a folk hero in Japanese revenge literature.

The cynicism underlying Akutagawa's iconoclasm is also found
in 'The Handkerchief' ('Hankachi', 1916), the earliest of his
tales with a modern setting. A professor of colonial policy at the
University of Tokyo, known for his advocacy of *bushidō* (the
traditional warrior spirit of Japan), and married to an American,
herself sympathetic to Japanese culture, is evidently modelled on
the celebrated Nitobe Inazō (1862–1933), the sometime influ-
ential principal of the First National College and Japanese dele-
gate to the League of Nations.[12] The story centres on the visit of
the mother of one of his students, to inform the professor of her
son's death. While she is doing so, she maintains self-composure
even with a smile on her face. In trying to pick up a fan dropped
on the floor, however, the professor notices under the table that
'probably due to the endeavour to suppress the agitation of her
emotion, her hands, as they trembled, grasped the handkerchief
on her knees so hard that they all but tore it in two'.[13] The lady's
self-restraint strikes the professor as the paragon of *bushidō*.
Later, while reading a Strindberg play, the professor comes across
an episode about an actress who, stricken with grief, at once smiles
and tears a handkerchief in two. Strindberg calls her act 'clap-

trap'. Thus the authenticity not only of *bushidō* but also of the professor who believes in it is undermined by Akutagawa's cynicism. Similarly, 'The General' ('Shōgun', 1922) denigrates the traditionally heroic image of General Nogi by showing how his soldiers' lives were sacrificed to the general's noble cause, how his shrewdness entailed his soldiers' sadistic cruelty to enemies and how naïvely sentimental the general was as a person. Akutagawa's cynicism thus lashes out at the sanctified popular myths of the good, heroic and virtuous.

Most of the stories so far discussed are characterised by the intellectual power of Akutagawa's analysis of human affairs in objective and even ruthless terms. There are a few exceptions in which his feelings win out over his intellectual concerns. In 'The Ball' ('Butōkai', 1920), he exhibits an ability to seize a particular moment of life – the encounter of a young Japanese woman with Pierre Loti, the French novelist known for his *Madame Chrysanthème* (1887). She remembers this encounter throughout her life with its initial emotional intensity. Highly-charged emotion also permeates 'Autumn' ('Aki', 1920), a tale in which the elder sister gives up her beloved cousin to her younger sister. The renunciation on the part of the elder sister and the reciprocation of sympathy between the sisters achieve a cathartic effect. Likewise, the pervasive sense of decay and pathos of the deserted heroine differentiates 'Princess Rokunomiya' ('Rokunomiya no Himegimi', 1922) from other Akutagawa stories in the *ōchō-mono* genre.

It is clear from the foregoing discussion that Akutagawa was more at ease when writing stories with historical settings than those based on his own life and that therefore he dissociated himself from the naturalist or realist tradition. However, there are a few works that have an exceptionally realistic vein. 'A Clod of Earth' ('Ikkai no Tsuchi', 1924) is concerned with the hopeless life of a resilient peasant widow, although its realism never compares with that of full-scale agrarian literature such as *Earth* (*Tsuchi*, 1910) by Nagatsuka Takashi. Another and perhaps the best example of Akutagawa's realist stories is 'Genkaku's House' ('Genkaku Sanbō', 1927), in which Akutagawa ruthlessly examines a nauseating set of human relations: Genkaku, now fatally ill and bed-ridden; his wife O-Tori, also bed-bound for years; their daughter O-Suzu, son-in-law Jūkichi and their son

Takeo; O-Yoshi, once the maid servant and later Genkaku's mistress, and her son Buntarō begotten by Genkaku; and the nurse Kōno as a malicious observer of the domestic scene. Jūkichi bears no love whatsoever for his father-in-law; indeed, he is only repelled by and afraid of his tuberculosis. The arrival of O-Yoshi with Buntarō causes the two children to fight and O-Tori to become jealous of O-Yoshi. Kōno, herself a woman with an unhappy past, derives sadistic pleasure from grinning cynically at O-Suzu's blunders and the children's fights, yet she pretends to reconcile the domestic rifts. She flirts with Jūkichi, who becomes aware of her approaches and timidly withdraws himself. Genkaku is at once consoled and harassed by O-Yoshi's presence. He cannot help admitting that although he was once attached to O-Yoshi and Buntarō, he now feels at times tempted to kill them.[14] Even Genkaku's death, preceded by his pathetically flawed attempt to strangle himself, is greeted with stinginess by Jūkichi. Knowing that the first-class funeral is fully booked up, he feels free to order it instead of the second, and, in the end, is given the super-class funeral at the price of the first. This picture of hell on earth in a realistic setting is as powerful and coherent as any of the stories with a historical setting.

Whether they concern the historical past or modern times, the Akutagawa stories so far discussed, in marked contrast with the I-novels, do not deal directly with personal experience. However, even Akutagawa could not help writing about himself, in either a straightforward or a thinly disguised manner. There are some stories in which the main character is called Yasukichi but is unmistakably the author himself (for example, 'From Yasukichi's Notebooks' ['Yasukichi no Techō kara', 1923] and 'A Cold Day' ['Samusa', 1924]). In others, mainly devoid of plot and action, Akutagawa in his own person depicts aspects of his own life (for example, 'The Illness of a Child' ['Kodomo no Byōki', 1923], 'Bowing' ['Ojigi', 1923], 'Mirage' ['Shinkirō', 1927] and 'Winter' ['Fuyu', 1927]). In 'Mirage', for instance, Akutagawa creates a world in which the feelings of the characters (the author, his wife and their friends) are so refined that their lives become more nebulous than the mirage which they think they are watching.

In his autobiographical recollections, too, unlike Shiga Naoya who reconstructed his life history into the lengthy *A Dark Night's Passing*, Akutagawa specialised in the short form. 'My Life in Those Days' ('Anokoro no Jibun no Koto', 1919) recounts his happy association with his university friends, all aspiring to literary renown. The quasi-autobiographical 'The Early Life of Daidōji Shinsuke' ('Daidōji Shinsuke no Hansei', 1925), written two and a half years before his death, looks back on his earlier life with ambivalence, a blend of nostalgia and resentment. His native district of Honjo in Tokyo is seen as squalid, yet more charming than the traditional *shitamachi* or, for that matter, *yamanote*;[15] we read of the loss of his mother, the poverty covered up by his vain foster-parents, his precocious contempt for school and teachers, his use of books to substitute for real experience, and his inability to make friends except through intellectual excellence – all of these may well have been responsible for his insecurity and alienation from reality.

By 1927, except for these semi-autobiographical pieces, Akutagawa had long ceased to write works with a fictional structure. 'Kappa' (1927) is practically the only exception to this development of his fiction. An allegorical satire, it has obvious similarities to *Gulliver's Travels* and Anatole France's *Island of Penguins*. Further comparison may be made with such Western works as *News from Nowhere* and *Erewhon*. The author uses a double narrative structure in which a lunatic tells a story about his experiences in the country of the *kappa*, an imaginary amphibian in Japanese folk-lore. Ironically enough, the lunatic speaks rationally about the irrational, absurd and repulsive aspects of the *kappa* country which is supposed to be more advanced than human society. The keynote of the story is one of pessimism. In the *kappa* land it is customary for a father to ask the foetus whether or not it wants to be born. One foetus replies: 'I do not wish to be born. In the first place, it makes me shudder to think of all the things that I shall inherit from my father – the insanity alone is bad enough. And an additional factor is that I maintain that a Kappa's existence is evil' (section 4).[16] Akutagawa also partly projects himself into the character of Tok the poet who believes the family bond is the source of suffering. In his view the supreme concept of art is that of art-for-art's sake; an artist must be a superman who transcends the distinction between good and evil. Akutagawa apparently borrows the idea of superman from G. B. Shaw as well as from Nietzsche. Shaw's ideas are also echoed in the practice of courting which lets the female take the initiative. Akutagawa's satirical blade touches upon such subjects as police censorship of art and employers' exploitation of labourers, who are dismissed and then butchered. *A Fool's Words*, a collection of aphorisms by the philosopher Mag, echoes Akutagawa's own 'A Dwarf's Words' ('Shuju no Kotoba', 1923–5) and 'A Fool's Life' ('Aru Ahō no Isshō', 1927). It contains, for instance, a pungent remark on rationalism: 'If we live our lives by reason, then, as a matter of course, we would negate our own existence. The fact that Voltaire, who made a god out of reason, ended his life happily indicates that a human being is not evolved as a Kappa' (section 11).[17] Thus cynicism is particularly relevant to the poet Tok. Like the author himself, Tok eventually commits suicide. This is attributed to his chronic stomachic atony and melancholia, while others think that 'he realized he was burnt out as a poet as well' (section 13). By recounting his experiences in the imaginary *kappa* country, the narrator is explicitly making a criticism of human society. 'Insane' in the eye of society, he has to be judged sane by the reader since what he says makes sense as regards the absurdities of the *kappa* country, the land which is in fact human society.

Tok's suicide in 'Kappa' obliquely hints at Akutagawa's own fate. In his 'A Note to an Old Friend' ('Aru Kyūyū e Okuru Shuki', 1927) Akutagawa attributes his suicide to 'vague anxiety about future'. He discloses in this note that he was thinking of suicide for two years; that he once conceived of a platonic double suicide with a woman but abandoned the idea out of consideration for his wife. A supplementary account is also available in 'A Dialogue in Darkness' ('Anchū Mondō', 1927), in which the two interlocutors may well represent the strife in a split personality between the self and anti-self, ego and super-ego, conscious and unconscious. Once again he mentions his attempt at a double suicide with a woman he loved, and he gives four causes for his suicide: (1) hereditary, (2) environmental, (3) accidental and (4) intentional. 'Hereditary', of course, means his mother's insanity which he always feared he had inherited. 'Environmental' suggests his involvement with his relatives, e.g. the suicide of his brother-in-law who was suspected of having set his own home on fire to receive insurance benefits (cf. 'Winter'). The words 'accidental' and 'intentional' suggest that there existed in his mind contradictions which he himself could not fully explain. His suicide was intentional since it was a voluntary act. Yet, it seems possible that he was involuntarily driven to it by powers beyond his control.[18]

Earlier it has been mentioned that in the so-called *kirishitan* stories Akutagawa's concern was neither to defend nor to reject Christian faith and that he merely used Christian material for the framework of his stories just as he did with historical material. The case is slightly different with 'The Western Sage' – meaning Christ ('Seihō no Hito', 1927), in which he attempts a personal interpretation of some Christian doctrines. His treatment of the subject is not comprehensive, nor is his argument thorough-going. Like 'A Fool's Life' it consists of a series of aphoristic observations full of ironies and paradoxes. Moreover, it seems to pay little respect to the orthodox theories of Christianity. How it deviates from orthodoxy, however, is not of primary importance. More interesting is the psychological motive behind these devia-tions. Throughout 'The Western Sage' he sympathises whole-heartedly with Christ's Passion. His arguments are based on two central ideas. First, Christ's tragedy originates from the split in him between the spiritual and the material: Christ's renunciation of the glory on earth entails his perpetual alienation from the material world. Secondly, Akutagawa identifies Christ with various types of people such as a 'journalist', a 'poet' and a 'rationalist'. In his over-simplified view, both Christ and these people sacrificed their lives to spiritual values. Thus they all suffered from the fracture of personality or a kind of schizo-phrenia. Furthermore, by finding parallels between Christ and these people, the author seems to identify himself with Christ. This kind of self-identification is in itself typical of a schizoid character.[19]

That towards the end of his life Akutagawa suffered from acute neurosis is proven by 'Cogwheels' ('Haguruma', 1927). It reads like a stream of consciousness story with the key image of 'semi-transparent cogwheels' continually turning in his mind's eye. He is harassed by a series of hallucinations, obsessions, phobias and paranoid feelings, which are all associated with a mysteriously Kafkaesque sense of death. The memory of a worm which he finds on his meat plate at a wedding feast later returns when he detects the skull under the skin of his gaunt face as reflected in a mirror. He tries in vain to write his work, only to find himself continuously writing 'all right', the phrase he imagines to have been spoken by invisible hotel waiters. In reading a Tolstoy story he sees it as a caricature of his own life. A mere paranoiac feeling of being stared at coldly by the hotel staff grows out of all proportion into a sense of damnation. Even a passer-by's casual remark 'how irritating' jars his nerves. Avoiding yellow-coloured taxis as they tend to involve him in accidents he takes a green taxi to Aoyama and finds himself in front of the crematorium instead of the mental clinic which he wants to visit (one as ominous as the other). In the taxi he senses a profound unreality around him – 'politics, business, art, science – all these are nothing but the multi-coloured enamel covering up the terrifying life' (section 2). In Ginza, overwhelmed by a huge crowd, he hurries into a bookshop, where even the reference to Nemesis in a children's book of Greek mythology scares him. A picture of 'cogwheels' drawn by a German lunatic horrifies him. He opens one book after another, but they all prove equally threatening. A book on Eastern religion cites 'four arch-enemies – doubt, fear, pride and carnal desire', which is what he considers 'sensibility and reason' to be. Thus Eastern religion is no more help than modern Western thought in relieving his distress. A portrait of Napoleon in a café reminds him of the story that Napoleon as a student wrote down in his notebook the words 'St Helena' as if he had had prescience of his fate. Then what about his own words in 'A Dwarf's Words' – 'Life is even more infernal than the inferno', or the fate of Yoshihide in 'The Hell Screen'? Does it not look as if he had forecast in these writings his own agonies and his own fate (section 3)? Apparently he is aware of the Freudian concept of the slip of the tongue, for his failure to pronounce certain names makes him uneasy about his mental state. Towards the end of the story his paranoiac sense of persecution increases beyond his control. The sound 'mmm...' repeatedly mumbled to him by a stranger over the telephone becomes associated in his phantasy with 'la mort' (section 4). A letter from a German publisher requesting an article on 'modern Japanese women' somewhat like a sketch in 'black and white' reminds him of a bar where he had Black and White whisky, and felt that the news reporters were gossiping about him. He tears the letter to pieces. Another letter from his nephew about Saitō Mokichi's (1882–1953) collection of poems *Red Light* (*Shakkō*, 1913) scares him as it reminds him of the red lantern in Ginza which, reflecting his own shadow, frightened him (section 5): 'That someone or something has been trying to persecute me made me uneasy at every step I walked. Thereupon the semi-transparent cogwheels began to obstruct my sight one after another. Fearing that the last moment was drawing near, I walked with my neck straight.'

One may wonder whether 'Cogwheels' is an accurate record or an artistic representation of what Akutagawa actually suffered. The details of abnormal psychology and behaviour look too real to be artificially invented by someone who has not actually experienced them. On the other hand one may be struck by the coherence of the details and wonder how this work could be written by a sick mind. Admittedly schizophrenic phantasy has its own rational coherence. Yet one may still be tempted to detect in this work some deliberate contrivances for artistic effect. And, if 'Cogwheels' was not an exact record but a deliberately modified version of what Akutagawa actually suffered, it is likely that it owes its coherence to some theoretical sources of psychology, such as the works of Mainländer whom Akutagawa mentions in 'A Note to an Old Friend'. One should remember that recourse to some psychological and philosophical theories as a moral prop can be in itself symptomatic of an abnormal psychological state.[20] Possibly he resorted to theoretical sources because he was partly aware of what was wrong with him, and such self-awareness on his part would indicate that his abnormality was not so much one of psychosis as of neurosis. One may question the common belief that self-awareness and self-analysis with the aid of theoretical sources actually help to relieve pain. Unfortunately, self-awareness and self-analysis alone are ultimately not enough to prevent the suffering person from committing suicide.

Akutagawa had a unique sensibility with which he investigated the facts of life, its intricacies and complexities. His unwillingness to reconcile himself with these facts indicates at once his moral scrupulousness and his lack of tolerance towards the weakness in others and in himself. In coping with these facts he turned to the faculty of reason, as had modern European masters, especially Voltaire. Yet he parted company from Voltaire. ('A Dwarf's Words'): 'I despise Voltaire. If one sticks to reason, one must curse one's own existence through and through. Yet how happy is the author of *Candide*, who is absorbed in praising the world! What reason taught me after all was its own futility.' In rejecting Voltaire, Akutagawa aligns himself with the writers of the European *fin de siècle*, for whom morality founded on a belief in rationalism and individual autonomy had gone bankrupt ('A Fool's Life'):

> It was on the first floor of a book-shop. He (at the age of twenty) climbed a Western style ladder hung on the book-shelf and was looking for new books. Maupassant, Baudelaire, Strindberg, Ibsen, Shaw, Tolstoi, . . .
> . . .He kept on reading intently the letters on the backs of books. They were not so much books as the *fin de siècle* itself: Nietzsche, Verlaine, the Goncourts, Dostoevski, Hauptmann, Flaubert, . . .
> . . .The books began sinking in the gloomy darkness. . . .Then an uncovered lamp was lighted suddenly over his head. Standing on the top of the ladder, he looked down over the shopkeepers and customers moving among books. The human figures all looked dwarfed. Moreover, they looked paltry.
> 'Life is not worth a line of Baudelaire.'

After the collapse of morality based on individualism there remained only an infernal vision of life, which he shared with the writers he cites. The ghost of Nietzsche beckoned him to transcend the distinction between good and evil. Failing this, he had nowhere to go. Yet, was he really qualified to denounce Voltaire? Not only was he far short of Voltaire's stature, but they had different notions of reason. To Akutagawa reason was rather the hypersensitive 'intellect' which 'was immediately at the tips of the senses':[21] 'I have not a bit of consciousness; all I have is my nerve' ('A Dialogue in Darkness'). His adoption and later rejection of Voltaire's reason illustrate the impasse in which modern Japanese writers have often found themselves. By resorting to European values in the abstract, they lose touch with Japanese reality and the real substance of life. Furthermore they find that the abstract principles which they have built up according to European models are of no use in coping with the realities of their lives. Akutagawa's failure to grasp tangible reality and his ultimate alienation from it made the mode of his life almost schizophrenic. In this respect he contrasts with Shiga Naoya and with Tanizaki Jun'ichirō as well. Clearly he did not possess the resilience with which Shiga got out of his impasse as described in *A Dark Night's Passing* and other stories, let alone the hedonistic gusto with which Tanizaki relished the pleasures of life.

These features of Akutagawa's attitude to life link up naturally with the form of his writing. Here again there are interesting interrelations between Shiga, Akutagawa and Tanizaki. In 1927, from April to the time of his death, Akutagawa was embroiled in a series of controversies with Tanizaki in the magazine *Chūō Kōron*. Akutagawa entitled his articles 'Artistic, too Artistic' ('Bungeitekina Amarini Bungeitikina'), echoing Nietszche's 'Human, too Human'. One of Tanizaki's main arguments was that Japanese novels, unlike their Western counterparts, lacked an organic structure. Tanizaki further asserted that novels must have a coherent plot. Against this, Akutagawa, while admitting that stories with a plot were certainly more interesting, defended those without one, stories which were 'pure' in the sense that they did not flatter popular taste. As examples of his kind of 'pure' fiction he cited Shiga's stories and extended his definition of 'pure' to such terms as (1) Shiga's moral sincerity; (2) realistic description of details; (3) realism mixed with a poetic spirit, e.g., the scene in *A Dark Night's Passing* (chapter 2, section 14) where the protagonist shouts 'Harvest! Harvest!' as he touches the breast of a prostitute; (4) the effective technique of ending a story with picturesque accuracy and concentration; and (5) freedom from imitation of Western stories despite the apparent resemblance. Akutagawa thus deviates from his original purpose in arguing with Tanizaki in order to eulogise Shiga's works with a mixture of respect and envy. His defence of 'plotless' and 'pure' fiction is also a justification of the kind of stories he himself came to write after he had ceased to bother with historical settings.

All this bears on his plight in his last years. Beginning his literary career in conscious reaction to the naturalist tradition of self-exposure, he succeeded in creating stories which had an autonomous world independent of the author's own life. Yet towards the end of his career he seems to have exhausted whatever talent he had for creating fiction and ended up drawing material in a rather straightforward way from his own life. With his perceptive insight he must have been aware of the fact that he was heading for a dead end. He could not allow himself to expose his real life in the sado-masochistic manner of the Japanese naturalists. Nor could he emulate Shiga who produced works of art based on life experiences, and who, while inheriting the tradition of the naturalists, nevertheless distinguished himself from them by producing a record of overcoming his plight instead of being defeated by it. With his talent for creating historical fiction drained of the real content of life, Akutagawa was left with only a high-powered intellect abstractly fashioned according to Western models. This ultimately proved inadequate for his survival.

5

The eternal womanhood:
TANIZAKI JUN'ICHIRŌ and KAWABATA YASUNARI

I

Both Tanizaki Jun'ichirō (1886–1965) and Kawabata Yasunari (1899–1972) are still fresh in our memories. Tanizaki had more than once been a candidate for the Nobel Prize for Literature before he died in 1965. The prize instead went to Kawabata in 1968. Shortly afterwards Kawabata gained attention for his involvement in the election campaign for the governor of Tokyo, and subsequent suicide. Yet, the literary careers of these two masters spanned three eras. Tanizaki's 'Tattoo' ('Shisei'), for instance, was written as early as 1910, and his reputation was already secure by the end of the Taishō era. Kawabata's literary activity by the early years of Shōwa was also noteworthy. Both writers were, therefore, masters of the prewar period who continued to produce important works in the postwar period. Furthermore, their works show interesting parallels as well as differences from one another.

Throughout this book I have assumed that a work of literature should be treated as an autonomous entity. While it is certainly wrong to treat the contents of a novel as a direct reflection of its author's life (except perhaps in the case of some I-novels), there is no use denying that the life of an author – particularly a modern Japanese author – in many ways affects the nature of his works. Tanizaki – the man and his works – is no exception to this rule. His immediate ancestors were for generations the natives of Edo. Being of merchant rather than samurai class, they were interested not so much in the affairs of state as in enjoying themselves. Secondly, despite the patriarchal structure of Japanese society, Tanizaki's grandfather and father are said to have been feminists. His father is said to have doted on Tanizaki's beautiful mother. Tanizaki, in turn, felt drawn to her with an almost Oedipal force: 'Not only her face, but also the skin of her thighs was so fair and fine that I was often struck with its beauty when we shared a bath.'[1] The image of eternal womanhood was thus indelibly impressed on Tanizaki's mind not through his phantasy but through the flesh and blood memory of his own mother. Thirdly, Tanizaki was a handsome little boy, often vulnerable to the masculine violence of his school mates and sometimes sought after by older bullies as a sexual object. These experiences may well have fostered a potential masochism in him. Fourthly, at his primary school a perceptive young teacher noticed in Tanizaki a promising talent and gave him special instruction in the Japanese and Chinese classics, an education which undoubtedly helped him to develop a refined understanding of the oriental cultural tradition.

It is a well-attested part of the Tanizaki legend that he was the brightest pupil ever to graduate from the First Municipal Secondary School of Tokyo. He then followed a path which many a bright young man had taken before him – the First National College and the University of Tokyo. While a university student in the Department of Japanese Literature, he joined the *Shinshichō*, the literary magazine of the University, and began publishing short stories, some of which were lauded by his literary elders, including Mori Ōgai (1862–1922) and Nagai Kafū (1879–1959). He did not finish his university course – simply because he did not pay the fees. The disruption of his university education, however, did not matter very much to him, for by then his works were beginning to gain ground in the literary world. His earlier works are characterised by a variety of features: Gothic, grotesque, decadent, hedonistic, sex-maniacal, immoral, diabolic, and so on. Some of these features may well be traced back to the Japanese tradition, but Tanizaki also used European models of the mid-nineteenth century and the *fin de siècle*, for example Edgar Allan Poe, Charles Baudelaire and Oscar Wilde. His move from Tokyo to the Kansai (Kyoto, Ōsaka and Kōbe) area after the Great Earthquake of 1923 had more than accidental significance, for it coincided with his more conscious cultivation of Japanese sensibilities and treatment of Japanese subjects. His personal life remained as sensational as the decadence of his earlier works. In 1930 he divorced Chiyoko, his wife for fifteen years, so that she could marry Satō Haruo (1892–1964), his friend and fellow writer. Tanizaki was then free in 1931 to marry another woman,

Tomiko, a literary disciple. He divorced her in 1934 and then married in 1935 for the last time. His new wife was Nezu Matzuko, the alienated wife of an Ōsaka millionaire and a patron of artists and writers, including Tanizaki himself. From 1935 to 1938 he was engaged on the translation into modern Japanese of *The Tale of Genji*. The time was unpropitious. Japan was coming under the rule of totalitarianism and militarism, and Tanizaki was forced to expurgate the amorous passages from his translation of *Genji*. Furthermore, even the publication of *The Makioka Sisters* was interrupted, because it also dealt with amorous matters, which the military government regarded as incompatible with the purpose of carrying out the 'sacred war'. However absurd this may seem now, we must bear in mind the earnestness with which such things were regarded in those days.

Tanizaki would have deserved renown for his earlier works alone. But *The Makioka Sisters* (*Sasameyuki*, 1943–8) truly established his position among the greatest of modern Japanese writers. It stands out not only among his own works but also among the whole corpus of modern Japanese literature. In the light of his own works it sounds a note quite different from that of his earlier, decadent and diabolic pieces. How these different notes are intermingled in the development of Tanizaki's literary art will be seen in the following pages.

'Tattoo', which Tanizaki wrote while still a university student, illustrates the characteristic features of his earlier works. The protagonist, a tattooer, has long wished to find a beautiful girl on whom to tattoo a spider. The girl must look identical with the one in a picture he possesses, entitled 'Victims', which portrays a beautiful girl leaning against a cherry tree and surrounded by men's corpses lying on the ground. Obviously the girl is a *femme fatale* and the dead men her victims. On finding an ideal girl, the tattooer works on her body while she is drugged. When he finishes the work he says:

> 'To make you truly beautiful I have poured my soul into this tattoo. Today there is no woman in Japan to compare with you. Your old fears are gone. All men will be your victims.'
>   As if in response to these words a faint moan came from the girl's lips. Slowly she began to recover her

senses. With each shuddering breath, the spider's legs stirred as if they were alive.[2]

Ironically enough, her first victim, as the reader would probably guess, is the tattooer himself. The story thus amounts to the protagonist's quest for ideal beauty or eternal womanhood, in this case not something intangible, but instead the tangible flesh of a woman.

The theme in Tanizaki's works of the yearning for an irresistible *femme fatale* is sometimes supplemented by another theme – that of the yearning for motherhood as in 'Yearning for Mother' ('Haha o Kouru Ki', 1919). This short story consists of a poignant and imaginary dream in which the author-narrator is a boy of seven or eight who searches for his lately deceased mother. In the first half of the dream he finds himself in the middle of a desolate marshland, and he walks towards a light flickering in the distance. The old woman whom he meets there and takes for his mother, however, heartlessly rejects him. In the second half of the story he finds himself in a moonlit landscape, where the sound of a samisen reminds him of his infancy. The samisen music turns out to be performed by a woman walking by. In the climactic recognition scene, although the narrator feels uncertain about her identity, the woman reveals herself to be his mother. Unlike the old woman in the first half, this second one is portrayed as exquisitely beautiful. The narrator particularly admires the sole of her foot which he feels tempted to nibble. This description ranks as one of the earliest examples of foot fetish in Tanizaki's works. The quest for eternal womanhood either through a *femme fatale* or through the idealised mother figure proved to be the keynote in many of Tanizaki's works. So different from the quests for virtues praised in the Marian woman in many Western medieval romances, this essentially masculine worship of the female senses represents throughout Tanizaki's work the persistent source of manly joy, an obsession he relishes without guilt or sin.

Like 'Tattoo', *A Fool's Love* (*Chijin no Ai*, 1924–5) is a story about its narrator's quest for an ideal woman. While 'Tattoo' is set in the Tokugawa period, the setting of *A Fool's Love* is thoroughly modern. The narrator, a kind of modern Pygmalion, meets fifteen-year-old Naomi, a novice waitress at a coffee shop.

He takes her home and looks after her with the intention of marrying her in a few years' time. He tries to bring her up according to his ideal – that is, the so-called 'modern girl' of the early Taishō period. Thus Naomi is made to dress herself in Western fashion and to practise the piano, English and social dancing. Their house in Yokohama boasts, of course, a fashionable European style. Towards the end of the story, Naomi leaves him after a quarrel. In the end they are reconciled, but only precariously.

Some Prefer Nettles (*Tadekuu Mushi*, 1928–9) is about a marital relationship on the verge of breaking up. The estranged couple, Kaname and Misako, have long ceased to be sexually interested in each other. He encourages her to have an affair while he himself gratifies his sexual desires with a Eurasian prostitute named Louise. Yet this married couple is more resigned than bitter about its grim situation. While his peculiar marital relationship anticipates to some extent Tanizaki's own divorce and yielding of his first wife to Satō Haruo, the author's technique and intention in this novel should not be confused with an I-novelist's. Tanizaki is concerned not so much with making a public confession about his personal plight, as with making a detached observation through fictional narrative.

Being a typical Tanizaki protagonist, Kaname is in search of the eternal womanhood, whether she is a *femme fatale* or an ideal mother figure. But his quest is in vain. The Eurasian Louise does not embody it although she gratifies his desires. Nor does Misako, who is spared from merely serving Kaname's desire. The estrangement between Kaname and Misako is contrasted with the perfectly harmonious relationship between Misako's father and his mistress, despite an age gap of thirty years between them. The old man's cultivated taste for *Bunraku* (Japanese puppet theatre) introduces into the novel another theme which proves in the end to be tightly interlocked with the main theme. This new theme reflects Tanizaki's growing interest in the traditional culture of Japan, which he praised later in the essay 'In Praise of Shadows' ('In'ei Raisan', 1933–4), at the expense of what he regarded as Western culture. In formulating a perhaps over-simplified theory or pseudo-theory, Tanizaki contrasted Western and traditional Japanese cultures in terms of the light and shade, explicit and implicit, and liberated and repressed.

In *Some Prefer Nettle*s it is just these features of traditional Japanese culture that the puppet theatre comes to represent. Towards the close of the novel the image of the old man's mistress, O-Hisa, merges with a puppet in Kaname's phantasy:

> Kaname crawled under the net himself when O-hisa had gone. . . .He tried to make out the picture in the alcove beyond the light-green netting. Something in modest, neutral colors, a landscape it seemed to be, wider than it was high. With the light inside the net, however, the rest of the room lay in deep shadow, and he could make out neither the details nor the artist's signature. Below it in a bowl was what he took to be a blue and white porcelain burner. There was a faint smell of incense through the room – he noticed it for the first time. Plum blossom, he judged. For an instant he thought he saw O-hisa's face, faint and white, in a shadowy corner beside the bed. He started up, but quickly caught himself. It was the puppet the old man had brought back from Awaji, a lady puppet in a modest dotted kimono.[3]

Although in this novel the protagonist is led to no definite goal in his relationship with women, this ending suggests Tanizaki's willingness to cultivate more of the traditional Japanese values in order to aid and, indeed, achieve his quest for the ideal woman.

Tanizaki took great pains to disguise *A Portrait of Shunkin* (*Shunkinshō*, 1933) as a biography of a blind *koto* teacher. But the theme that emerges from this novel is unmistakably Tanizaki's. The heroine, the daughter of a wealthy Ōsaka merchant, is blinded at the age of nine probably by a jealous nurse, and later becomes a virtuoso at playing the *koto*, a kind of Japanese harp. The story centres round her relationship with Sasuke, originally a servant apprenticed to her father but then her attendant after she becomes blind. Not only does Sasuke learn the art of the *koto* from serving her while she is taking lessons from her teacher, but also he secretly becomes intimate with her. The domineering and proud Shunkin, however, never officially acknowledges the devoted and subservient Sasuke to be her husband. She even disowns their children who are adopted by a local farmer. Sasuke in turn is perfectly content to be enslaved to her as a disciple. Later, after having attained mastery and herself become a teacher in the art of *koto*, Shunkin is disfigured a second time, when her beautiful face is burnt by boiling water poured on her by someone either jealous of her relationship with Sasuke or resentful of her extremely strict method of teaching. Faithful Sasuke then proves his devotion by blinding himself. He pricks his eyes with a needle to blot out any vision of Shunkin's disfigured face and thereby eternally cherishes in his mind an image of her intangible, perfect beauty. At this climactic moment Sasuke paradoxically attains his enlightenment through self-inflicted darkness.

> As they sat facing each other in silence, Sasuke began
> to feel the quickening of that sixth sense which only the
> blind possess, and he could tell that there was nothing
> but the deepest gratitude in Shunkin's heart. Always
> before, even while they were making love, they had been
> separated by the gulf between teacher and pupil. But
> now Sasuke felt that they were truly united, locked in a
> tight embrace. Youthful memories of the dark world of
> the closet where he used to practice came flooding into
> his mind, but the darkness in which he now found
> himself seemed completely different. Most blind people
> can sense the direction from which light is coming; they
> live in a faintly luminous world, not one of unrelieved
> blackness. Now Sasuke knew that he had found an inner
> vision in place of the vision he had lost. Ah, he thought,
> this is the world my teacher lives in – at last I have
> reached it! He could no longer clearly distinguish the
> objects around him, or the way Shunkin herself looked;
> all he could detect was the pale, blurred image of her
> bandage-swathed face. But he had no thought of the
> bandages. It was Shunkin's exquisite white face – as it
> had looked until only two months ago – that hovered
> before him in a circle of dim light, like the radiant halo
> of the Buddha.[4]

This episode is supplemented by a touching account of their later years:

> Now that Sasuke had taken over all the teaching and
> was in effect supporting the household, why did he not

become Shunkin's legal husband? Was her pride still the obstacle? According to Teru, Sasuke told her that Shunkin had become quite dejected, and that it grieved him – he could not bear to think of her as pitiable, someone to feel sorry for. Apparently the blind Sasuke had given himself up to his imperishable ideal. To him, there was only the world of his old memories. If Shunkin had actually changed in character because of her misfortune she would no longer have been Shunkin. He wanted to think of her as the proud, haughty girl of the past; otherwise, the beautiful Shunkin of his imagination would have been destroyed. And so it seems that it was he who had the stronger reason for not wishing to marry.

Because Sasuke used the real Shunkin to call to mind the Shunkin of his memories, he was careful to observe the proper etiquette between servant and mistress. Indeed, he humbled himself more than ever, serving her with the utmost devotion so that she might soon forget her misery and regain her old self-confidence.

Tanizaki had thus successfully created a character who with willing masochism devotes himself to his ideal of eternal womanhood in which the tangible and intangible are intricately merged together.

From these works of Tanizaki's emerges the theme of his pursuit of the ideal woman, a quest undertaken with a precarious psychological balance not totally free from an underlying morbidity. Was it possible for him to represent beauty that obsessed him in a more positive form? The answer is to be found in *The Makioka Sisters*, which is concerned with the history of a wealthy Ōsaka merchant family. Its heyday is already over and the four sisters are trying hard to maintain a remnant of the past glory against the declining fortune. As a family chronicle *The Makioka Sisters* is reminiscent of Tōson's *The House* and *Before the Dawn*, although the authors' narrative techniques and their ways of treating their subjects are entirely different. One may seek an analogy with and yet will find it different from some family chronicles in Western literature such as Thomas Mann's *Budden-*

brooks and John Galsworthy's *The Forsyte Saga*. *The Makioka Sisters* is constructed in such a way that it does not move towards only one conclusion – Yukiko's final successful *miai* or marriage arrangement after a series of unsuccessful ones. Instead, it consists of a multi-layered quilt of episodes and emotions that create a social and psychological texture rare in modern Japanese fiction.

The Makioka Sisters focuses on the characterisation of the four eponymous sisters and their interactions as much as with a series of events. The Japanese title, *Sasame-yuki* or fine flakes of snow, refers to the sister Yukiko, whose unsuccessful series of *miai* provides the background for the novel. But Sachiko, the second eldest, plays, with the aid of her compassionate and resourceful husband Teinosuke, the more explicitly significant role of intermediary who joins together the various characters and incidents. Without her, the Makioka family, like the novel itself, would split up, each of the sisters drifting as her own inclinations dictate: the eldest and conservative Tsuruko with her mediocre, unimaginative husband; Yukiko, despite her delicate beauty and resourcefulness, ineffectual in coping with the world; and the youngest, Taeko, despite her talents and intelligence, dabbling in licentiousness.

The Makioka Sisters successfully conveys a sense of beauty, first by representing it in the context of modern *haute* bourgeois culture and secondly by suggesting to the reader its precariousness and transience. Specifically rooted in *kamigata* (the Kyoto and Ōsaka area), this culture retains in genuine form traditional Japanese sensibilities, while also successfully assimilating Western culture. In this novel preference is given explicitly to *kamigata* against Tokyo. Tatsuo, Tsuruko's husband, becomes the manager of the Tokyo branch of his bank, and the family moves from Kansai to Tokyo. Tsuruko is disturbed by this move, and thereafter she is portrayed in a less sympathetic light. The major characters speak the most elegant Ōsaka dialect, with which the Tokyo speech – not the dialect of the native Edo people but the so-called *yamanote* speech – is unfavourably contrasted. This typifies Tanizaki's own predilection, despite his upbringing in Tokyo, for the genuinely Japanese *kamigata* culture. The authenticity of Tanizaki's references to Kabuki and Japanese dancing derives from his close familiarity with these traditional arts. It is also worth noticing that the contact with Western culture represented in such episodes as the piano recital, the acquaintance with the Russian *émigrés* and the neighbouring German family, and the habit of wine-tasting, is entirely in keeping with the main characters' way of life. In this connexion, one may in passing say that unlike Tōkoku, Sōseki and Akutagawa, Tanizaki saw the confrontation between the East and the West in sensuous, not intellectual, terms. Such famous scenes as that of viewing the cherry-blossoms or the firefly hunt illustrate the keynote of *The Makioka Sisters* – the realisation and transcience of beauty.

Those weeping cherries just beyond the gallery to the left as one steps inside the gate and faces the main hall – those cherries said to be famous even abroad – how would they be this year? Was it perhaps already too late? Always they stepped through the gallery with a strange rising of the heart, but the five of them cried out as one when they saw that cloud of pink spread across the late-afternoon sky.

It was the climax of the pilgrimage, the moment treasured through a whole year. All was well, they had come again to the cherries in full bloom. There was a feeling of relief, and a hope that next year they might be as fortunate, and for Sachiko, at least, the thought that even if she herself stood here next year, Yukiko might be married and far away. The flowers would come again, but Yukiko would not. It was a saddening thought, and yet it contained almost a prayer that, for Yukiko's sake, she might indeed no longer be with them. Sachiko had stood under these same trees with these same emotions the year before and the year before that, and each time she had found it hard to understand why they should still be together. She could not bear to look at Yukiko.

The willows and oaks beyond the cherry grove were sending out new buds. The oleanders had been clipped into round balls. Sending the four ahead, Teinosuke photographed them at all the usual spots: White Tiger Pond, with its iris-lined shore; the stepping stones called the Bridge of the Reclining Tiger, reflected from the water with the four figures. He had them line up under the truly glorious branches that trail down over the path from the pine-topped hillock to the west of the Pond of the Nesting Phoenix. All sorts of strangers took pictures of the Makioka procession. The polite would carefully ask permission, the rude would simply snap. There the family had had tea, here they had fed the red carp – they remembered the smallest details of earlier pilgrimages.

(Book 1, chapter 19)

They turned off the flash lights and approached in silence. Fireflies dislike noise and light. But even at the edge of the river there were no fireflies. 'Maybe they are not out tonight', someone whispered. 'No, there are plenty of them. Come over here.' Down into the grasses on the bank, and there, in the delicate moment before the last light goes, were fireflies, gliding out over the water, in low arcs like the sweep of the grasses. On down the river, and on and on, were fireflies, lines of them wavering out from this bank and the other and back again, sketching their uncertain tracks of light down close to the surface of the water, hidden from outside by the grasses. In the last moment of light, with the darkness creeping up from the water and the moving plumes of grass still faintly outlined, there, far as the river stretched – an infinite number of little lines in two long rows on either side, quiet, unearthly. Sachiko could see it all even now, here inside with her eyes closed. Surely that was the impressive moment of the evening, the moment that made the firefly hunt worth-while.

A firefly hunt has none of the radiance of a cherry-blossom party. Dark, dreamy, rather – might one say? Perhaps something of the child's world, the world of the fairy story in it. Something not to be painted, but set to music, the mood of it taken up on piano or koto. And while she lay with her eyes closed, the fireflies, out there along the river, all through the night, were flashing on and off, silent, numberless. Sachiko felt a surging inside her, as though she were joining them, soaring and

dipping along the surface of the water, cutting her own
uncertain track of light.

(Book III, chapter 4[5])

For the characterisation of Sachiko and her sisters, Tanizaki
admittedly gained an inspiration from his third wife and her
family. It is as likely that his translation of *The Tale of Genji*
into modern Japanese made a significant contribution to the composition of *The Makioka Sisters*. The hypothesis can be sub-
stantiated by pointing out the parallels between the two works.
First, the refined life style in Tanizaki's work corresponds with
the *miyabi* or grace of *Genji* despite the difference in social background between a modern bourgeois family and the Heian
imperial court. Secondly, both works succeed in portraying a
group of charming women. Thirdly, in linking one after another
of Yukiko's *miai* in a series, the organisation of Tanizaki's novel
has an episodic quality similar to that of *Genji*. Fourthly, one
should differentiate the prose style of *The Makioka Sisters* from
that of his earlier work: in this novel, long clauses link up with
one another in a way somewhat reminiscent of the elaborate style
of *Genji*. Fifthly, events in *The Makioka Sisters* correspond with
the seasons and this is also a prominent feature of *Genji*. Finally,
both works are free from didacticism, and their primary objectives
are the aesthetic representation of reality.

One feels enriched by reading *The Makioka Sisters*, where
Tanizaki gives a picture of life in its most integral and complete
form. There is little trace of the morbidity, actual or potential,
which was characteristic of his earlier works. Even Taeko's affairs
which from time to time cast ominous shadows on the destiny of
the Makioka family are happily embraced within an ultimately
harmonious picture of life. One may conjecture that in the process
of creating his earlier works Tanizaki's personality was as yet not
fully integrated. The sense of equilibrium achieved in *The
Makioka Sisters*, however, suggests a personal dilemma largely
resolved; a blessing not only to himself but to his readers.

Unlike Sōseki who produced his major works within the last
decade of his life, or Akutagawa who came to a dead end in both
his writing and life in his mid-thirties, or Mishima who timed
the end of his life to coincide with a calculated completion of his
art, Tanizaki continued to mature over time, producing works in

keeping with various phases of his life. His works of the postwar period clearly illustrate his ripened maturity as a man and artist. In *The Mother of Captain Shigemoto* (*Shōshō Shigemoto no Haha*, 1949–50), for example, he demonstrates his virtuosity at historical fiction, a skill in using historical sources which he no doubt mastered while translating *Genji* into modern Japanese. Against the background of the late Heian period when power was in the hands of the Fujiwara family, we read of the imperial court official Kunitsune's beautiful aristocratic wife – admired and loved by a host of dandies, eventually being snatched away from him by Fujiwara Shihei, his superior younger in age. The underlying theme, however, is not this woman's fate but her deserted son's lifelong yearning for her. Two experiences in the life of this woman's son, Captain Shigemoto, are juxtaposed. As a child he watches his decrepit father, after being deserted by his beautiful wife, practise the Buddhist discipline of *fujōkan* (purging of impurity) by observing in a desolate moonlit field the worm-eaten corpse of a woman. By observing the sordid in a woman the old man tries to transcend his attachment to the beauty who has betrayed him. At the climax of the story Captain Shigemoto strays into a suburb of Kyoto, enters a dilapidated house and encounters his mother, old yet beautiful, after years of yearning for her. The story thus represents a further variation of the 'Yearning for Mother' theme artistically cloaked this time in historical garb.

The pattern of Tanizaki's artistic development, however, is complicated by yet another kind of work written in the last decade of his life. In both *The Key* (*Kagi*, 1956) and *Diary of a Mad Old Man* (*Fūten Rōjin Nikki*, 1961–2), Tanizaki concentrates on obsessions with sex in old age,[6] which is to some extent a variation of the earlier themes. The main characters of *The Key* are a 56-year-old university professor and his 45-year-old wife. The title concerns the key which the protagonist uses to keep his diary secret from his wife – though he actually intends her to read it at her leisure – and may also symbolise the key to the secret world of sex psychology. He dotes on his wife, who, however, does not seem to respond adequately. His behaviour approaches morbidity when he develops the habit of observing and even taking detailed photographs of his wife stark naked and drugged with brandy. Kimura, a university student betrothed to the protagonist's daughter, serves at first as an assistant who helps him to pursue his sexual obsession but gradually he falls deeply in love with the wife, who reciprocates his feelings. The daughter, Toshiko, serves as an intermediary and promotes these amorous relations. The protagonist also encourages the relationship between his wife and Kimura in the belief that his resulting jealousy will further stimulate his appetite and hence increase his sexual satisfaction. In presenting the intricate psychology of the characters concerned Tanizaki makes effective use of their separate diaries, the one written in *katakana* script and the other in *hiragana* script. The protagonist and his wife pretend to keep their diaries secret from each other, and yet in actual fact both know that not only is the other's diary easily accessible, but that both hope the other will read it. Ikuko, the wife, pretends in her diary that she has never gone beyond the bounds of fidelity and only keeps friendly with Kimura to arouse her husband's jealousy and hence increase his appetite. In fact she favours Kimura in preference to her husband. She can disguise these facts successfully in her diary until after her husband dies of a stroke. That Tanizaki, with his bold treatment of the amorous, actively pioneered the fashion of greater freedom in the literary expression of sex is in itself noteworthy. However, the elements of perversion in *The Key*, which might repel some readers, are clearly distinguished from pornography by the artistic detachment with which they are treated.

Diary of a Mad Old Man, too, consists of a diary written by the protagonist. He is even older and more decrepit than the one in *The Key*; he suffers from high blood pressure and is carefully watched by a nurse. He is sexually impotent and yet still attracted by Satsuko, his coquettish daughter-in-law, who is alienated from her husband and is having an affair with another man. The way in which he takes pleasure in her is often perverse, for example, kissing her feet or biting her toes in the shower room. His perversion reaches its climax when towards the end of the story he identifies her with a *Kan'non* figure (a Buddhist divinity recognised as Goddess of Mercy) and takes print after print of her foot dabbed in red ink to be carved on his tombstone. The old man indulges in a masochistic phantasy of being trodden by a *Kan'non*-like *femme fatale*. The detachment with which Tanizaki depicts the absurdity of a decaying and yet still sensual man releases the story from possible repulsion. Tanizaki's pursuit of eternal womanhood through the conflicting images of idealised mother and *femme fatale* reappears in the old man's phantasy:

September 5

Early this morning I dreamed about my mother.

. . .

Unfortunately she neither looked at me nor spoke to me. I didn't attempt to talk to her either. Perhaps I was afraid she would scold me.

. . .

Mother knew her grandson Jokichi, but because she died in 1928, when Jokichi was four, she never knew the girl who became his bride. Since even my wife had so violently opposed his marriage to Satsuko, I wonder what my mother might have done. Probably the marriage would never have taken place. No, from the very first an engagement with a former chorus girl would have been unthinkable. Supposing she had known that such a marriage was followed by the infatuation of her own son with her grandson's wife, by my squandering three million yen to give her a cat's-eye in return for the privilege of 'petting' – Mother would have fainted with horror.

. . .

People called Mother a beauty, when she was young. I remember her very well in those days – until I was fourteen or fifteen she was as beautiful as ever. When I compare that memory of her with Satsuko, the contrast is really striking. Satsuko is also called a beauty. . . . But between these two beauties, between the 1890's and now, what a change has taken place in the physical appearance of the Japanese woman! For example, Mother's feet were beautiful too, but Satsuko's have an altogether different kind of beauty. They hardly seem to belong to a woman of the same race. Mother had dainty feet, small enough to nestle in the palm of my hand, and as she tripped along in her straw sandals she took extremely short, mincing steps with her toes turned in.

.   .   .

All Meiji women had that pigeon-like walk, not just beauties. As for Satsuko's feet, they are elegantly long and slender; she boasts that ordinary Japanese shoes are too wide for her. On the contrary, my mother's feet were fairly broad, rather like those of the Bodhisattva of Mercy in the Sangatsudo in Nara.

.   .   .

Suppose Mother knew that her son Tokusuke, born in 1883, is alive today and is shamefully attracted to a woman like Satsuko – to her granddaughter at that, the wife of her own grandson – and finds pleasure in being tantalized by her, even sacrificing his wife and children to try to win her love! Could she possibly have imagined that now, thirty-two years after her death, her son would have become such a lunatic, and that such a woman would have joined our family?[7]

.   .   .

Noteworthy of this dream is that two prototypal Tanizaki figures, the protagonist's mother on the one hand and his daughter-in-law as a *femme fatale* on the other, are not only juxtaposed but also linked together through his fetishism of the female feet which are identified with those of the Buddhist's deities. The dream of the mad old man thus sums up Tanizaki's lifelong preoccupation with the quest for eternal womanhood. The sex-ridden protagonists in *The Key* and *Diary of a Mad Old Man*, however, should not be directly identified with the author himself in his old age. The eroticism in these novels appears morbid, but Tanizaki treated it with a kind of detachment and objectivity which could be achieved only after the harmonious vision of life in *The Makioka Sisters*.

2

Among some biographical facts that may bear on the development of Kawabata's literary talent the most notable is that in infancy

he became an orphan. His father died when he was two and his
mother when he was three. He was then looked after by his
maternal grandfather and his elder sister was looked after by
an aunt. His grandmother died when he was seven, then his
elder sister a few years later, and finally his grandfather when he
was sixteen. The psychological effect of early parental deprivation, whether actual or imagined, has already been mentioned
with regard to Sōseki and Akutagawa, both of whom suffered
from acute neurosis. Compared with them, there is little reason
for treating Kawabata as pathologically abnormal.[8] However, it is
at least true that the early loss of his parents seems responsible for
the unique quality which one perceives in his life and work –
a peculiar tension between life and death, detachment and attachment, the abstract and sensuous, whence derives a very special
awareness of beauty bordering on sorrow.

In the lifetime of many writers there is a period in which
they draw heavily from other writers for their ideas. In his
early years Tanizaki found the source of inspiration in some
European models; so did Kawabata. In September 1924 some
twenty young writers founded the magazine called *Bungei Jidai*
(The Age of Literary Arts). The members included such people
as Kataoka Teppei (1894–1944), Nakagawa Yoichi (1897–)
and Kon Tōkō (1898–1977), but it was Yokomitsu Riichi
(1898–1947) and Kawabata himself who played leading roles.
One critic called this group of writers 'Shin-kankaku-ha' (New
Perceptionists), the term still used for them by literary historians.[9]
They cultivated a very particular perception of the external world
and prose style with which to express it.[10] For their models they
turned to European modernism; for example, the poetic method
of Paul Morand as translated by Horiguchi Daigaku (1892–).
The Shin-kankaru-ha as a literary movement, however, was rather
short-lived. The crisis of sensibility and culture that led to European modernism was peculiarly European. No such historical
shift in Japan supported the continuation of this literary clique. In
fact, the uniqueness of Kawabata's style is not its imitation of
European modernism but rather its use of quintessentially Japanese
poetic sensibility in the once prosaic genre of the novel.

Snow Country (*Yukiguni*, 1935–47) was composed in a most
peculiar fashion, even when one thinks of the extended magazine
serialisation of many a Victorian novel. The first portion,

originally entitled 'The Mirror for an Evening Scene', was published in the *Bungei Shunjū* in January 1935. The rest appeared portion by portion, under separate titles, over a twelve-year period, until it was completed in October 1947. Considering its medium length, its creation was a slow process, typical of Kawabata's entire work. Apparently, he had in mind no original plan for the plot. Accordingly, *Snow Country* comprises a series of episodes, each of which evinces very concisely Kawabata's refined sensibility.

Despite such a process of composition, *Snow Country* has a coherent structure. Shimamura, a married man with no particular profession, is attracted to two different types of women in the snow country of north-western Japan. Yōko is intangible or inaccessible to Shimamura, and in this respect an extension of Kawabata's famous Izu dancer (*The Izu Dancer* [*Izu no Odoriko*, 1926]). In contrast Komako, a snow country geisha, willingly gives herself to Shimamura. The past lives of the two women are quite different. Komako became a geisha to pay the medical expenses of her invalid fiancé, who is now looked after not by Komako but by Yōko. Shimamura lives in unresolved tension with the ironic distinctions between the tangible, fully embodied Komako and intangible, ethereal and, as it were, disembodied Yōko.

Near the opening of the novel there is a striking scene in which Shimamura sees Yōko in a train for the first time. It is worth noting Kawabata's symbolic use of the forefinger of Shimamura's left hand, with which he sensuously recalls Komako's physical presence. With the same finger he then wipes the window, which has misted over, and finds the reflected mirror image of Yōko. So, ironically, the same finger points to the intangible as well as the tangible. In fact the irony goes deeper. Shimamura views Yōko as an ethereal, intangible entity, but, objectively, she is very much flesh and blood as we see later on when she is nursing the invalid young man: 'Yōko stepped lightly over the samisen box, a glass chamber-pot in her hand.'[11] Komako is certainly tangible to Shimamura, because they have a physical relation, but that does not make their relationship any less transient. Only by synthesising the paradoxical dualities of the tangible and intangible is Shimamura able to attain an enduring sense of beauty. As it is, he has only momentary glimpses of it in the snow country.

Furthermore, the vision of beauty borders on death, as is illustrated by Yukio's death and finally Yōko's probable death in a fire. The fire which in the opening chapter is associated with beauty in the mirror image of Yōko thus becomes the fire that brings death.

Thousand Cranes (*Senba Zuru*, 1949–51) begins with two striking images, a birthmark and cranes. On his way to a tea party organised by Chikako, once the mistress of his late father, the protagonist Kikuji vividly remembers having once as a child seen her cutting the hair on the birthmark covering half her breast. The grotesqueness contrasts sharply with the picturesque beauty of Inamura Yukiko, who is carrying a pink kerchief decorated with the pattern of a thousand cranes, shining brightly in the sunlight. These two key images reappear later in the novel, one ominous and the other beautiful, innocent and decent. The initial situation involves ironies. First, ominous Chikako plays the role of a mediator to introduce Kikuji to the innocent Miss Inamura as his prospective bride. Secondly, at Chikako's party Kikuji meets Mrs Ōta who replaced Chikako to become the last mistress of his father. Kikuji has no fore-knowledge that he is going to have an affair with Mrs Ōta and, after her death, with her daughter Fumiko. And thirdly, the tea ceremony, which is supposedly a ritual for spiritual discipline, is going to contribute to the development of amorous relations.

Chikako's birthmark is a grotesque image that evokes the ominous in Kikuji's subconsciousness but she is not so much an embodiment as a reminder of what is truly ominous – the unmanageable power of fate that dominates the amorous relations of these men and women. The reciprocal love between Mrs Ōta and Kikuji is no doubt under the spell of such a power. Their relation is in a sense incestuous because she was originally the mistress of his father. However, Kawabata completely releases his characters from moral reproach. With all her dotage, Mrs Ōta is not entirely free from compunction about her quasi-incestuous relation, whereas Kikuji not only shows no resentment about his late father's affair, but also seems to think that his relation with Mrs Ōta will redeem his father's sin.

As this affair develops, any possibility for Kikuji to marry Miss Inamura naturally recedes. One may wonder, then, why the thousand cranes are used as a key image and in fact as the title of the book. Had this work been composed in the carefree manner of many other Kawabata novels, it would probably have lacked any predetermined ending before starting its serialisation. But since the period during which *Thousand Cranes* was serialised was much shorter than that of *Snow Country*, Kawabata quite possibly from the start used the image of the thousand cranes to symbolise the innocence and decency embodied by Miss Inamura to contrast with the darkness that befalls Kikuji. It is not that Kikuji does not like her. On the contrary he is attracted to her, as can be seen from a description of the effect of her visit to his house: 'He had not slept the night before. He had felt that the scent of the girl would still be in the cottage, and he had wanted to go out in the middle of the night.' (part II, chapter 2).[12] His attraction to her, however, is counterbalanced by his recognition that 'she will always be far away'. More than anyone else, Kikuji is aware that the stainless decency of Miss Inamura is incompatible with the fact that the morally-stained Chikako is their go-between and that the family fate ties him inextricably to Mrs Ōta.

One must not overlook the subtleties of Kawabata's techniques, for instance, in his treatment of the visit of Miss Inamura to Kikuji's house through Chikako's officious intervention. The visit takes place in part II, chapter 1, even though there is no straight narrative account of the details. Instead, they are narrated in the next chapter as a flashback. Presented thus as Kikuji's recollection, Miss Inamura becomes crystallised in the depth of his consciousness as a pure image transcending all corporeality. Another structural ingenuity of the second chapter is that the account of Kikuji's imaginative crystallisation of Miss Inamura leads directly into and contrasts with the unexpected visit of Mrs Ōta. This, their last, meeting is followed by her suicide from an overdose of sleeping pills. Part II then ends with his recollection of the day that he had his first rendezvous with her, a flow of thoughts composed of the vivid images describing the antithetical elements in his life (part II, chapter 3):

Kikuji sat by the telephone with his eyes closed.
He saw the evening sun as he had seen it after the night with Mrs. Ota: the evening sun through the train windows, behind the grove of the Hommonji Temple.

The red sun seemed about to flow down over the branches.

The grove stood dark against it.

The sun flowing over the branches sank into his tired eyes, and he closed them.

The white cranes from the Inamura girl's kerchief flew across the evening sun, which was still in his eyes.

One may find in *Thousand Cranes* Kawabata's unique ability to represent the supra-sensory powers which are kept in balance with the sensory. The language he uses is compact and evocative like that of traditional *haiku* poetry. He gives hints and suggestions instead of stating everything in explicit and realistic terms. In brief, his language is symbolic. One example is his effective use of the tea ceremony, to serve as the way the characters in the novel meet each other. Kikuji's father developed his relation with Mrs Ōta when she asked him to dispose of tea vessels after her husband's death. At the ceremony held by Chikako, tea is served in an antique bowl, which was originally possessed by Mr Ōta, but changed hands from him to Mrs Ōta, to Kikuji's father and finally to Chikako. Watching Miss Inamura serving tea, Kikuji is struck by her innocent beauty which contrasts sharply with the history of the bowl invested with the dark passions of its owners.

The symbolic use of tea vessels gains further importance in the latter half of the novel. The Shino water jar, which Fumiko gives Kikuji, enables him to duplicate his love for Mrs Ōta in his love for Fumiko, just as Mrs Ōta duplicated her love for his father in that for Kikuji. There is an irony in the fate of this jar, as there is in that of Mrs Ōta's Shino bowl offered by Fumiko, which Kikuji places side by side with his father's favourite bowl (part v, chapter 3):

Kikuji could not bring himself to say that the Shino bowl was like her mother. But the two bowls before them were like the souls of his father and her mother.

The tea bowls, three or four hundred years old, were sound and healthy, and they called up no morbid thoughts. Life seemed to stretch taut over them, however, in a way that was almost sensual.

Seeing his father and Fumiko's mother in the bowls, Kikuji felt that they had raised two beautiful ghosts and placed them side by side.

The tea bowls were here, present, and the present reality of Kikuji and Fumiko, facing across the bowls, seemed immaculate too.

Kikuji had said to her, on the day after the seventh-day service for her mother, that there was something terrible in his being with her, facing her. Had the guilt and the fear been wiped away by the touch of the bowls?

'Beautiful', said Kikuji, as if to himself. 'It wasn't Father's nature to play with tea bowls, and yet he did, and maybe they deadened his sense of guilt.'

'I beg your pardon?'

'But when you see the bowl, you forget the defects of the old owner. Father's life was only a very small part of the life of a tea bowl.'

Irony derives from the way in which antitheses become fused: the tea bowls and jar are made of inorganic materials, unlike the passions and desires of the people who possess them. Their history, spanning three or four hundred years, far surpasses the brief life of their owners. As art objects they are appreciated through the senses, but ultimately they attain an aesthetic quality which transcends the senses. Despite these differences, Kawabata creates a symbolic effect that hinges on the parallels between the tea vessels and human relations. The two pairs of bowls and cups are emblematic of the relations between Mrs Ōta and Kikuji's father, and Fumiko and Kikuji. The stain of Mrs Ōta's lips furnishes the cup with a sensuous quality, and her sensuousness is thus eternalised on a supra-sensory art object. By the superb use of such symbols Kawabata fuses the organic and inorganic, the human and non-human, the sensory and supra-sensory.

After the consummation of love, which is only implicitly hinted at, Fumiko shatters the Shino cup to pieces. The destruction of the cup stained by her mother's lips signals the end of the fate to which Kikuji has been bound. His consummation of love with Fumiko, paradoxically enough, seems to release him from this fate (part v, chapter 4):

There had been no resistance from Fumiko, only from the cleanness itself.

That fact, one might think, told how deep he had sunk into the meshes of the curse, how complete the paralysis was; but Kikuji felt the reverse, that he had escaped the curse and the paralysis. It was as if an addict had been freed of his addiction by taking the ultimate dose of a drug.

Yet that consummation must be the first and last consummation, and Fumiko, like the morning star which Kikuji sees at dawn, must disappear from his sight. Kawabata never says explicitly, but only implies, that she too chooses to take her life like her mother. The ultimate paradox, then, is that by ceasing to exist physically, Fumiko becomes crystallised as a permanent image in Kikuji's mind – even more permanent than the tea cups and bowls. Thus at the end of the novel Kikuji is left unable to reach both the ethereal beauty represented by Miss Inamura and the shadow of love, in which reality and phantasy, life and death meet.

The serial publication of *The Sound of the Mountain* (*Yama no Oto*, 1949–54) extended to over four years and partly over-lapped with that of *Thousand Cranes*. Kawabata projects his central concerns into the character, Shingo, who is older than the author was himself at the time of writing the work (instead of being a younger man as in *Thousand Cranes*). Since it concentrates on the relations between fewer characters, *Thousand Cranes* is relatively limited in scope, whereas the introduction of more characters furnishes *The Sound of the Mountain* with the scope of a realistic novel. Yet Kawabata seems to aim not so much at describing the complicated relations of these characters in realistic terms as at representing the symbolic effects that derive from their relations. Just as *Thousand Cranes* centres round the consciousness of Kikuji, so does *The Sound of the Mountain* focus on the consciousness of Shingo. More important, the quasi-incestuous relations in *Thousand Cranes* are transformed into a platonic affair between Shingo and Kikuko, his daughter-in-law. Also, though Kawabata's treatment of the ethically immoral relations is, as it were, amoral, the platonic relationship between Shingo and Kikuko occurs under moral restraint and is set off against the immorality of Shingo's son, Shūichi. In other words, in *Thousand Cranes* the sins of the fathers are handed down to the son, whereas in *The Sound of the Mountain* the sins of the son are partly redeemed by the self-control of the father.

Shingo's family, with each member impaired in a different way, is in danger of falling apart: Shingo is becoming decrepit and is apparently suffering from involutional dementia; Shūichi is neglecting his wife Kikuko and having an affair with a war-widow; both Kikuko and Shūichi's mistress become pregnant at about the same time, but Kikuko terminates her pregnancy; Fusako is estranged from her drug-addicted husband and comes with her two infant daughters to Shingo's household. The situation is made more complicated by the reciprocal affection between Shingo and Kikuko. Kawabata seems to attribute the present predicament to the fate of this family, just as he did in *Thousand Cranes*. In the case of *The Sound of the Mountain* it originates in Shingo's unfulfilled desire for the beautiful elder sister of his wife. Accordingly his marriage is from the very beginning an anti-climactic act of expedience. His lack of love for his mediocre daughter Fusako is almost responsible for her broken marriage. On the other hand, Shingo favours and spoils his hand-some son Shūichi. Shingo's pity for Kikuko, in turn, derives partly from his awareness that he cannot talk Shūichi out of his affair. More important, Shingo seeks, whether consciously or unconsciously, in Kikuko the image of beauty which he once found in his wife's sister. In *The Sound of the Mountain* Kawabata seems to stress the concept of love that is handed down for numerous generations – not for only two generations as in *Thousand Cranes*. As an indication of this, he refers twice to an elderly botanist who acquired fame by growing and bringing to blossom a 2,000-year-old lotus seed found during an archaeological excavation. What Kawabata seems to be driving at in this episode is the Buddhist concept of reincarnation transcending time.[13]

Kawabata consciously makes use of other flora and fauna symbols to parallel human affairs. For instance, the scene in which Shingo feels male virility in a sunflower ('The Wings of the Locust', section 2) represents the unconscious wish-fulfilment of a man with a declining sexual power. Similarly, the untimely budding in autumn of an old ginko tree ('A Blaze of Clouds', section 1) coincides with the awakening of Shingo's unconscious affection for Kikuko. However, that Shingo's wish for rejuvenation is unlikely to bear fruit is suggested when the sunflower falls during a storm (*ibid.*). The two pine trees which Shingo had overlooked for years and has only recently discovered ('The Kite's House', section 2) look like two human beings drawn to each other, suggesting Kikuko and himself. The scene in which Shingo and Shūichi collaborate in cutting a *yatsude* tree so that the young branches of a cherry tree may grow ('The Scar', section 1) hints at the possibility that Shūichi and Kikuko are gradually going to be reconciled. One of the animal symbols concerns the episode of a stray dog giving birth to puppies ('A Dream of Islands', section 1). While conveying a sense of fertility in its own right, it also suggests the pregnancy of Shūichi's mistress and contrasts with Kikuko's abortion. Other animals live in their home. A snake is regarded by them as the soul of their family. So is the kite, which may be the same one seen for years but could be an offspring of the original one, thus suggesting the continuity and reincarnation of life.

No less important than the symbolism of flora and fauna are Shingo's dreams. They are partly the product of the fading libido of an old man. For instance, Shingo dreams of embracing a young woman on one of the Matsushima islands. Having read a newspaper article about promiscuity, pregnancy and abortion in teenagers, Shingo has another dream about a fourteen- or fifteen-year-old girl's abortion. In his dream the girl 'has become an eternal saint'. Although Kawabata makes no explicit comment, the reader may be free to take this dream as a forecast of Kikuko's pregnancy and abortion. It may also be the projection of Shingo's sympathy for her. Shingo wonders whether the girl in this dream may be the projection of his wife's elder sister whom he once loved. It seems, however, more plausible to say that the girl in the dream represents eternally innocent femininity, such as Shingo once found in his wife's sister and is perhaps finding in Kikuko. It may be reincarnated in future generations, but the girl's abortion suggests that it remains after all a disembodied and intangible entity. On another occasion, Shingo dreams a more libidinous dream in which he touches the breasts of a young woman who becomes identified with the younger sister of Shūichi's friend. The fact that she had once been a candidate for Shūichi's bride provides the key to the interpretation of the dream ('The Scar', section 3):

Asking for the first time who she was, he saw that she had become the younger sister of a friend of Shuichi's; but the recognition brought neither excitement nor feelings of guilt. The impression that it was the sister was a fleeting one. She remained a dim figure. . . .

Had not the girl in the dream been an incarnation of Kikuko, a substitute for her? Had not the moral considerations after all had their way even in his dream, had he not borrowed the figure of the girl as a substitute for Kikuko? And, to coat over the unpleasantness, to obscure the guilt, had he not made her a less attractive girl than she was?

And might it not be that, if his desires were given free rein, if he could remake his life as he wished, he would want to love the virgin Kikuko, before she was married to Shuichi?[14]

However, Shingo is consistently portrayed by Kawabata as a stoic old man who purges himself of his libidinous feelings. This dream of Shingo's is preceded by another one (*ibid.*):

It may have been because of the electric razor that Shingo had a dream of chin-whiskers.

He was not a participant but a spectator. In a dream, however, the division between the two is not clear. It took place in America, where Shingo had never been. Shingo suspected that he had dreamed of America because the combs Kikuko had brought back were American.

In his dream, there were states in which the English were most numerous, and states in which the Spanish prevailed. Accordingly, each state had its own characteristic whiskers. He could not clearly remember, after he awoke, how the colour and shape of the beards had differed, but in his dream he had clearly recognized differences in colour, which is to say in racial origins, from state to state. In one state, the name of which he could not remember, there appeared a man who had gathered in his one person the special characteristics of all the states and origins. It was not that all the various whiskers were mixed in together on his chin. It was rather that the French variety would be set off from an Indian beard, each in its proper place. Varied tufts of whiskers, each for a different state and racial origin, hung in sprays from his chin.

The American government designated the beard a national monument; and so he could not of his own free will cut or dress it.

This dream is probably aroused by the electric razor given him by Kikuko as a homecoming present but its contents are entirely absurd. Its hilarious absurdity adequately neutralises the sombreness of the other dream. Shingo relieves himself by thinking: 'A dream. And the national monument was a dream too. Don't put faith in what dreams decide for you.' (*Ibid.*) Another of Shingo's significant dreams is that of two eggs, one an ostrich's and the other a serpent's, from which a baby serpent is thrusting its tiny head. The dream can only be the product of Shingo's subconscious obsessions with the simultaneous pregnancy of both Shūichi's mistress and Kikuko. Shingo wonders which egg represents which, but the tiny serpent may well represent both the imaginary offspring born of Kikuko as the product of Shingo's wishful thinking and the reincarnation of the family spirit.

Comparable to Kawabata's symbolic use of tea bowls in *Thousand Cranes* is his use of the Noh mask in *The Sound of the Mountain*. Shingo buys from the bereaved family of his friend two Noh masks representing boys' faces to which he feels unusually attracted. There are a number of paradoxical implications. The episode of Shingo's buying these masks immediately follows that of his dream about his embracing a young woman in Matsushima. The paradox about dreaming is that it arouses sensations rooted in the subconscious libido, yet it is nothing more than a substitute for an actual experience. A Noh mask, on the other hand, is a paradoxical synthesis, which at once represents human emotions and yet transcends the sensory. The irony of the present situation is that Shingo is attracted to the potentially sensuous in the supra-sensuous mask. Another irony is that although the mask is that of a boy, it is neither entirely masculine nor entirely feminine; it represents at once the angelically neuter and feminine beauty ('A Dream of Islands', section 3):

The *kasshiki* was masculine, the eyebrows those of a man; but the *jido* was neuter. There was a wide space between eyebrows and eyes, and the gently arched eyebrows were those of a girl.

As he brought his face towards it from above, the skin, smooth and lustrous as that of a girl, softened in his ageing eyes, and the mask came to life, warm and smiling.

He caught his breath. Three or four inches before his eyes, a live girl was smiling at him, cleanly, beautifully.

The eyes and the mouth were truly alive. In the empty sockets were black pupils. The red lips were sensuously moist. Holding his breath, he came so close as almost to touch his nose to that of the mask, and the blackish pupils came floating up at him, and the flesh of the lower lip swelled. He was on the point of kissing it. Heaving a sigh, he pulled away. . . .

He felt as if he had looked behind the lower lip of the *jido*, to where the antique red faded away inside the mouth. The mouth was slightly open, but there were' no teeth ranged behind the lower lip. It was like a flower in bud upon a bank of snow.

To bring one's face so near as to touch it was probably, for a No mask, an inexcusable perversion. It was probably a way of viewing the mask not intended by the maker. Shingo felt the secret of the maker's own love in the fact that the mask, most alive when viewed at a proper distance from the No stage, should all the same be most alive when, as now, viewed from no distance at all.

For Shingo had felt a pulsing as of heaven's own perverse love. Yet he sought to laugh at it, telling himself that his ancient eyes had made the skin more alluring than that of a real woman.

These paradoxical implications of the Noh mask are developed later on in the novel. When Kikuko wears the mask in front of Shingo, she becomes identified with the mask. Only with the aid of the mask can she express her feelings to the paternal in Shingo. Paradoxically enough, the apparently placid Noh mask is even more expressive than her real face ('The Bell in Spring', section 4):

> He took up the *jido*. 'This one is a sprite. A symbol of eternal youth. Did I tell you about it when I bought it?'
> 'No.'
> 'Tanizaki, the girl who was in the office. When I bought it I had her put it on. She was charming. A great surprise.'
> Kikuko put the mask to her face. 'Do you tie it behind?'
> No doubt, deep behind the eyes of the mask, Kikuko's eyes were fixed on him.
> 'It has no expression unless you move it.'
> The day he had brought it home, Shingo had been on the point of kissing the scarlet lips. He had felt a flash like heaven's own wayward love.
> 'It may be lost in the undergrowth, but while it still has the flower of the heart...'
> Those too seemed to be words from a No play.
> Shingo could not look at Kikuko as she moved the glowing young mask this way and that.
> She had a small face, and the tip of her chin was almost hidden behind the mask. Tears were flowing from the scarcely visible chin down over her throat. They flowed on, drawing two lines, then three.
> 'Kikuko,' said Shingo. 'Kikuko. You thought if you were to leave Shuichi you might give tea lessons, and that was why you went to see your friend?'
> The *jido* Kikuko nodded.
> 'I think I'd like to stay on with you here and give lessons.' The words were distinct even from behind the mask.

The reciprocal sympathy between Shingo and Kikuko, however, never trespasses into the realm of immorality. The angelic neutrality of the mask of the boy is in itself a guarantee of this. From Shingo's point of view it may be 'perverse love' but 'heaven's own perverse love' ('A Dream of Islands', section 3).

In *The House of Sleeping Beauties* (*Nemureru Bijo*, 1960–1), written a decade afterwards, Kawabata presents the amorous life of an old man in a different light. Though he has long been impotent, the protagonist, an old man Eguchi, finds pleasure in a house where he is provided with a beautiful young girl naked and made insensible with drugs. One may easily find the setting analogous to that of Tanizaki's *The Key*, in which the elderly protagonist watches his wife naked and drugged with brandy. However, the difference is as obvious. In Tanizaki's work, the protagonist's motives and behaviour are geared towards amorous fulfilment; in Kawabata's *Sleeping Beauties*, fulfilment is out of reach for the old man who only indulges in recollections of his affairs in the past while lying beside the sleeping girl. External reality, therefore, becomes somehow disembodied for him. Even the boundary between life and death becomes indistinct, with his erotic vision verging on necrophilia, for indeed one of the girls sleeping beside him turns out to be dead the following morning.

The parallels and differences between the writings and lives of Tanizaki and Kawabata should now be clearer. In their earlier years they both looked to European literature for their models but the genuinely Japanese sensibilities were what eventually found expression in their major works. They were both concerned with the search for eternal womanhood, which in Tanizaki's case originated in his memory of his beautiful mother, and in Kawabata's case in his lonely orphaned childhood. Tanizaki achieved his aim in some of his works, especially in *The Makioka Sisters*. Kawabata was less successful as suggested by the insoluble coexistence of the tangible and intangible womanhood in his works, a failure of fusion which might indicate some kind of insecurity in his relationship with outer reality. However, he had some resilience, or what may be called 'negative capability', with which he managed to counterbalance his insecurity during his long career as a writer. The balance was broken only late and abruptly. The paradoxical nature of his suicide, however, is that, propped on such a perilous and delicate balance, Kawabata lived in a realm where life and death always bordered on one another. His suicide involved no dramatic gesture and in this respect differed from the death of Mishima Yukio.[15]

A phantasy world:

MISHIMA YUKIO

I

Mishima Yukio (1925–70) killed himself on 25 November 1970 at the age of forty-five in the traditional Japanese warrior manner of *seppuku* after a vain attempt to incite a unit of the Self-Defence Forces to a coup d'état. The event shocked and alarmed not only the Japanese but also people abroad. Many were reminded of the 1936 coup by young army officers, and some, especially abroad, became worried about a possible revival of Japanese militarism. But the jeering by the rank and file troops whom Mishima tried to rouse to action proves that such a possibility was very slight. The Japanese government, including Mr Nakasone, the Minister of Defence, positively disapproved of Mishima's action. The then prime minister, Mr Sato, was anxious lest such scandalous behaviour on the part of an eminent writer might tarnish the country's reputation founded on economic prosperity. Neverthe-less, the prime minister's statement that Mishima had 'gone mad' needs some qualification. In every detail Mishima's suicide was an act calculated well in advance. In its political implications it was a challenge to the kind of stability and prosperity of present-day Japan of which the prime minister himself was the repre-sentative. Mishima detested the progressive or left-wing Japanese intellectuals, but he did not align himself with the Liberal Demo-cratic Party either. Nor was he prepared to link with the estab-lished right-wing organisations, in spite of the ultra-nationalism of his own Shield Society. Ironically enough, Mishima could have agreed with the dissident students of the New Left who played the leading role in the 1968–9 university upheavals. For despite their different views on such matters as the Imperial authority both Mishima and those students aimed their criticism at the order and prosperity of Japan, which was marching towards the attainment of a spectacular economic growth in the late 1960s.[1]

Politics, however, was just one facet of the multifarious implications of Mishima's suicide. It was rooted in what may be called his personal and aesthetic motives. No explanation, in either purely political or aesthetic terms, is adequate: the truth may be seen only from a due balance between the two. For Mishima's whole career was one of paradox built on an extraordinary tension between spirit and body, words and action, and artistic creation and commitment to the world. It is practically impossible within a limited space fully to explain such a complex phenomenon, and the following will be merely an attempt to trace the development of Mishima as a man and writer and to find the logical connexion, if any, between his aesthetics and its confrontation with the world which culminated in his suicide.

2

Mishima's contribution to modern Japanese literature was immense. In embracing both traditional Japanese literary sensibilities and knowledge obtained from European literature he was as masterly as Sōseki and Akutagawa. In Mishima's case, however, the mode of amalgamating the two elements was far more complex than in his predecessors. The philosophy underlying his *seppuku* was definitely Japanese. The last phase of his vindication of Japanese cultural identity was fanatically nationalistic. The literary past and present, or Japanese tradition and Mishima's individual talent, were superbly synthesised in his *Five Modern Noh Plays* (*Kindai Nōgaku Shū*, 1956). On the other hand Mishima was well versed in European literature. Raymond Radiguet and François Mauriac, for instance, are among those writers to whom the young Mishima looked for inspiration. Again, one of his plays was adapted from Racine's *Phèdre*. It is easy enough to detect in his work literary elements of European origin, such as the Greek idealisation of physical beauty, sadism, satanism of Baudelaire's type, and so on. Further, in its logical clarity and rhetorical richness his prose style is by far the most distinguished in modern Japanese literature; he is one of the few Japanese writers whose prose can equal the best of European prose in these qualities. In his achievement, after all, Mishima surpassed many of his Japanese predecessors.

Mishima's place in the history of modern Japanese literature may best be clarified if we compare him with the I-novelists and especially with a typical example of their kind, Dazai Osamu (1909–48). The major characters of his novels are reflections of the author himself. They are all at odds with society and violate the code of respectability. It is as if Dazai had to demoralise his own life in order to project it into his work. There is thus a curious confusion between life and work. Eventually, in 1948, Dazai committed suicide, trailing behind him a cloud of immorality and disgrace.

Mishima began his career as a writer under the influence of the Nihon-rōman-ha or Japanese School of Romanticism, of which Dazai was a member. The fact is noteworthy in a double sense. First, some members of the School were renegades converted from Marxism to nationalism who now advocated the Japanese cultural tradition and indirectly contributed to the propaganda put out by the militaristic government during the war. Secondly, a more important point is that Mishima soon became an opponent of Dazai. Between the two there were both repulsion and affinity. Dazai indulged in sentimentality and self-commiseration, which Mishima could not tolerate. The almost deliberate morbidity in Dazai's real life was unforgivable to Mishima. And yet Mishima shared with Dazai certain characteristics such as physical frailty, in his youth at least, and a sense of enmity towards the world. Mishima, however, differed from Dazai in that he was a man of extraordinary stoicism who continually transformed his own self into its opposite. Furthermore, Dazai's confusion between life and art led to the failure of the latter. This had a curious result. First, a sensitive and frail young Mishima tried to disguise his real life under a mask of wholesomeness. Secondly, he allowed room in his work for the gloom of his mind's abyss, but made every effort to make the created world of his work independent of his life. It will be my purpose to trace in Mishima's work a hidden morbidity somewhat like Dazai's, and to see at the same time how he succeeded, unlike Dazai, in maintaining the autonomy of his work through his perfect artistic method.

Confessions of a Mask (*Kamen no Kokuhaku*, 1949) is a short example of a *Bildungsroman*, in which the hero's personal history is traced from his childhood to his adolescence. One of its peculiar features is the author's uninhibited treatment of sexual perversion. What matters, however, is not sexual perversion as such, but its wider implications. Curiously enough, one of the earliest childhood memories of the frail, well-bred hero is a 'night-soil man', to whom he is attracted because he represents 'a marvellous mixture of nothingness and vitality'. He is drawn to Joan of Arc, whom he misconceives as a man. How disappointed he is to discover that Joan was a woman! The sensitive hero is also attracted to soldiers through the smell of their perspiration. In this case, significantly enough, the soldiers fascinate him because they are destined to die. Still another example is the memory of a portable shrine carried by sturdy young men, whose ecstasy arouses in him a yearning. All these examples of the hero's childhood response to the external world foreshadow his infatuation with a physically precocious but unintelligent boy at school. The precociously intelligent but physically frail hero thus aspires to physical strength, the antithesis of his own condition, and it is all the better if the object of his aspiration lacks intelligence.

It is worth noticing that the hero's sexual perversion is curiously connected with his attraction to death as has already been hinted at by his fascination with soldiers. In reading fairy tales the hero does not like princesses but only princes, especially those who are destined to die. The hero is obsessed not only with the death of other people but also with his own. He exults in the idea of his imaginary death and once pretends to be killed on the battlefield. The references to death are legion: a circus youth shot in the chest, the fractured skull of a tight-rope walker, and so on. But the most important is the picture of St Sebastian's Martyrdom by Guido Reni, which evokes in the hero the combined effect of fascination with death and erotic feeling, the latter leading to his first experience of 'ejaculation'. Another such experience takes place by the sea, which stands for eternity as opposed to the worldly order and serves as the setting for mental exaltation. One may find here the elements that recurrently constitute the trinity in Mishima's novels: death, love (either perverted or not) and eternity.[2]

The hero's obsession with death, furthermore, is placed in a historical setting. He feels his future to be a burden. Accordingly the prospect of death on the battlefield and even in an air-raid is attractive to him. Ironically enough, however, he is dismissed from the army on the very first day of recruitment. This intensifies his desire for death: he looks forward to the time when the American troops will land and devastate his native soil. The defeat in the war therefore deprives him of his hope and brings him back to normal life. Thus for the hero of *Confessions* there are antithetical values: war against peace, abnormality against normality, and inability against necessity to love women. One constitutes reality and the other mere fiction. In other words the hero stands at odds with the society of postwar Japan, which is fictitious only; reality lies in the products of his own phantasy.

From the hero's character there emerge the following features: his sexual perversion and inability to love women, a disbelief in the existing order of the world, an aspiration to the vast or eternal as symbolised by the sea, a wish for the end of the world and an inclination towards suicide. In a word the hero is a nihilist who cannot find any meaning in life and in a sense inherits the characteristics of the I-novelists in general and Dazai in particular. What then is the relation between the hero and the author? Is the former a mere reflection of the latter and, if so, would it follow that there is little to choose between Dazai and Mishima and that Mishima's dislike of Dazai is that of one's own counterpart? The question leads us to consider the meaning of the title of the novel: *Confessions of a Mask*.

At first sight the title appears self-contradictory. A confession must be the true voice of feeling, which indeed was the case with the I-novelists, but in Mishima's case it is spoken by a mask. What then is the meaning of the mask? Is it merely a device for the author to disguise himself? If so, the confession would be made by the disguised self of the author. But this author-hero identification does not explain the self-contradiction of the title. There must be something more in the implication of the mask. First, in the context of the novel, the mask could mean the hero who is unable to, and yet pretends to, love a woman. Contrary to the ordinary concept of a stoic who restrains what he actually desires, Mishima's hero forces himself in vain to like what he does not actually desire. It seems irrelevant to identify the hero with the author and to consider whether or not Mishima himself was homosexual. Certainly homosexuality in itself is an important theme, but it is also the means of presenting a larger theme.

The stoicism of the hero who tries unsuccessfully to love a woman becomes a stoicism in putting up with the existing order of the world which he actually does not accept. The second meaning of the mask therefore, is the disguised self of the hero who is at odds and yet must somehow come to terms with the world. It is not the first but the second meaning of the mask that makes possible identification of the hero with the author and hence the third meaning of the mask. So long as Mishima shares with the hero nihilism and stoicism, the hero is the mask of Mishima himself. But the author is so well disguised under the mask of the hero that the confession is not as straightforward as that of the I-novelist. Viewed in this way, the title is not self-contradictory at all, but is a superb artistic device which made it possible for the author of this novel to detach his work from life as the I-novelists had never done before. And yet the fact remains that the nihilism of the hero inevitably reveals the abyss in the mind of the author himself, which made the artistic device all the more necessary. The author's own nihilism and his urgent need to disguise it under the highly artistic device were to become Mishima's major preoccupations.

Mishima's aim in *The Temple of the Golden Pavilion* (*Kinka-kuji*, 1956) was to show the logical consistency of the protagonist's act of setting fire to the Golden Pavilion by enriching his character. On the surface the protagonist looks so defective that one might well call him an anti-hero. Nevertheless he is equipped with some important qualities. The theme of alienation from society is as dominant as in *Confessions*. The protagonist is handicapped in many ways: his natural habit of stammering, physical frailty, impoverished background and so on, all of which are both the fact and symbol of the barrier that intervenes between him and the external world. Rejected by the world, the protagonist reacts to it in two ways. One alternative, as he envisages, would be to take vengeance on the world by becoming a despot presiding over it. In this respect the protagonist shares certain characteristics with such typical devilish figures as Richard III, some of the Byronic heroes and, more generally, Satan himself. The other alternative would be to confine himself voluntarily to his solitary inferno and to compensate for his deprivation by adhering to a set of aesthetic values. Herein originates his obsession with the Golden Pavilion as the symbol of beauty.

By worldly standards the protagonist is a mere criminal and not at all heroic, but he is the master of his inner world, which is fundamentally amoral, and where good and evil are reversible. He is confronted with the choice between life and aesthetic beauty, in which there is no room for compromise. So long as he adheres to beauty as an ideal aesthetic value, he cannot attain the fullness of life. This is superbly illustrated by the protagonist's inability to make love to a woman. There are two such occasions; just when he is on the verge of tasting the honey of life, he is prevented from action by a haunting vision of the Golden Pavilion. As exemplified in many words of literature, satanic solitude or alienation from the world entails such states of mind as self-love, narcissism and inability to love a woman. This is just another variation of the sexual perversion in *Confessions* and testifies to Mishima's preoccupation with the theme. Once again, it is irrelevant to speculate about whether Mishima himself was perverted. Perversion in Mishima's novels is simply the means of presenting a larger theme, that is, the clash between fulfilment of life and pursuit of aesthetic values, and the necessity to sacrifice the former to the latter. Again, the theme is presented in a historical context. Curiously enough, the protagonist becomes unable to conceive the beauty of the Golden Pavilion except as something destined to be burnt down by an American air-raid. This perverted vision of apocalypse increases the aesthetic value of the Golden Pavilion just as it gives meaning to the otherwise meaningless sequence of the protagonist's life. We should notice here the parallel to *Confessions*, in which the end of the war only adds to the hero's sense of the futility of life. The Golden Pavilion must be an absolute aesthetic value in itself; it must not be a part of the existing order of the world to which the protagonist is hostile; or else it must be destroyed.[3]

From the analysis of *Golden Pavilion* there emerge such important features as the protagonist's estrangement from life, his nihilism or inability to find any positive meaning in life, and his obsession with beauty as an absolute value. In fact, these are all relevant to Mishima himself. And yet Mishima's art is so perfect that the created world of *Golden Pavilion* is completely autonomous. The work certainly reveals Mishima's own preoccupations, but there is no confusing the world of art with Mishima's own life. The world of his work in itself is a reality, perhaps even more real than life, and by attaining such a reality Mishima is able to survive his own enmity towards life. In simplified terms phantasy dominates over reality.

Nihilism or the concept of life as fiction still continues in Mishima's work in the 1960s. The precocious boy of thirteen and his companions in *The Sailor Who Fell from Grace with the Sea (Gogo no Eikō,* 1963) despise life as boring, hypocritical, sentimental, fictitious and ultimately meaningless. There are a few exceptions, however. In contrast to the ephemeral nature of ordinary life, the sea represents eternity.[4] Naturally enough, the boys find for a time an ideal in the sailor, a solitary wanderer on the sea uncontaminated by the world and embodying virile strength. By the time Mishima wrote this novel, he had already found, in *The Sound of Waves (Shiosai,* 1954), a positive value in the Greek perfection of physical beauty. The boy watches through a peephole the love-making of his widowed mother and the sailor, an ideal union in which physical power is untainted by any sentimentality. Thus there exists a curious parallel or link between the boy and the sailor. The sailor, however, undergoes a fatal disintegration of personality. The boy's mother becomes fond of him not as the incarnation of eternal value but as a part of the existing order of the world. When both are ready to get married, in the normal way, the boy and his companions no longer tolerate him as their hero and must kill him. There is an irony in the way in which the sailor's obsession with the Wagnerian idea of *Liebes-Tod* is materialised when he is ultimately murdered. In fact, according to the standard set by the precocious boys, the relative value of life and death is reversed. Before killing a cat, which foreshadows their murder of the sailor, the leader of the boys says: 'They [ordinary people] don't even know the definition of danger. They think danger means something physical, getting scratched and a little blood running and the newspapers making a big fuss. Well, that hasn't got anything to do with it. Real danger is nothing more than just living.'[5] The passage is perhaps as revealing about Mishima himself, as it is about these boys.[6] Finally it must be noted that the nihilism of the boys is the obverse of their cult of physical strength. The novel is an autonomous work of art detached from Mishima's own life even more perfectly than *Confessions* and *Golden Pavilion* and yet the curious fact is that worship of physical power is exactly what Mishima had been practising since the mid-1950s in order to transcend his fundamental nihilism.

What is particularly interesting about Mishima is the extraordinary tension between his life and works. In some of his works, such as *Confessions* and *Golden Pavilion*, the major characters, handicapped in various ways, cannot accept the external world except as mere fiction, and their hunger for eternity, coupled with their death-wish, makes them desire the end of the existing order of the world. In others, for example, *The Sound of Waves*, the major characters embody the fullness of life through their ideal physical strength. Here we have in fact the two sides of one coin: the former represents Mishima's own nihilism disguised under the highly artistic device of fiction and the latter Mishima's wish-fulfilment or search for his anti-self. In both cases it is characteristic of Mishima that in contrast to the I-novelists there is no simple confusion between his own life and the artistically created world of his work. Mishima was successful in creating a world of fiction not only as real as life, but even more real. To create such an autonomous world of fiction was the means of compensating for his sense of enmity towards the external world and hence of mastering life. In a word, writing novels as a kind of phantasy-making was for Mishima a means of survival and salvation.

There is no doubt that Mishima conceived of *The Sea of Fertility* (*Hōjō no Umi*, 1965–71) as the culmination of his creative work. The tetralogy treats the period extending from 1912 to 1975. It is noteworthy that in the last volume written in 1970, the year of his suicide, Mishima saw five years into the future, which is rather unusual for a realistic novel. Each volume has its own protagonist, but there is one character, Honda, who appears throughout the whole of the tetralogy as the witness of the history of the sixty-odd years. It is Honda, as well as Mishima's use of the concept of reincarnation, that links one volume of the tetralogy to another.

At the beginning of volume 1, *Spring Snow* (*Haru no Yuki*, 1965–7) both the aristocratic protagonist, Matsugae Kiyoaki, and his friend Honda are eighteen years old and attend Peers' School. At the end of the volume Kiyoaki dies just before he becomes twenty-one. The love relationship between Kiyoaki and Ayakura Satoko, his elder cousin, ends in catastrophe. Because of youthful pride and his reluctance to be treated by Satoko as a younger pet, Kiyoaki obstinately pretends to be indifferent to her love. It is only when the arrangements for Satoko's prospective marriage with Prince Tōin are well advanced that Kiyoaki reveals his love for Satoko. When she becomes pregnant, both her own and Kiyoaki's parents attempt to cover up the secret in order not to jeopardise the royal match but Satoko renounces the world by entering a nunnery, Gesshūji (temple of the moon and learning). Kiyoaki tries in vain to see Satoko for the last time and dies of pneumonia contracted in the cold weather of early spring (accompanied by snow – hence the title of the volume). Throughout the volume Kiyoaki and Honda are good friends and represent opposite personalities: while Kiyoaki uses up his energy with his impassioned love, Honda is by nature a rationalist and prepares himself to pursue a lawyer's career. Mishima portrays minutely the lives of such people as imperial courtiers, aristocrats, leading businessmen, students at Peers' School, the Thai princes studying at Peers' School, and so on. Honda's rationalistic temperament, however, is gradually challenged by his attraction to the irrational. As the framework of the tetralogy Mishima resorts to the Buddhist idea of reincarnation, which is hinted at by the three moles on Kiyoaki's left side and by the last words in his feverish dream: 'Just now I had a dream. I'll see you again. I know it. Beneath the falls' (chapter 55).[7] And finally Honda is entrusted with Kiyoaki's diary which gives an account of the future in the form of dreams.

Volume II, *Runaway Horses* (*Honba*, 1967–8) is set in the 1930s. Kiyoaki's death-bed prophecy is fulfilled when Honda, now a prominent judge, meets Iinuma Isao, a champion in Japanese fencing, who turns out to be the eighteen-year-old son of Kiyoaki's former tutor. When standing beneath a waterfall (significantly enough), Honda finds three moles on Isao's left side. Iinuma, his father, is now in charge of a group of young right-wingers. Isao himself is a devotee of the *Shinpūren*, a group of Shintoist patriots in Kyūshū revolting against the Europeanist policy of the Meiji government. It is dangerous for Honda, as an advocate of law, to be involved with right-wing patriots, but he is irresistibly attracted to Isao because of the possibility that he could be the reincarnation of Kiyoaki. The main part of volume II is concerned with an abortive attempt by Isao and his group to assassinate leading businessmen and to achieve a coup d'état. Honda resigns his post and volunteers to act as defence counsel. Thanks to his efforts, the accused are acquitted. At the end of volume II, however, Isao assassinates a leading businessman and commits ritual suicide. Needless to say, *Runaway Horses* ominously foreshadows Mishima's own fate.

Towards the end of volume II, Isao speaks in his dream: 'Far to the south. Very hot. . .in the rose sunshine of a southern land' (chapter 38).[8] This remark of Isao's anticipates another reincarnation in volume III, *The Temple of Dawn* (*Akatsuki no Tera*, 1968–70). Honda, now a flourishing solicitor, visits Thailand as an adviser for the Itsui Company – of course, the fictitious name for Mitsui – and happens to meet Ying Chan (Princess Moonlight), the seven-year-old youngest daughter of Prince Pattanadid, a contemporary of Kiyoaki and Honda at Peers' School in volume I. She is reputed to be insane, as she insists that she is Thai only in body and Japanese in soul. In the first half of volume III, covering the prewar period, the princess remains in Thailand, and it is only in the latter half, which deals with the postwar period, that she comes to Japan. Honda becomes emotionally involved with her. However, she must remain unattainable so long as she is the reincarnation of Kiyoaki and Isao. He may love her only if she is proved otherwise. Volume III moves towards an embarrassing scene, in which Honda peeps through a hole in the wall of his study into the next room. He witnesses not only the three moles on the left side of the princess's naked body, but also the lesbian relationship she is having with a Japanese woman. At the end of the volume, the princess goes back to Thailand and, before reaching the age of majority, dies after being bitten by a cobra.

In volume IV, *The Decay of the Angel* (*Tennin Gosui*, 1970–1), Honda encounters an orphan, Tōru, who also has three moles, and adopts him as his heir. As Honda becomes decrepit Tōru becomes uncontrollable. The latter attempts suicide, but succeeds only in blinding himself and, unlike the heroes or heroine of other volumes, lives to the age of majority. He also burns Kiyoaki's diary. The grounds on which Honda's faith in reincarnation and his otherwise rationalistic life itself have been founded are now jeopardised. Furthermore, at the end of the novel when Honda visits the Gesshūji Temple, Satoko, now the abbess, denies

having ever known Kiyoaki. This is another blow to Honda.
This last scene seems to be full of subtle ironies. With his dreams
shattered, Honda is left with the stark fact of paltry and futile old
age. One might argue that Honda's wish to have his faith in
Kiyoaki's reincarnation confirmed by Satoko could be misguided,
for he seeks the confirmation for the sake of his security, which is
nothing but a confusion between reality and dream. When his
request is denied by Satoko, Honda can no longer link his
memories of Kiyoaki with reality, but he still retains them
independently in a dream-like form. That such a realisation
comes about at the Gesshūji Temple is also relevant to the title of
the novel. The sea of fertility is the name of a moon crater.
The moon has nothing to do with the fertility of organic life, yet
it has its own autonomy irrespective of life.

The Sea of Fertility is much wider in scope, both thematically
and structurally, than *Confessions* and *Golden Pavilion*. But it
readily links up with the earlier works. The theme of alienation
from life is represented even more dramatically by being reduced
to the antithesis between life and death. Such characters as
Kiyoaki and Isao, although one is socially immoral and the other
a criminal, seem to demonstrate that death is absolute, eternal
and pure, whereas life involves absurdity, banality and impurity.
Honda, on the other hand, is essentially a rationalist, succeeding
as a lawyer and attaining wealth. But he is also under the spell
of the irrational: his faith in the idea of reincarnation and interpretation of Kiyoaki's diary and dreams. The ultimate physical
decay of Honda and the futility of his life throw into relief the
absoluteness of dream and death, which can be even more real
than life itself.

3

The obsession with death and apocalyptic vision of the end of the
world are pervasive elements in Mishima's novels. However, if
we adopt the view that Mishima's work constitutes an autonomous world, these elements in themselves do not account for his
own tragic death. What of the trilogy that deals with the coup
d'état of 26 February 1936: 'Patriotism' ('Yūkoku, January
1961), 'Kiku on the Tenth' ('Tōka no Kiku', acted November;
published December 1961) and *The Voices of the Heroic Dead*

(*Eirei no Koe*, 1966)? Even in these works Mishima's aim is not to treat the historical incidents as such but to create out of them situations in which the consciousness of individual characters is revealed. In 'Patriotism', for instance, the 26 February incident is in the background, while in the foreground are the lieutenant and his wife, whose integrity through death is curiously identified with their passionate love-making (another example of Mishima's preoccupation with the concept of *Liebes-Tod*). But we should notice a change in the relation between Mishima's life and art. In his earlier works the apocalyptic wish for the end of the world is conceived by negative characters who are handicapped in various ways and cannot master life. In the army mutineer, however, Mishima represents a character who is no longer handicapped but fulfils his personal integrity through physical strength. Curiously enough, this is exactly what Mishima practised in his own life.

In the last years of his life, martial activities were becoming conspicuous: from 1967 on he took part on several occasions in training exercises with the units of the Self-Defence Forces. The Shield Society was founded in October 1968. More than a decade before that Mishima's personal behaviour had already become the subject of popular gossip. It was in 1955 that the then frail-looking Mishima started weightlifting. This was just a prelude to his later feats of physical training, which included boxing, traditional Japanese fencing, karate and so on. By these means Mishima changed himself into a muscular figure. At first it might have looked to many like a mere ostentatious gesture. Now, however, nobody can doubt the logical consistency underlying these acts, which is endorsed, for instance, by *Sun and Steel* (*Taiyō to Tetsu*, 1965–8). The remarkable fact was that Mishima's physical training proved useful for his mastery of life as much as the act of writing his novels. Thus Mishima came to find complementary to each other those things which had originally seemed antithetical: the world and words, life and art, body and spirit. As a corollary to this Mishima asserted the Japanese tradition of the union of literary and martial arts and Wang Yang-ming's concept of the unity of knowledge and action.[9] Formerly, the created world of Mishima's art was a compensation for his disenchantment with his unmanageable life. Now Mishima was the master of both spheres of art and life, and, paradoxically enough, the two spheres came to encroach upon each other in a way they did not with the I-novelists. Now the muscular and masculine Mishima could realise his desire for an apocalypse in the sphere of action, and did so in his final attempt at a coup d'état and his own suicide.

In explaining Mishima's death, therefore, it is necessary to draw attention to two facets, personal and social, aesthetic and political, inseparable from each other. One may naturally wonder whether Mishima really believed in the success of a coup. He certainly rehearsed the attack on the Self-Defence Forces headquarters, but it is unlikely that a man of such foresight as Mishima could have imagined in the given circumstances that the coup would be successful. It is even more difficult to guess what he could have done if it had been successful. His rehearsals also included the ceremony of *seppuku*. It seems more likely, therefore, that Mishima had envisaged the failure of the coup and that he was fully determined to kill himself. Or to put it another way, his determination to die was the primary cause and his attempt at a coup its by-product.

In retrospect there is a fair amount of proof of Mishima's firm determination to die. He held an unusual exhibition at a department store in Tokyo displaying not only all his published works, but manuscripts including his school exercises and photographs of himself since childhood. In a letter written to his former schoolteacher about a week before the incident of 25 November Mishima referred to volume iv of his tetralogy, saying: 'the end of this work will mean the end of my world'.[10] There is a longer and more important explanation of the matter in one of his series of essays on the novel contributed to a magazine entitled *Nami* (The Waves) from the spring of 1968 until just before his death. Referring again to the process of writing his last masterpiece, Mishima says:

> While I am engaged in writing this long novel, my life comprises two kinds of reality. As exemplified by the episode that Balzac on his death-bed called the doctor whom he created in his work, writers very often confuse the two kinds of reality. But it has been my essential principle of life and art never to confuse the two. . . .
> So long as I do not commit myself ultimately to either

of the two kinds of reality but seek the source of the
impulses for creation in the tension between the two,
the act of writing does not mean to be always under the
spell of the inspiration inherent in the created world, but
on the contrary to confirm the basis of my own freedom
at every moment. This freedom is not the so-called
freedom of a writer: it is the freedom to choose at any
moment either of the two kinds of reality. I cannot keep
on writing without this sense of freedom. Briefly, the
alternative for my choice is to dismiss either literature or
life. I keep on writing in the extremity of suspending
the choice. A confirmation of freedom at a certain
moment warrants this suspension, which is equivalent
to the act of writing.

A writer can never express adequately his painful
feeling when he becomes confined to the created world
of his own work.

I still have a volume, the last volume, to write. I
forbid myself to ask 'What will become of me when
I complete this novel?' I cannot conceive of the world
after I finish this novel.[11]

The passage might have escaped the readers' attention when it
was first published, but evidently it anticipated his forthcoming
death. It is endorsed by Mishima's quotation of a letter written
by Yoshida Shōin, a patriot towards the end of the Tokugawa
period, who was executed in prison on 25 November 1859:[12]
'Some perish in body but live in soul; it is useless to live with a
dead soul; one loses nothing by dying physically so long as one's
soul is alive.'[13] Mishima comments on the passage: 'Whether
alive or dead, a writer's life cannot be compared with that of a
man of action like Yoshida Shōin. Nothing can be more accursed
than a writer's life if, while alive, he is forced to suffer the death
of his soul and observe its dying process.'[14] Prior to the fatal
incident on the morning of 25 November, Mishima had handed
in the last portion of the fourth and final volume of *The Sea of
Fertility*. The completion of that work meant the breaking
of the delicate balance between the created world of his work
and commitment to life. He had to confront the 'freedom to
choose'.

As a phenomenon Mishima's death reminds us of Dazai and Akutagawa. But Mishima's case must be distinguished from theirs. Akutagawa belonged to that type of frail intellectual whom Mishima felt it necessary to transcend. Akutagawa's suicide was not so much the mastery of life as defeat by it. So was Dazai's. Mishima's death, on the other hand, was no mere passive defeat since he had the will to control his own life. The situation was one of paradox. If Mishima had remained the type of writer who, as in his earlier years, felt handicapped in life but compensated for it by creating his work, he would have kept on living in that mode. Now he had acquired physical strength, by means of which he could extinguish his own body so that his soul could live. It seems likely that for all his success as a great literary figure the external world remained alien to him and that the content of his life, even including his last attempt at a coup, was a product of his phantasy. He lived all along in a phantasy world, which could never be authentic except through serving the ultimate purpose of being transformed into an art form.

In search of identity:
ABÉ KŌBŌ and ŌE KENZABURŌ

The award to Kawabata Yasunari (1899–1972) of the Nobel Prize for Literature in 1968 brought Japanese literature into the international arena for the first time. Tanizaki Jun'ichirō (1886–1965), who had been reputed to be a candidate for the prize for many years, did not survive to witness the event. Kawabata himself ended his life by a rather anti-climactic suicide in 1972. This had been preceded eighteen months earlier by Mishima's more dramatic and ostentatious ritual suicide. With the death of Shiga Naoya in 1971, we have scarcely any writer of importance left who began his career in the Taishō period (1912–26). Of the writers who started working before the Second World War, Ibuse Masuji (1898–) and Ishikawa Jun (1899–) deserve special mention, but the major roles in the contemporary literary scene are played by postwar writers. Among these, we choose for discussion here two men whose choice of themes and innovation in literary methods make them particularly relevant to an understanding of modern Japan: Abé Kōbō (1924–) and Ōe Kenzaburō (1935–). They are writers who have already produced important works and are likely to produce more in the years to come.

Despite the gap in their ages (Ōe being eleven years the younger), there are interesting similarities as well as differences between the two. Both are concerned with the solitude of men and women alienated from contemporary society and suffering from a loss of identity. Besides the thematic parallels in their works, Abé and Ōe agree in their deliberate deviation from the dominant trend of the prewar Japanese novels. They are completely free from the sentimentality or self-commiseration characteristic of the I-novelists. Their prose style is also a mark of their deviation from the Japanese tradition. Abé's style is objective, logical and lucid. Ōe, on the other hand, deliberately distorts the traditional syntax, but is incomparable in his use of vivid imagery. Comparisons are often odious, but Abé's literary world has a closer kinship with that of Kafka and some contemporary European writers than that of his countrymen. It is also evident that Ōe is greatly indebted to and has absorbed much of the writings of Jean-Paul Sartre, Henry Miller and Norman Mailer.

I

Except for a collection of poems privately printed in 1947 Abé's first published work is *The Road Sign at the End of the Road* (*Owarishi Michi no Shirube ni*, 1948). This work is inferior to his major works, but its significance is borne out by his own words:

> On re-reading it I have come to feel that after all I must acknowledge this work as my point of departure.
> Although I do not like the view that a writer inevitably returns to his first piece of work, I cannot deny that this is the beginning of an important thread that even now runs through my work.[1]

The protagonist of this novel is in self-imposed exile in Manchuria, captured by a bandit in a border village and suffering from tuberculosis and opium addiction. The setting is important not only because Abé spent the sensitive years of his boyhood in Manchuria but also because many of his characters are deracinated either voluntarily or involuntarily. In this novel the 'homeland' is used in a double sense. There is the homeland of Japan, where the protagonist was born; and another homeland to which he had escaped to find himself. But the ultimate consequence is his confinement and deprivation of freedom. Finally he is cut off from the external world and loses his identity completely. The novel thus embodies the themes of deracination, confinement, deprivation of freedom, alienation and lost identity.

From the point of view of literary technique Abé explored a new and unique possibility for prose fiction in his 'The Wall: The Crime of Mr S. Karuma' ('Kabe – S. Karuma shi no Hanzai', 1951), for which he was awarded the Akutagawa Prize in 1951. This story is concerned with the metamorphosis of human beings, a theme which he also treats in 'Dendrocacalia' ('Dendorokakariya', 1949), 'Red Cocoon' ('Akai Mayu', 1950), 'A Badger in the Tower of Babel' ('Baberu no Tō no Tanuki', 1951), 'The Magic Chalk' ('Mahō no Chōku', 1951) and 'Stick' ('Bō', 1955). These bear a resemblance to Kafka's *Metamorphosis*, where the technique is far removed from realism. From the thematic point of view, however, the author is still concerned with the problem of lost identity. The alternatives for Abé were whether to employ a realistic method or a method which one may call allegorical, symbolic and even surrealistic. The difficulty of the latter alternative lies in the extent to which the use of the irrational and absurd can be plausible in rationalistic terms. There was in this sense a limitation to the highly allegorical stories of metamorphosis. It was natural enough that instead of the purely surrealistic or absurd, Abé came to deal with the realistic situation while still charging it with implications that are above mere realism.

Of Abé's major themes, that of deracination is in the foreground of *The Beasts Go Homeward* (*Kemonotachi wa Kokyō o Mezasu*, 1957). The hero, a boy of seventeen, is left alone in Manchuria at the end of the war with all his relatives dead and abandoned by his countrymen. The Manchurian wilderness is the setting in which the lonely, disorientated boy is left to wander, accompanied by a fraudulent half-caste, in search of his homeland and lost identity. Its symbolic effect prefigures that of the dunes in *The Woman in the Dunes* (*Suna no Onna*, 1962). At the end of his futile journey the hero finds himself confined in the bowels of a smugglers' ship. The effect of the work depends so much on minute details that it does not yield itself to paraphrase, but its theme is epitomised by the hero's internal monologue in the concluding paragraph.

> Damn it! it is as if I were circling round and round in the same place. . .however far I go, I cannot get out of the wilderness. . .maybe there does not exist a Japan at all. . .as I walk along, the wilderness moves along with me. Japan runs farther and farther away. . . .For a moment I had the flash of a dream, a dream of my childhood in Bakhalin. Over a high wall my mother is washing clothes. Crouched beside her the child is

amusing himself by squashing bubbles in the tub one
after another with his fingers. . . .Timidly watching this
scene from the other side of the wall is the other self,
worn out and quite unable to cross the wall. . . .Do I
have to be loitering like this outside the wall all my life?
Outside the wall man is lonely and must live, baring his
teeth like a monkey. . .one can live only like a beast.[2]

This passage is instructive in many ways. There is little to choose
between the tantalising situation over the wall and loitering in a
wilderness outside. In the dream episode, the wall divides the
childhood self, which is protected by maternal love in a paradisiacal garden encircled by a wall, from the mature self which is
outside the wall. The divided self symbolises the loss of identity.
The passage also clarifies the meaning of the title: in a state of
deprivation man embodies beast-like instincts devoid of reason
and confronts his fellow men as enemies.

With Western audiences the film version of *The Woman in the
Dunes* has become as popular as the novel itself. The novel represents all of Abé's major themes and reveals a highly ingenious
technique. The protagonist is cut off from his home and society,
and caught in the labyrinth of the dunes. In ordinary society he
maintains his identity through his profession as a schoolmaster
and through his legal relationship with his wife. In the dunes his
identity is completely lost. The dunes in their symbolic effect are
equivalent to the wilderness in *The Beasts Go Homeward*. They
function, in this case, as a setting for confinement, in which the
protagonist is deprived of freedom. The novel is built up on a
series of ironies and paradoxes. The protagonist is not aware of
the similarity between himself and the insects which he collects.
Furthermore, though he himself is not aware of it, his excessive
curiosity about the insects might be a symptom of his social maladjustment. In fact, in the course of the development of the novel
it becomes clear that there existed an unbridgeable gap between
him and his wife. It is an irony that he wishes to return to society
where his identity is only an illusory one and that he tries to
threaten the villagers of the dunes with this illusory identity.
A further irony is found in his gradual realisation of the futility
of his attempt to escape. In his attempt he only finds himself

caught in a worse trap of quick-sands. At the end of the novel he shows no wish to escape by means of a rope ladder to which he now has access.

What then emerges from *The Woman in the Dunes*? It exhibits Abé's penetrating view of such concepts as home, identity and freedom. In the first half of the novel the protagonist shares the conventional and illusory idea that he maintains his identity with his home and society, and that confinement in the dunes is the antithesis of freedom. But at the end of the novel he seems determined to stay in the dunes. His determination of course cannot be satisfactory in every respect. Certainly there exists a feeling of sympathy between him and the woman in the dunes. They develop a sexual relationship and the woman becomes pregnant. This pregnancy, however, is extra-uterine and thus symbolic of abnormality in the relationship. The only positive sign of hope, though still faint, is his discovery of water accumulated from the sand by capillary action. In the terms which Abé uses in *The Road Sign at the End of the Road* the protagonist parts company from the homeland of his birth and finds himself in another homeland, the equivalent of Manchuria. His identity is not established in either. Abé seems to say that identity cannot be found anywhere, but consists in a continuous search in the new homeland, which in this case is symbolised by the dunes. Since the dunes never stay stable but move continuously, man, as in the myth of Sisyphus, can never cease in his toil, for then he ceases to exist at all.

The theme of alienation and lost identity is further elaborated in *The Face of Another* (*Tanin no Kao*, 1964), which focuses on the relations of one individual with another and tries to define precisely the nature of individual identity. The protagonist, a chemist, has a face covered all over with a leech-like mass of keloid scars as a result of a laboratory explosion. The novel consists of his private notebook or diary in which he writes down the process of his making a mask and the subsequent psychological effect on both himself and his wife with whom he wants to re-establish a rapport by wearing the mask.

The protagonist's estrangement derives from the assumption on the part of society that one's face is one's identity and that ugly disfigurement deprives a person of his claim to be a member of that society. One of the many ironies in this novel, however, is that the protagonist, as a result of his unfortunate disfigurement, discerns the falsity of this common assumption. He becomes aware that the normal face is as unreal as a mask and that it can conceal beneath it a self which is far uglier than a disfigured face. Another irony is that the initial success of the mask comes to nullify, or at least temper, the hero's fearful obsession with his keloid scars:

> when I returned to my room, took off the mask, washed away the adhesive material, and again looked at my real face, the merciless scar webs seemed less real. The mask had already become just as real as the webs, and if the mask was a temporary form, so were the webs. . . . Apparently the mask was safely beginning to take root on my face.[3]

On one occasion, to test the use of his mask, the protagonist tries it at a Korean restaurant. What matters is not so much the subconscious racism or his conviction that he can easily dupe the Koreans, as the intensified realisation on his part of the extent of his hopeless alienation, which is comparable to that of the Koreans unjustly discriminated against in Japanese society.[4]

With the use of the mask the protagonist gains insight not only into other people but into himself. Once in a crowded train he is squashed close to a woman but his mask conceals his embarrassment. In his notebook, however, he confesses that his sexual desire was aroused on that occasion. The irony of the situation is that the mask conceals but does not change his real self. The problem has a deeper implication as developed in the protagonist's afterthought: it has to do with man's helpless solitude in contemporary society. The author seems to say that human beings are enemies of one another and that philanthropism is a fiction to disguise this very fact. The sexual desire that the protagonist feels towards the woman in a crowded train is a facet of such sterile human relationships in contemporary society.[5]

> Surely one may say that an aimless erotic act is a sexual tangent to the abstract human relationship. As long as the definition of 'other people' is confined to abstract relationships, those people are merely something in abstract opposition, one against others, enemies; and their sexual opposition is, in short, the impersonal erotic act.

For example, as long as the abstract idea of womanhood
exists, free-floating masculine eroticism is an unavoidable
necessity. Such eroticism indeed is not the enemy of
women, as is usually thought; rather woman herself is
the enemy of its impersonality. If that is true, an erotic
existence is not deliberately distorted sex, but may be
considered a typical form of sex as it exists today.

Anyway, today the line of demarcation between
enemy and fellow man, which in other times was easily
and clearly distinguishable, has become blurred. When
you get on a street-car, you have innumerable enemies
around you rather than fellow men. Some enemies come
into your house disguised as letters, and some, against
which there is no defense, infiltrate into your very cells in
the guise of radio waves. In such circumstances, enemy
encirclement becomes a custom to which we are already
inured, and 'fellow man' is as inconspicuous as a needle
in a desert. We have coined concepts of succor, such as
'All men are brothers', but where is such a vast,
imaginary repository of 'brothers'? Wouldn't it be more
logical to reconcile oneself to the fact that others are
enemies and abandon such highflown, misplaced hopes?
Wouldn't it be safer to hurry up and produce some
antibody for loneliness?

And why shouldn't we men, surfeited with loneliness,
become involved in impersonal eroticism even with our
wives, not to mention other women? My own case
cannot be exceptional. If, as a function of the mask, I
acknowledge a considerable abstracting of the human
relationship – indeed, I am probably addicted to empty
fancies precisely because of this abstracting – I, who am
trying to find some solution, had best shelve my own
problems and shut up. Yes, no matter how clever I am,
the very subject of my plans is perhaps merely erotic
fancy.

If that is so, the plans for the mask were not my own
special desire alone, but merely the expression of a
contemporary, detached man's common craving. Even
though it seemed at first blush that I had again lost to the
mask, in reality I had not at all.[6]

From the protagonist's realisation that the use of a mask can allow free play of his libidinous impulse there follows the generalisation that the mass production of masks would create an immoral as well as an amoral society. Abé's vivid imagination is employed in his fantastic picture of the world in which manufacturers of masks prosper by meeting the demands of people and in which one crime after another is committed.

> Some people would suddenly vanish. Others would
> be broken up into two or three people. Personal
> identification would be pointless, police photographs
> ineffective, and pictures of prospective marriage partners
> torn up and thrown away. Strangers would be confused
> with acquaintances, and the very idea of an alibi would
> collapse. Unable to suspect others, unable to believe in
> others, one would have to live in a suspended state,
> a state of bankrupt human relations, as if one were
> looking into a mirror that reflects nothing.
> . . . And when it became common practice to constantly
> seek new masks, the word 'stranger' would become
> obscene, scrawled in public toilets; and identification
> of strangers – like definitions of family, nation, rights,
> duties – would become obscure, incomprehensible
> without copious commentary.[7]

Abé can also be humorously ironical about the possible plight of his own profession:

> On balance, of course, some things would be definitely
> negative. The popularity of detective stories would
> naturally decline to a shadow, and novels of family
> affairs dealing with double and triple personalities
> would be popular for a while; but since the purchasing
> of masks would occur at the rate of five or more different
> kinds per person, the resultant complexities of plot
> would exceed the limits of the readers' patience. For
> some the *raison d'être* of the novel except for fulfilling
> the demands of lovers of historical fiction, would possibly
> disappear.[8]

The ultimate end of the protagonist's plan to seduce his wife under a mask is partly to take vengeance on her because she has rejected him and partly to re-establish a relationship with someone other than himself, but the execution of his plan is bound to take the form of raping his wife. He can perceive this much, but cannot foresee the consequences it will entail. His wife's apparently unresisting acceptance of his seduction under the mask appals him, but the actual fact is that his wife is aware of his identity. The vulnerability of the mask is indeed hinted at by the irony that a mentally retarded girl easily identifies him under the mask. No wonder his wife, too, knows him. She overcomes her initial embarrassment by trying to see his scheme as being based on his consideration towards her. She is morally innocent so long as she knows that the mask is a mere fiction and that she is actually re-establishing a rapport with her husband. The protagonist, on the contrary, is testing her and fostering distrust of her, which proves not only tormenting to himself but also injurious to her goodwill towards him. It is inevitable that the gap between the two becomes more deeply felt. The ultimate irony is that the mask which the protagonist invents to restore a tie with his wife actually contributes to an irrevocable break.

What *The Face of Another* amounts to may be summed up as follows: according to the common assumption, one's face represents one's identity and disfigurement means a damaged personality; the creation of a mask seemingly compensates for disfigurement and helps to restore one's identity, but, in actual fact, the mask is false and can be no more one's identity than can one's face; ironically enough, the mask helps the process of introspection and brings with it a realisation that, whether one wears a mask or not, the real self is ugly, helpless, lonely, and unable to commune with another individual; the search for one's lost identity inevitably leads to the recognition that the ideal self does not exist. *The Face of Another* was followed by *The Ruined Map* (*Moetsukita Chizu*, 1967), which is another novel about a search for identity: a private detective, while engaged in looking for a man who has disappeared into thin air, loses his own identity. Thus Abé does not give any easy solution to the search for identity. However, this may not be so much a pessimistic philosophy as a realistic acceptance of the human condition. It reminds us that to dream of release from our impasse must prove illusory. The lost identity is not to be discovered, and yet life is meaningful only if the search is continued: the cessation of the search means death. If we use Abé's own metaphor, we are surrounded by desert or dunes, and there is no other place for us.

2

The link between Abé Kōbō and Ōe Kenzaburō is evident from the latter's remark in his introduction to the selected works of Abé:

> When I first started writing novels, there was nothing
> for me but to imitate Abé Kōbō. I tried my best to
> imitate his way of thinking, but naturally I never
> attained the clarity characteristic of the world he created.
> I soon gave up imitating him and wrote a short story.
> Its publication in the newspaper of the University of
> Tokyo marked the beginning of my literary career. Soon
> after that I was asked to review for that newspaper *The
> Beasts Go Homeward* – my first-ever book review.
>   Abé Kōbō was thus very important for me to start
> my career as a writer. This is still true even now when
> I can talk face to face with him.[9]

Between the two writers there are parallels in more ways than one. Abé's earliest work came to be published through a recommendation by Haniya Yutaka (1910–) who was then a member of the magazine *Kindai Bungaku*. Practically the earliest of Ōe's short stories, 'A Strange Job' ('Kimyōna Shigoto', 1957), was chosen for the University of Tokyo Newspaper Prize by Ara Masahito (1913–), who was also a founding member of *Kindai Bungaku*. Abé and Ōe thus share the qualities that must have appealed to the literary taste of their elders, who constituted one of the main forces of postwar Japanese literature. But these circumstances are in a way incidental. The link between the two must be defined in more fundamental terms. In Ōe's earliest short stories such as 'A Strange Job' and 'The Arrogance of the Dead' 'Shisha no Ogori', 1957), the main characters are university students who are engaged in humiliating hack work for their livelihood. Unable to resort to political activities as their fellow students do, they find no way out from their present impasse.

In this respect their condition may most appropriately be described as one of confinement, alienation and deprivation of freedom, which are all unmistakably Abé's major themes.

'The Catch' ('Shiiku', 1958), for which Ōe was awarded the Akutagawa Prize for the first half of 1958, has many merits and, despite its limitation as a short story, reveals his literary talent at its best. Instead of the baffled youths suffering from mental inertia and feelings of estrangement in the metropolis, as in 'A Strange Job' and 'The Arrogance of the Dead', the major characters are country boys. The story in fact owes its vigour to the vivid picture of the Japanese countryside, with which Ōe, coming from the province of Shikoku, is well acquainted. In this respect he differs from Abé who, born in Tokyo but brought up in Manchuria, is essentially a déraciné. While the fact of deracination and solitude in the Manchurian wilderness is the framework of Abé's *The Beasts Go Homeward*, Ōe's story is built around the boys' sense of oneness with the natural surroundings of the Japanese countryside. It is also possible that Ōe might have obtained from Abé the idea of using the boy as the point of view. Furthermore, *The Beasts Go Homeward* and 'The Catch' reflect the impact of wartime experience on the authors, one in his adolescence and the other in his boyhood.

The setting of the story is intriguing. From the common-sense point of view the captured Negro American pilot represents the enemy country. From another point of view (though this is never explicitly stated), the Negro belongs to a minority group alienated within American society and cannot be entirely identified with the enemy country. From yet another point of view, Ōe may anticipate a recently fashionable idea that black is beautiful. The first point of view is represented by the adults, while it is on the tacit understanding of the second and the third that the boys' actions are based. For them the captured Negro is the object of their admiration, for he embodies the life force of organic Nature which they also find in the natural surroundings of their native village.

What Ōe creates through the eyes of the boys is an almost paradisiacal state of innocence in which man and Nature are organically united.[10] Harmony seems to pervade the whole community, so that there no longer exists a barrier even between the adults and their captive. However, the harmonious state of the community proves vulnerable to the code of the external world: the Negro must be handed over to the local authorities. Ironically enough, when the protagonist discloses the news to the captive, he finds himself held as a hostage. The story ends tragically: the Negro is killed, and the boy's hand wounded by his father's axe; thus the dream of innocence is completely shattered.

Ōe's first novel, *Plucking Buds and Shooting Lambs* (*Memu-shiri Kouchi*, 1958), is an extended version of 'The Catch'. In 'The Catch' the antithesis between innocence and experience, juvenile spontaneity and social restraint, is only gradually realised in the course of the story, but in this novel the antithesis is presented from the outset in that the protagonist and his companions are stigmatised as juvenile delinquents. They are outsiders, unlike the boys in 'The Catch' who are natives of a local community. But in the course of the story it becomes evident that they are in fact variations of the boys of 'The Catch', and that in spite of their social stigma, paradoxically enough, they represent potential innocence, while the villagers embody malignity, hypocrisy and injustice.

Ōe succeeds to the fullest extent in bringing home the theme of confinement and alienation from the outside world, which he shares in common with Abé and with which he was concerned in his earliest short stories. The hero and his companions find themselves not only deserted by the villagers, who run away for fear of an epidemic, but also locked up in a shed. One can also recognise here a caricature of wartime Japanese society: the juvenile delinquents share their lot with a Korean boy, the daughter of an evacuee, and an army deserter. Their initial animosity towards one another changes to a sense of fellowship which arises from their common lot.

The author's sympathy lies with the juvenile delinquents, but do they embody any positive value? They are certainly akin to the boys of 'The Catch', but the fact of their deracination and alienation makes their rapport with the external world weaker than in the case of their prototypes. The utmost they can achieve is reduced to a kind of primitivism: for instance, their curious affinity with animals. Another aspect of the potential good that they could represent is their uninhibited life force. But again there is an ambivalence about it: their uninhibited spontaneity can manifest itself, for instance, in sexual perversion as practised by one of the boys.[11] Perhaps the only positive moment of communion is achieved between the hero and the deserted girl. Only this act embodies genuine human solidarity and therefore a positive value.[12]

Both 'The Catch' and *Plucking Buds and Shooting Lambs* reveal Ōe's wish-fulfilment for envisaging a universe pervaded with pantheistic harmony. Two approaches are therefore discernible in Ōe's work so far: those which directly treat confinement, estrangement and lack of freedom against the background of urban society, and those which envisage an aspiration to the potentially pastoral. These are in fact two sides of the same coin. Since the latter is not easy to achieve, as illustrated by *Plucking Buds and Shooting Lambs*, it was natural for Ōe to concentrate on the former in his subsequent writings, producing such works as 'Leap Before You Look' ('Miru maeni Tobe', 1958), *Our Age* (*Warera no Jidai*, 1959) and *The Youth Who Arrived Late* (*Okurete Kita Seinen*, 1960–2). All these are concerned with the theme of how to get out of a state of humiliation and restraint.

The sense of confinement in Ōe's earlier short stories and novels is an expression not only of an existential anxiety but also of an intuitive apprehension about the postwar political situation at large. When the Pacific War ended, Ōe was in the fifth form of a primary school. He listened to the emperor's speech on the acceptance of the unconditional surrender, but he did not understand a word of it, nor the reaction of his elders. Unlike Mishima, for whom the end of the war was almost the end of the world, Ōe belonged to the generation that accepted the postwar 'democratisation' initiated by the American occupation. For him as well as Oda Makoto (1932–) the postwar 'democratisation' and the New Constitution which proclaimed the renunciation of war formed the bases of their political views and activities. They are thus in a sense the best pupils of the postwar American policy; and yet the irony of the situation is that they came to feel at odds with many products of the American presence in Asia.[13] It is against this background that Ōe wrote the works which express his sense of helplessness and humiliation such as 'The Human Sheep' ('Ningen no Hitsuji', 1958), 'Today the Struggle' ('Tatakai no Konnichi', 1958) and *Our Age*.

Already in his earliest works Ōe's concern with sex is evident.

In the early 1960s he wrote three novels in which sex occupies an important place: *Seventeen* (*Sevuntiin*, 1961), *Outcries* (*Sakebigoe*, 1962) and *The Sexual Man* (*Seiteki Ningen*, 1963). In his treatment of sex two features stand out clearly. The first is his complete freedom from any kind of inhibition. This partly reflects the change of attitude to sex in Japanese society at large. This freedom is also shared by Ishihara Shintarō (1932–), who was awarded the Akutagawa Prize for his *The Season of the Sun* (*Taiyō no Kisetsu*) in the first half of 1956. But the parallel does not go very far. Ishihara treats sex as an end in itself and goes no further than the sensationalism of the Japanese naturalistic tradition. The detailed description of sexual scenes in Ōe's novels, however, is characterised by the author's callousness. Sex almost becomes an abstract object as we often find in Abé's novels. In spite of such detail, however, sexual description in Ōe's novels arouses no pornographic interest.

This is due to another feature of Ōe's treatment of sex: the sexual impulse in his novels is relevant not in its own right but as a symptom of an unfulfilled, repressed social ego. In *Seventeen*, for instance, the protagonist's habitual masturbation is a compensation for his discontent with the external world. In criticising the political and social situation of Japan the protagonist appears to be a potential left-wing radical. Curiously enough, however, he becomes indoctrinated by the right wing instead of the left. The sequel to this novel, *The Death of a Political Boy* (*Seiji Shōnen Shisu*, 1961), which echoes the assassination of the chairman of the Japan Socialist Party by a right-wing youth, provoked threats to Ōe and his publisher from the right. Ōe's position in these novels is extremely complex. The process by which the protagonist's sexual impulse is sublimated into a political passion is an extension of the reaction of the juvenile delinquents to the hypocritical adults in *Plucking Buds and Shooting Lambs*. In drawing a parallel between the sexual impulse and right-wing fanaticism, *Seventeen* and its sequel resemble Mishima's story 'Patriotism'. And yet Ōe himself is no ally of the right wing. Ōe's works in question parallel Mishima's story only superficially and are at best a parody. Ōe wrote them with tongue in cheek and their effect is one of irony. He commits himself neither to the left nor to the right, but is concerned with the curious fact that the sexual impulse as a symptom of a repressed social ego can reveal itself either as left-wing radicalism or as right-wing patriotism and that the two are interchangeable.

The theme of *Seventeen* is taken over with a slight variation in *Outcries*.[14] The four central characters, including the narrator, are all social misfits in one way or another but united by their common intention to build a yacht and run away from their present state of maladjustment. Their social inadaptability is presented in the form of lost identity due to their racial background. A half-caste, born of a black American and a Japanese–American, nicknames himself 'Tiger' as the colours black and yellow are mixed in his skin. As a misfit in Japanese society, his dream is to go to Africa in search of his lost identity. Another character, Takao, is born of a Korean father and a Japanese mother. An interesting feature in both Tiger and Takao is the curious interlocking of their social alienation with their sexual life. For instance, Takao, like the protagonist of *Seventeen*, finds self-sufficiency in masturbation. That he can be neither Japanese nor Korean is shown by the fact that he finds himself a stranger in a Korean ghetto. He writes down in his diary the French words '*l'homme authentique*', by which he means man secure within society, the exact antithesis of himself. After Tiger's death his previously self-sufficient masturbation proves inadequate and he fails to achieve a sense of mastery over the external world. As an alternative, he kills a female high school student, whom he sees as an example of '*l'homme authentique*', under the guise of raping her. Ōe bases this on the actual murder of a female high school student by a Korean boy, which is known as 'the Komatsugawa Incident'. He transforms, as Mishima did in his *The Temple of the Golden Pavilion*, a criminal into a coherent character. Takao is an extension of the hero in *Seventeen* and represents a socially repressed and alienated ego who seeks release in either sexual activity or in the destruction of a symbol of the established social order.

Preceded by *Seventeen* and *Outcries*, *The Sexual Man* looks like the final part of a trilogy dealing with the human condition in terms of sex. At the end of the novel the protagonist, who has had only a sterile relationship with his wife, tries to achieve a sense of presiding over society by means of his sexual misconduct in public. Here again we see the author's use of the sexual act as a means of revenge on the society from which one is cut off.

This novel has little to add to *Seventeen* and *Outcries*, but one notable feature is the author's sense of the primitive, which is not unfamiliar in his earlier works such as 'The Catch' and *Plucking Buds and Shooting Lambs* and which was to play a more important role in *The Football Match in the First Year of the Man'en Era (Man'en Gannen no Futtobōru*, 1967). In a fishing village where the protagonist and his company are staying to make a film *Inferno*, the villagers happen to be suffering from poor catches, which they attribute to some supernatural cause. The village is thus a miniature of the waste land. In the meantime the protagonist and his company feel the presence of 'a pair of eyes' in the villa where they are staying. They turn out to be the eyes of a village boy who has been hiding in the villa and who witnesses the protagonist's sterile intercourse with his wife. The boy runs out through a window crying in a local dialect, 'I've seen ogres.' There is an ironical effect that the protagonist and his company themselves have been playing both the real and fictitious roles of infernal characters. The villagers' attempt to regain fertility, and the sterile sexual life of the city dwellers who are uprooted from the sources of life are starkly contrasted. It may follow from all this that except for the momentary synthesis of the primitive and life force in 'The Catch' the sexual pursuit in Ōe's novels is a vain compensation for the characters alienated from the root of life.

In the whole corpus of Ōe's works *The Football Match in the First Year of the Man'en Era*[15] is monumental in that it synthesises all the elements of his earlier works in a new and wider perspective. The major character suffers from a sense of being cut off from reality and the story opens with him sitting at the bottom of a hole, an act which is symptomatic of his anxiety about existence itself. This has been caused partly by the birth of an abnormal and defective child, and the subsequent impotence of himself and frigidity of his wife. He is also haunted by the memory of his activist friend, who, after the failure of the 1960 campaign against the Security Treaty, went mad and committed suicide in a grotesque fashion. The author as elsewhere resorts to the older-and-younger brother pattern: while Mitsusaburō is a brooding, impractical intellectual, his younger brother Takashi is an active man. Ōe also places the setting of the novel in the familiar countryside of Shikoku. That these characters are in search of their identity is evident from the visit they pay to their native village, as well as their family name Nedokoro, which means 'where the root is'. Ōe's description of the village where the protagonists' ancestors used to be the local headmen is as masterly as in 'The Catch'. In addition to his superb sense of place the author employs his historical imagination: the political situation in which Takashi becomes involved overlaps with that of the first year of the Man'en era, 1860. In that year a revolt by the peasants against the great-grandfather of the Nedokoro family was led by his younger brother. The revolt was a failure and the younger brother is said to have escaped to Edo and later made his career under the Meiji government. It is with the younger brother of the great-grandfather that Takashi identifies himself. In 1960 the Nedokoros are no longer powerful in the province. The village economy is under the control of an upstart Korean who owns a large supermarket. Conflict arises between him and the native villagers whose lives he makes unbearable. As might be expected, Takashi becomes the leader of the villagers' strife against the upstart millionaire or 'the emperor of the super-market' as he is called. But Takashi becomes isolated and deserted by the villagers as a result of his raping a girl. He commits suicide and the villagers' battle fails. Takashi's death is preceded by his confession that he had incestuous relations with his idiot sister many years ago. It is followed by a further recognition that the younger brother of the great-grandfather actually did not escape from the village but was kept imprisoned till his death in a dungeon on the Nedokoro estate.

What emerges from this gloomy family chronicle in which the past and present overlap? Are Ōe's characters able to re-discover their lost identity? The answer is no. As shown in 1860 the family of Nedokoro contained within itself two antithetical elements: the great-grandfather, as the retainer of the family tradition and patriarchal authority; and his younger brother, who rebelled against him in collaboration with the peasants and was eventually defeated. In 1960 the relationship between Mitsusaburō and Takashi corresponds to that of the great-grand-father and his younger brother. Mitsusaburō as an urban intel-lectual, however, has already been cut off from his ancestors, while the object of Takashi's rebellion is the commercialism that destroys the village community. But Takashi himself cannot embody an absolutely positive value, for he is responsible for the death of a village girl and his own idiot sister. He functions only as a mediator for discovering the identity which is universal and unchanging throughout history. It seems that Ōe wants to say that such an identity is embodied in the nature of the country-side, the belief in the spirit of the forest, and rituals such as the *nenbutsu* (invocation) dance, all shared by the people of the village community. Such is the identity that Mitsusaburō and Takashi should be searching for. It could have existed in an ideal com-munity where there was harmony between man and man and between man and Nature. Unfortunately, however, for neither Mitsusaburō nor Takashi, living in the industrial society of 1960, is it possible to attain this state without some sacrifice: in Takashi's case, his own death; and in Mitsusaburō's case, patience to come to terms with reality, reconciling himself with his adul-terous wife and bringing up Takashi's baby. It is far from heroic, but that is the only alternative for Mitsusaburō.[16]

While producing a number of novels year after year, Ōe has also for some time been an active political orator. In 1960 Ōe, Ishihara Shintarō and Etō Jun (1933–) all collaborated to organise the Wakai Nihon no Kai (the Young Japan Group), which criticised the way in which the government handled the revision of the Security Treaty and expressed deep concern over the subsequent political chaos.[17] In the same year Ōe visited the Chinese mainland and vigorously praised the communist regime until the first Chinese nuclear tests, which he criticised. In 1963 he paid a visit to Hiroshima, the record of which was published as *Hiroshima Notebook* (*Hiroshima Nōto*, 1965). His concern with Hiroshima is not based on any specific ideological standpoint but derives from his genuine compassion for the survivors who have suffered from the same kind of humiliation and existential anxiety as represented in his novels. For these people neither the government's aid nor the ideologically biased anti-nuclear cam-paign would suffice. The *Hiroshima Notebook*, however, does not end with complete pessimism about the situation but with admiration and hope for the attempt on the part of the survivors to recover from the persistent after-effects of radiation and the effort of half a dozen conscientious local intellectuals to help them.

The *Hiroshima Notebook* was followed by the *Okinawa Notebook* (*Okinawa Nōto*, 1970), which was in a way a logical development from the previous book. Here again the author looks at the situation from his unique position. At that time, while the Japanese government was doing its best to get Okinawa back from America, the opposition parties and various left-wing groups were protesting against the presence of the American bases. But they all overlooked the fact that whoever governed Okinawa, whether the Japanese government (1868–1945) or the postwar American administration, there always existed the indigenous populace who were sacrificed for some external aim. It was with these people that Ōe sympathised. His sympathy is at one with his aspiration to the communal identity shared by the local people in *The Football Match in the First Year of the Man'en Era*.

We are entering the sphere where literature and politics meet. Ōe's aspiration to the communal identity shared by the indigenous people involves a difficult question: how could it transcend its own specificity and attain universality? A tentative answer to this question may be found in Ōe's account of his trip to South-East Asia in the autumn of 1970:

> After staying a few weeks in India, I became aware that I was beginning to take my Japanese identity as something of only relative importance. This awareness of mine appeared in the forefront of my consciousness in the holy land of Benares in the valley of the Ganges when I heard on the B.B.C. radio news about how a Japanese writer committed *seppuku* after crying 'Long Live the Emperor'. For the last few years I have been preoccupied with Okinawa and obsessed with an overwhelming and shameful question: 'what is it to be a Japanese? how can I transform myself into a Japanese different from what he is now?'...
>
> When from India I look back upon Japan, it becomes crystal clear that the view of the Emperor given by that writer who committed suicide was nothing but a fiction, a personal mysticism.
>
> Also I cannot but realise how we are bound by a false Japanese identity. Yes! it is not so much that we are dissatisfied with our false identity as that we are proud

of it. Are we ever ashamed of ourselves as 'economic
animals'? Have we sufficiently disapproved of having
ourselves defined as 'an economic power'?[18]

In India Ōe came across a gregarious, poverty-stricken people.
Instead of recognising them as Indians, he sees in them humanity
at large driven to extreme deprivation. He goes on to say:

> In the climate of India and surrounded by the people
> there I became more and more aware of the falsity
> of the assumption that Japan is an economic power and
> will predominate in the twenty-first century.
> . . .Japan is wrapped in 'ethnocentricism', which,
> however, looks so illusory as to fade away in the eyes of
> the 'human beings' in the streets of Calcutta.[19]

According to Ōe, Japan as an economic giant, and Mishima's
suicide are both based on a false standard of values. Perhaps
he is over-simplyfying the matter. That Mishima's idealism
was not compatible with the recent material prosperity of Japan
is well-known. But Ōe's sin of over-simplification is venial. It
is more important to note the different ways in which Mishima
and Ōe seek Japan's identity. Mishima's search moves upward
towards the idealised concept of the emperor, while Ōe's moves
downward towards the populace; Mishima's imagination binds
itself within the framework of the national polity, while Ōe's
releases itself beyond and transcends the boundary of the state.
The indigenous populace embodies a medium through which Ōe
can search for his identity, yet he is capable of transcending
geographical particularities and attaining identity in a universal
perspective: 'Through my Indian experience the voice of
"humanity" free from the illusion of "ethnocentricism" indicates
where a new hope exists, yet curiously intermingled with deeper
despair. I find myself on the threshold of a new vista at the end of
my trip to India, Asia and Okinawa.'[20]

In this chapter an attempt has been made to show how Abé Kōbō
and Ōe Kenzaburō are both concerned with the search for identity,
each in his own way. Abé's unique position may become clear by
comparison with his predecessors. The Japanese I-novelists, for
instance, believed or at least tried to believe that there was the ego
or the core of individual personality to be searched for through

their attempts to write novels, although their purpose was never really fulfilled. Even Mishima, who was an opponent of the tradition of the I-novels, treated the growth of his own ego under the guise of a mask. Abé, on the contrary, seems to suggest that, whether disguised under a mask or not, there is no personal identity other than that which is inevitably bound to the material world. In this Abé represents the truly existentialist standpoint that existence precedes essence.

The search for identity presupposes a community in which the ego is to be realised as a social self. For Abé, however, a community is an illusory idea which he rejects outright. His works provide a picture of life in which man is utterly lonely, deprived of communication with his fellow men and determined by physical reality. And yet what Abé intends to prescribe in his works is not despair but tough reasonableness with which to accept the inescapable reality of life; only by doing so can man justify his own existence. In contrast to Abé, Ōe seems to aspire to a community in which the personal identity is to be realised. The difference between the two in this respect is probably due to the fact that as a child one lived the life of an expatriate while the other was deeply rooted in his native rural community. However, it is extremely difficult for Ōe, now living in the midst of industrial society, to celebrate the pastoral. As a result he portrays characters overwhelmed by the strain of urban society, or else he is 'of the Devil's party': in depicting a tension between the social restraint and spontaneous impulse, he represents the latter by anti-social characters, such as juvenile delinquents, sexual perverts and criminals, who are apparently intended to be fallen angels. Ōe's dream of a pastoral community is expressed in such a way as to show the difficulty of its realisation.

The history of modern Japanese literature, as in other aspects of culture, has been streaked with the cross-currents of the native tradition and Western influence. There were writers, such as Tanizaki and Kawabata, who represent an almost spontaneous example of the traditional sensibility. Mishima's artificially acquired Western taste, on the other hand, was deliberately counterbalanced by his fortified Japanese consciousness. Abé differs from any of these predecessors. He was brought up as an expatriate in a place somewhat like a barren wilderness, where neither the culture of his homeland nor that of the West was available in tangible form. In such circumstances there was nothing for him but to conceive of culture, of whichever hemisphere, in the abstract. This could have been a disadvantage, but, in Abé's case, it enabled him to create a literary universe which transcends the author's nationality. He is probably the first Japanese writer whose works, having no distinctly Japanese qualities, are of interest to the Western audience because of their universal relevance.

With Ōe it is a different matter. On the one hand he is Westernised in his attempts to assimilate various features of contemporary European and American authors. On the other, however, he presents his themes in a specifically Japanese context. Attention has been drawn in this chapter to his concern with the communal identity to be sought in indigenous culture. This is likely to derive from his anxiety about his own and his country-men's precarious footing in contemporary Japanese society, where the native tradition is jeopardised by the ever-accelerating modern-isation which began under Western influence in Meiji and has perhaps got out of hand. A description of the situation in these terms might sound fictitious to Abé for whom there exists no distinction between the native and foreign cultures, while it is an overwhelming reality to Ōe. From this difference in their attitudes to the cultural milieu of present-day Japan emerge the two types of literature: one has so nearly effaced Japanese elements as to attain universality in both its themes and its tech-niques; the other, despite its Westernised façade, houses senti-ments that epitomise the present dilemma of the nation. In this sense, Ōe's is a search for the identity of the race as well as the individual.

Conclusion

From the foregoing discussion emerge some features that make modern Japanese literature markedly different from earlier Japanese literature of the preceding Tokugawa period. One of the most notable new elements is the strain – as unsettling as it was unending – that the writers had to suffer in struggling to cope with the rapidly changing realities of modern Japanese society. Contrary to a common sociological, if not literary, assumption that the modernisation of Japan should have coincided with these writers' freedom, both intellectual and spiritual, their lives and works bear out the blunt truth that they knew more discord than concord in their public and private lives. At the risk of over-simplification one may possibly explain this phenomenon by saying that the modernisation of Japan was meant to be pragmatic and utilitarian while the writers held on to their ideals which were often at odds with this political inclination. No wonder so many of these writers, so often apolitical, knew more of alienation, insecurity, mental breakdowns and even suicide than they did of any other kind of human experience.

One of the factors that contributed to these writers' insecurity was the cultural impact of the West. They went through a test which their Western models never had to experience. They had to be educated twice – an initial rearing in their own native cultural traditions and a later assimilation of cultural traditions hitherto unknown to them. With their expert knowledge of European languages and literature the leading modern Japanese writers were much more alive to the values and even the contradictory values of Western culture than their fellow countrymen. Yet, with their unusually perceptive insight these writers saw the traps that were set in the Westernisation of modern Japan. They were profoundly aware that their native traditions and those of the

West were not always compatible and that Japan's Westernisation was not modernisation and *vice versa*. Sometimes they realised the difficulties to which their own efforts to understand Western culture were subject. Worse still, they could not help noticing that by studying Western culture they were undergoing a split in their personal and cultural identities as they became afraid of losing their 'authenticity' in Japanese society.

Such phenomena as the writers' alienation and identity crises in the face of Western culture had an immediate bearing on the art form of modern Japanese literature. As precursors, both Tsubouchi Shōyō and Futabatei Shimei made efforts to refashion Japanese novels using modern European literature as their model, but the works they produced, as we have seen, were inevitably restricted by the literary heritage from the preceding Tokugawa period. As for highly autobiographical writers, they misinterpreted the concept of naturalism in European literature and distorted it by exposing the sordid realities of their own life. Experiencing at first-hand what might be called a psychologist's treasurehouse of neuroses and psychoses, they were never short of material for their work. Unfortunately, their self-flagellation in itself did not evolve into an authentic form of literary art.

Other writers, however, were seriously concerned with how to represent realities artistically. Natsume Sōseki, for instance, shaped fiction around some psychological problems he shared with his contemporaries. Worthy of special note is the way in which the concept of realism he learned from the nineteenth-century English novel became part and parcel of the artifice in his later works. Whether as a scholar or as a writer, he all along retained the integrity of an intellectual moralist. Akutagawa, though much more limited in his literary scope, inherited Sōseki's attitude, while Tanizaki and Kawabata had an entirely different approach to life and literature, which was, in brief, aesthetic, sensuous and amoral.

Tanizaki's attempts to establish a rapport with the external world through his search for eternal womanhood sometimes resulted in sado-masochistic morbidity as in his earlier works. *The Makioka Sisters*, however, marks his triumph by representing the life of fully authentic characters living in an authentically Japanese milieu, which its readers are cordially invited to join in and thereby have their sense of life enriched. Such a felicitous and harmonious picture of life is missing from Kawabata's work, which suggests that the relationship he maintained with external reality was precarious and insecure. Yet, paradoxically enough, he had what may be called a 'negative capability' with which to come to terms with and survive insecurity. This unique capability enabled him to attain the kind of 'authenticity' inherent in a writer embodying traditional Japanese sensibilities in a manner comparable to Tanizaki's.

Mishima Yukio had intellectual powers of great magnitude, somewhat comparable to Sōseki's, and aspired to the artisanship as exemplified by Tanizaki and Kawabata. He suffered invariably from alienation from the external world. It was partly the external world and partly his own existence that he felt to be unreal. His strong personality enabled him to put up with life while denying its significance. He had two ways of surmounting his predicament, either by releasing his phantasies in his work or by physically transforming himself into his antithesis. A closer look at Mishima, however, reveals the paradoxical fact that even his action which looks real enough is often a variation of his phantasy-making. Divorced from external reality, Mishima all along had a strong yearning for death and a wish for the end of the world. An even more catastrophic defeat of Japan in the last war might have realised his wish. As it was, he became completely disillusioned with postwar Japan, even though it had recognised him as a great literary figure. His ultimate suicide was an act of fulfilling his eschatological dream, in which he sacrificed the authenticity of his life to that of his art.

When we reach Abé Kōbō and Ōe Kenzaburō, we feel we have come a long way from the early Meiji writers. The barrier between the Western and their own traditions was felt to be immeasurably great by the earlier writers, who took nothing for granted in resorting to European models. Abé and Ōe now live in an environment where the pervasive Western influence is a matter of fact. And yet the discussion of these two writers has shown that they too are making their efforts to attain authenticity by means of their literary work. The search for authenticity has thus been one of the central concerns in modern Japanese literature and will remain so in the future.

Notes

Introduction

1 There are excellent book-length studies of Ōgai and Kafū.
  Richard J. Bowring, *Mori Ōgai* (Cambridge: Cambridge
  University Press, 1977).
  Edward G. Seidensticker, *Kafū the Scribbler* (Stanford, Calif.:
  Stanford University Press, 1965).

Chapter 1

1 Yanagida Izumi, *Meiji Bungaku Kenyū* (A Study of Meiji
  Literature), vol. I, *Wakaki Tsubouchi Shōyō* (The Young
  Tsubouchi Shōyō, Tokyo: Shunjūsha, 1960), pp. 68–135.
2 After graduating from Harvard University, Ernest Fenollosa
  arrived in Japan in August 1878. The courses he gave are
  marked with an asterisk. Those given by William A. Houghton
  are marked with two asterisks and those by Charles
  James Cooper with three asterisks. Cooper's course on Moral
  Philosophy dealt with Herbert Spencer, Henry Sidgwick,
  Walter Bagehot, Jeremy Bentham and J. S. Mill.
3 Fenollosa's theory of art was put into Japanese under the title
  Bijutsu Shinsetsu (The True Meaning of Art), which was later
  collected in *Meiji Bunka Zenshū* (The Collected Meiji Writings
  on Culture, Tokyo: Nihon Hyōronsha, 1928), vol. XII,
  pp. 157–74.
4 *Encyclopaedia Britannica*, 8th edn, 22 vols. (Edinburgh:
  Adam & Charles Black, 1853–60), vol. XIX (1859), pp. 253–69,
  269–93.
5 John Morley, 'George Eliot' in his *Critical Miscellanies*, 3 vols.
  (London, 1886).
6 Nakamura Mitsuo, *Futabatei Shimei Den* (The Life of Futabatei
  Shimei, Tokyo: Kōdansha, 1958).
7 Futabatei translated into Japanese one of Belinsky's essays,
  'The Idea of Art', under the title 'Bijutsu no Hongi', which was
  not published during Futabatei's lifetime but was collected
  posthumously in *Meiji Bunka Zenshū*, vol. XII, pp. 39–56.
8 Futabatei translated into Japanese the whole of *Fathers and*

Children, but unfortunately his manuscripts have been lost.

9 Natsume Sōseki has also created some 'superfluous characters' who have high ideals but are ineffectual in coping with the realities of life, e.g., Daisuke in *And Then*. . . .See ch. 3 below.

10 See, for instance, Sōseki's essay 'Hasegawa-kun to Yo' (Mr Hasegawa and I).

Chapter 2

1 Frank Kermode, *Romantic Image* (1957), John Bayley, *Romantic Survival* (1957), R. A. Foakes, *Romantic Assertion* (1958) and Graham Hough, *Image and Experience* (1960) all contributed to the reappraisal of romanticism in one way or another.

2 Arthur O. Lovejoy, 'On the Discrimination of Romanticisms', *PMLA*, xxxix (1924) pp. 229–53, later collected in his *Essays in the History of Ideas* (Baltimore: Johns Hopkins University Press, 1948).

3 See, for instance, René Wellek, 'Romanticism Re-examined', in *Romanticism Reconsidered*, ed. Northrop Frye (New York: Columbia University Press, 1963), pp. 107–33.

4 Frye, 'The Drunken Boat: The Revolutionary Element in Romanticism', in *Romanticism Reconsidered*, pp. 1–25, 24.

5 From the constitution of the Shinshisha (The New Poetry Society).

6 Samuel Taylor Coleridge, *Shakespearean Criticism*, ed. T. M. Raysor, 2 vols. (Cambridge, Mass.: Harvard University Press, 1930), vol. ii, p. 273.

7 'Jisei ni Kan Ari' (A Thought on the Present Time, 1890).

8 'Nakanka Warawanka' (Shall I Laugh, or Shall I Weep? 1890).

9 'Kokumin to Shisō' (The Nation and Thought, 1893).

10 *Mill on Bentham and Coleridge*, ed. with an introduction by F. R. Leavis (London: Chatto and Windus, 1950).

11 'Nihon no Gengo o Yomu' (On Reading 'The Japanese Language', 1889).

12 'Uta-nenbutsu o Yomite' (On Reading *Uta-nenbutsu*, 1892).

13 'Takai ni taisuru Kan'nen' (The Idea of the World Beyond, 1892).

14 *Ibid*.

15 'Tōseibungaku no Shiomoyō' (The Currents of the Present-day Literature, 1890).

16 'Isshu no Jōishisō' (My Chauvinism, 1892).

17 'The Nation and Thought'.

18 'My Chauvinism'.

19 'Ganshitsu-mōhai no Hei' (The Defects of Obstinate Attachment and Fanatic Repudiation, 1893).

20 'Banbutsu no Koe to Shijin' (The Universal Voice and the Poet, 1893).
21 See, for example, Emerson's poem 'The Harp'.
22 Samuel Taylor Coleridge, *The Collected Letters*, ed. Earl Leslie Griggs, 6 vols. (Oxford: Clarendon Press, 1956–71), vol. II, pp. 865–6.
23 'The Universal Voice and the Poet.'
24 For centuries the so-called *buraku-min* have been socially discriminated against and forced to engage in certain professions such as butchery and shoemaking and live in *buraku* ghettos. Presumably, the discrimination originally had something to do with Buddhist taboos about killing animals, the trade these people had to engage in. The discrimination came to be based on the assumption that they were racially different from ordinary Japanese – an assumption groundless and entirely absurd if one considers the multi-racial origins of the prehistoric Japanese. Apart from the discrimination against the *Ainu* (or the aborigines in northern Japan), this was the only racial problem in pre-modern Japanese society. The *buraku-min* were also called *eta*, the untouchable. The Meiji Restoration legally abolished the discrimination, but their registration as the *shin-heimin* (newly recognised non-warrior class), an analogy with the *heimin* (non-warrior class), was nothing less than an implicit sign of discrimination. The custom of registration ceased to exist only when other nomenclatures such as *shizoku* (warrior class) and *heimin* were abolished. The problem is far from being solved even at the time of writing. The situation may improve in the future in legal terms, but nobody can envisage a quick solution since the problem involves deeply rooted social prejudice.
25 See Itoh Sei, *Shōsetsu no Hōhō* (The Method of the Novel, Tokyo: Kawade Shobō, 1948). Also useful for the genealogy of the I-novel is Nakamura Mitsuo, *Fūzoku-shōsetsu-ron* (On the Novel of Manners, Tokyo: Kawade Shobō, 1950).

Chapter 3

1 Translated by Edwin McClellan in his *Two Japanese Novelists: Sōseki and Tōson* (Chicago: University of Chicago Press, 1969), p. 4.
2 Translation by Edwin McClellan.
3 In this essay Sōseki discusses Whitman in comparison with other poets, both English and American. It is ironical, in Sōseki's view, that some British poets such as Burns, Byron and Shelley are revolutionary, while some poets from the New World such as Longfellow, Bryant and Hawthorne stick to the older traditions. In this respect Whitman is really unique in that he

embodies the democratic spirit of the New World. Sōseki
especially draws his attention to the fact that the apparently
physical love which Whitman extols is in fact spiritual and
that it comprises not only the love between man and woman but
also 'manly love of comrades' ('For You O Democracy').
In writing this essay Sōseki is indebted to Edward Dowden's
'The Poetry of Democracy: Walt Whitman', *Studies in
Literature 1789–1877* (London, 1878). However, Sōseki's point
of view is uniquely Japanese in his comparison of Whitman
with Bashō, for instance. Also noteworthy is the fact that Sōseki
is not free from Confucian morality in being unable to approve
of Whitman's support for women's liberation and in rejecting
it as unsuitable for Japanese society.

4 The essay was originally a talk, which Sōseki gave at a literary
meeting at the University of Tokyo in January 1893. He was
hoping his *haiku*-poet friend Masaoka Shiki would attend the
meeting, but Shiki, who was soon to become bed-ridden with
tuberculosis, was too ill to come. In this essay Sōseki traces the
development of the concept of Nature in the British
pre-Romantic and Romantic poets such as James Thomson,
William Cowper and Robert Burns. However, he finds in
William Wordsworth, above all, a most philosophically profound
perceptiveness to Nature.

5 It is sometimes conjectured that Sōseki left Tokyo because of his
frustrated love. The post he took in Matsuyama was officially
meant for a native speaker of English, who was paid much
better than Japanese teachers. Sōseki therefore enjoyed the
superior position with a higher salary than that of his
colleagues.

6 Natsume Kyōko, *Sōseki no Omoide* (A Memoir of Sōseki,
Tokyo: Kaizōsha, 1928), ch. 3: 'The Wedding'.

7 The Reverend Andrews later became the Principal of Westcott
House, a theological college in Cambridge for Anglican
clergymen, and through his missionary activities in India came
to show sympathy with Mahatma Gandhi.

8 Translated by McClellan in his *Two Japanese Novelists*, p. 11.

9 Translated by Miyoshi Masao in his *The Accomplices of
Silence* (Berkeley: University of California Press, 1974). The
same applies to the next four quotations.

10 Sōseki moved from West Hampstead to 6 Flodden Road,
Camberwell New Road in December 1900 and then on to
81 The Chase, Clapham Common in July 1901.

11 Natsume Kyōko, *A Memoir of Sōseki*, ch. 16: 'The Official
Report Left Blank'.

12 *Ibid.*

13 'Jitensha Nikki' (A Bicycle Diary, June 1903).

14 See section 5 below.

15 The critic Etō Jun puts forward his theory that Sōseki's

romance as well as his later realistic novels are the expressions of
his obsessive guilt caused by the illicit love relations which he
had with his sister-in-law Tose. See Etō Jun, *Sōseki to Āsaō
Densetsu* (Sōseki and the Arthurian Legend, Tokyo: University
of Tokyo Press, 1975).

16 Translation by Aiko Itō and Graeme Wilson.

17 In 1897 Sōseki wrote an article on this novel and got it
published in the *Kōko Bungaku* (The Literature of the World).

18 Sigmund Freud, 'Jokes and their Relations to the Unconscious'
(1905).

19 Yo ga *Kusamakura* (On my *Pillow of Grass*, 1906).

20 Translation by Alan Turney under the title *The Three-Cornered
World*. The same applies to all the subsequent quotations from
Pillow of Grass.

21 Translated by Edwin McClellan in his *Two Japanese Novelists*.

22 See ch. 1 above.

23 Translation by Francis Mathy. The same applies to the two
subsequent quotations from *The Gate*.

24 Translation by Beongcheon Yu. The same applies to all the
subsequent quotations from *The Wayfarer*.

25 See section 5 below.

26 Translation by Edwin McClellan.

27 Translation by V. H. Viglielmo. The same applies to the next
quotation.

Chapter 4

1 A comparison may be made with Mishima Yukio, who was
separated in his infancy from his parents by his grandmother.
In Mishima's case this peculiar circumstance seems to have had
a lasting effect on his mental history.

2 Shiga's reaction to the new mother is narrated in his 'Haha no
Shi to Atarashii Haha' (Mother's Death and New Mother).
His attitude may be compared with Akutagawa's. See p. 88 below.

3 This episode too may be compared with Akutagawa's. The
different ways in which they reacted to similar circumstances
are worthy of note. See p. 88 and n.5 below.

4 The way in which as a child he mourns his mother's death
contrasts sharply with the placidity with which Shiga faces his
mother's death and welcomes his stepmother in his 'Mother's
Death and New Mother'. See p. 84 and n. 2 above.

5 This is illustrated by the episode of his wrestling with his
father. Knowing cunningly that his father would lose his
temper, Akutagawa as a child loses the match deliberately after
his first victory. This episode too compares with a similar one
in the prologue of Shiga's *A Dark Night's Passing* in which the

protagonist is tied up as a punishment for beating his father three times.

6 An equally vivid description of dead bodies observed at the Medical School of the University of Tokyo is attempted by Ōe Kenzaburō in his 'The Arrogance of the Dead'. See ch. 7, p. 162 below.

7 Translation by Glenn W. Shaw.

8 Sōseki's letter to Akutagawa dated 19 February 1916. Translated by G. H. Healey in his introduction to Geoffrey Bownas's translation of Akutagawa's *Kappa*.

9 'My Life in Those Days' (1919).

10 Translation by Glenn W. Shaw.

11 The title derives from Bashō's swan song:

> On a journey, ill –
> and my dreams, on withered fields,
> are wandering still.

(Trans. Donald Keene)

12 Cf. Nitobe Inazō, *Bushidō* (Tokyo: Shōkabo, 1900).

13 Translation by Glenn W. Shaw.

14 This is an example of Akutagawa's concern with the potential and actual wish to kill one's own relatives as the extreme case of egotism. As he says in one of his epigrams:

> I have often wished that other people die. And among these people are included some of my own relatives.

('Shuju no Kotoba') [A Dwarf's Words] Akutagawa's concern with this problem of course manifests itself in the relationship of the warrior and his wife in 'In a Grove' and also links up with the theme of Shiga Naoya's 'Han no Hanzai' (Han's Crime, 1913).

15 The words *shitamachi* and *yamanote* refer to the two different areas in Tokyo. The former literally means 'the low-lying town' and the latter 'the hilly part'. In addition, they denote the two opposing social and cultural concepts. *Shitamachi* is the area where the merchant class of the Tokugawa period and their descendants have lived for centuries. *Yamanote* is the area which has developed since Meiji with the new and increasing influx of white-collar workers.

16 Translation by Geoffrey Bownas.

17 *Ibid.*

18 Some Japanese critics like to explain Akutagawa's suicide in social and political terms. For instance, it incited Miyamoto Kenji, then a student in the Economics Faculty at the University of Tokyo and subsequently chairman of the Japan Communist Party, to write his celebrated essay 'Haiboku no Bungaku' (The Literature of Defeat, 1929), which won the first prize given by the magazine *Kaizō*. Miyamoto argued in this article that Akutagawa's suicide stood for the inevitable defeat of bourgeois culture which the younger generation should willingly transcend.

With his insight Akutagawa must have been aware of the
rising tide of the proletariat. It seems, however, as erroneous
to say that his suicide symbolised the collapse of bourgeois
culture as to say that Mishima Yukio's self-dramatising suicide
forecast the resurgence of Japanese militarism.

19 See, for instance, Charles Rycroft: 'Schizoid characters are
persons who "fancy themselves" and believe, consciously or
unconsciously, that they possess some attribute which sets them
a cut above the rest of the human race, but who half-realize
that their pretensions will not be endorsed by others.' (*Anxiety
and Neurosis*, London: Allen Lane, the Penguin Press, 1968,
p. 53). 'As a result he [a schizoid character] becomes suspicious
of all other human beings and instead of idealizing some actual
person and instating him or her as a protecting mother-figure,
he idealizes himself, imagining himself to be such an
omnipotent figure that the need for protection does not arise.
In extreme cases this leads to delusions of grandeur, in which
the patient asserts that he is some important though fictitious
personage.' (*Ibid*., p. 84).

20 See, for instance, Charles Rycroft: 'They [obsessional characters]
are also attracted by philosophical systems since they create the
illusion that it might be possible to discover a key to the universe
which would enable one to understand everything in general
and thus to become immune to anxiety-provoking encounters
with unknown particulars.' (*Ibid*., p. 78).

21 The phrase used by T. S. Eliot in his essay 'Philip Massinger',
Selected Essays (London: Faber and Faber, 1951), p. 210.

Chapter 5

1 From the chapter entitled 'Father and Mother' in *Yōshō Jidai*
(My Childhood, serialised in the *Bungei Shunjū*, April 1955–
March 1956).

2 Translation by Howard S. Hibbett.

3 Translation by Edward G. Seidensticker.

4 Translation by Howard S. Hibbett. The same applies to the next
quotation.

5 Translation by Edward G. Seidensticker.

6 One may find interesting parallels between these works of
Tanizaki's and two of Kawabata's. *The Key* might have
stimulated Kawabata to write *The House of Sleeping Beauties*
(*Nemureru Bijo*, 1960–1), while in writing *Diary of a Mad Old
Man*, Tanizaki might have been conscious of *The Sound of the
Mountain* (*Yama no Oto*, 1949–54) as a forerunning rival work.
(For discussion of these works of Kawabata's see below.) Despite
the resemblance in the subjects, however, one should also note
the different ways in which these two authors tackle them.

7 Translation by Howard S. Hibbett.

8 Some might like to explain away his suicide as a basically pathological act, but there also exists the possibility that it was caused by carelessly taking an overdose of sleeping pills.

9 This critic was Chilba Kameo (1878–1935).

10 For example: 'Ensen no keshiki wa koishi no yōni mokusatsu sareta'. Translated this reads ' [As the train ran faster,] the scenery along the line was ignored like pebbles.' (Yokomitsu Riichi, 'Atama narabini Hara' [The Head and the Belly]).
Or, the famous opening of Kawabata's *Snow Country*: 'Kokkyō no nagai ton'neru o nukeruto yukiguni de atta. Yoru no soko ga shiroku natta.' The literal translation of the second sentence is: 'The bottom of the night became white', while Seidensticker's translation reads: 'The earth lay white under the night sky.'

11 Translation by Edward G. Seidensticker.

12 Translation by Edward G. Seidensticker. The same applies to all the subsequent quotations from *Thousand Cranes*.

13 A full-scale treatment of the theme of reincarnation is attempted by Mishima Yukio in *The Sea of Fertility* (*Hōjō no Umi*, 1965–71).

14 Translation by Edward G. Seidensticker. The same applies to all the subsequent quotations from *The Sound of the Mountain*.

15 Kawabata's suicide is still veiled in mystery and critics have made various conjectures. In the spring of 1977 the critic Usui Yoshimi (1905–) ascribed it to Kawabata's frustrated yearning for his au pair girl in his *Jiko no Tenmatsu* (An Account of the Accident, Tokyo: Chikuma Shobō, 1977), which subsequently led to a fierce controversy with Kawabata's relatives.

Chapter 6

1 There was once a confrontation between Mishima and the students at the College of General Education, University of Tokyo, a record of which is available in *Mishima Yukio v. Tōdai Zenkyōtō* (Mishima Yukio v. the University of Tokyo Solidarity, Tokyo: Shinchōsha, 1969).

2 It is commonly observed that while the sea is the symbol used by Mishima to represent eternity, another important symbol in his works is evening, which stands for the glorious moment of apocalypse. The protagonist of *The Temple of the Golden Pavilion* associates the Golden Pavilion in his imagination with the sea and evening on various occasions. In *The Sailor Who Fell From Grace with the Sea* the significance of the sea as a symbol of eternity in contrast to the mundane life is self-evident.

3 There is a catechetic Zen problem, 'Nan Ch'üang Kills a Kitten' or 'Joshu Wears a Pair of Sandals on his Head'. This is

first cited by the Superior of the Temple of the Golden Pavilion on 15 August 1945, the day of Japanese defeat (ch. 3). The episode is rather ambiguous in its implication but is used deliberately by Mishima because of its very ambiguity. When it is mentioned for the second time (ch. 6) by Kashiwagi, a Mephistophelian counsellor and in a sense the counterpart of the protagonist, it becomes clear that the kitten, as much as the Golden Pavilion, is a symbol of beauty. And there seem to be three attitudes that one could adopt towards beauty. The first is a vulgar one adopted by the priests who dispute over possession of the kitten as a pet. This must be transcended by the two opposing attitudes: the one represented by Nan Ch'üang who kills the kitten as a solution to the dispute, and the other represented by Joshu who expresses his opposition to his master by wearing his sandals on his head. The former corresponds to Kashiwagi's attitude to beauty and the latter to that of the protagonist. When the episode is mentioned for the third time (ch. 8), however, there is a sign that the protagonist changes his position with Kashiwagi, moving towards his final act of setting fire to the Golden Pavilion. Further, in connexion with the episode, we may well pay attention to Nan Ch'üang's callousness in killing the kitten. This is a parallel with *The Sailor Who Fell from Grace with the Sea*. It has also to do with Mishima's unflinching readiness to shed his own blood for the sake of his aesthetic cause as demonstrated by his suicide.

4 See n. 2.

5 Part I, ch. 5. Translation by John Nathan.

6 See n. 3.

7 Translation by Michael Gallagher.

8 Translation by Michael Gallagher.

9 It is noteworthy that while Wang Yang-ming's philosophy was assimilated by such a conformist thinker as Kumazawa Banzan (1619–91), it also provided resources for a larger number of non-conformist radicals such as Ōshio Heihachirō (1794–1837) and Yoshida Shōin (1830–59). The influence of these latter two on Mishima is more than accidental.

10 A letter to Shimizu Fumio quoted by the addressee in his tribute to Mishima, the *Shinchō* (New Current), a special number (January 1971), p. 198.

11 'Shōsetsu Towa Nanika' (What is the Novel?), ch. 11, reprinted from the *Nami* (Waves), the *Shinchō* (New Current), a special number (January 1971), pp. 125–6.

12 The date adapted to the solar calendar. There is no doubt that Mishima chose the same day of the same month for his coup and suicide.

13 'What is the Novel?', the *Shinchō*, a special number (January 1971), p. 126.

14 *Ibid.*, 127.

Chapter 7

1 Postscript to the revised version of *Owarishi Michi no Shirube ni* (The Road Sign at the End of the Road, Tokyo: Tōjusha, 1965).

2 *Abé Kōbō Zensakuhin* (The Collected Works of Abé Kōbō), 15 vols. (Tokyo: Shinchōsha, 1972–3), vol. III, pp. 297–8.

3 *The Face of Another*, translated by E. Dale Saunders (New York: Knopf, 1966), pp. 109–10.

4 Ōe is also aware of the racial problem in Japanese society and deals with it in terms of lost identity. See the discussion of Ōe's *Outcries*, p. 167 below.

5 It is interesting to note that Ōe treats the psychology of the perverted characters who perform erotic acts in a train in *The Sexual Man*. See p. 167 below.

6 *The Face of Another*, pp. 146–7.

7 *Ibid.*, p. 162.

8 *Ibid.*, pp. 163–4.

9 Introduction to the selected works of Abé Kōbō in the *Warera no Bungaku* series, no. 7 (Tokyo: Kōdansha, 1966), p. 480.

10 The vision of this state includes the celebration of sexual power, with which Ōe becomes more and more preoccupied in his later works. It is noteworthy, however, that in his later works the sexual urge becomes increasingly perverted under the social strain and cannot be celebrated as in the present work.

11 Ōe's preoccupation with sexual perversion may be compared with Mishima Yukio's treatment of the subject. But the resemblance between the two in this and other matters is superficial. There are real differences between them, some of which will be mentioned later in this chapter.

12 One of the recurrent patterns in Ōe's fictional structure is the use of older and younger brothers as in *The Catch*, *Plucking Buds and Shooting Lambs*, *Today the Struggle*, *The Football Match in the First Year of the Man'en Era*, and so on. Ōe's use of this pattern is clearly intentional. In *Plucking Buds and Shooting Lambs* the young brother functions in a significant way. Unlike other boys, he does not originally come from a reformatory but, given up by his father, voluntarily participates in the juvenile delinquents' activities. Belonging neither to the delinquents nor to the hypocritical society of the adults, he is in a sense the representative of genuine innocence. He is therefore a mirror for his brother and his companions and functions as a point of view.

13 Each decade in the postwar history of Japan seems to have a marked character. For instance, in 1960 there was a vain and abortive attempt by the leftists to overthrow the direction of politics operated under the Japanese–American Security Treaty. The failure of their attempt made them realise that the reorientation of Japanese politics by means of abolishing the Treaty and the reformation of society at large along socialist lines

was an illusion. In the meantime, the Japanese economy was achieving a spectacular growth which led to a conflict between the respective economic interests of the United States and Japan, and the re-shaping of American policy towards East Asia. This new situation was typically symbolised by President Nixon's announcement of a new economic policy in the summer of 1971 and the accelerated Sino-American *rapprochement*. In the circumstances, the Japanese–American Security Treaty automatically lost part of its meaning. The irony was that it proved not only an error in postwar American policy towards East Asia, but also showed how illusory were the grounds for criticism by the Japanese left wing against the American policy.

14 Outcries are uttered twice in the novel: once near the beginning by a youth who dies in a car accident; later, by the girl whom one of the central characters strangles to death.

15 The first year of the Man'en era corresponds to 1860 in the Christian era. In fact football, which is played in the novel in 1960, did not exist in Japan in 1860. The author's intention is to overlap 1860 with 1960, thus drawing a parallel between past and present and implying continuity in history.

16 A similar kind of readiness to accept the reality is discernible in the hero of *A Personal Matter* (*Kojinteķina Taiķen*, Tokyo: Shinchōsha, 1964).

17 Soon afterwards they parted company. Etō harshly criticised Ōe's growing inclination to radicalism as well as his literary works. Ishihara became in 1968 an LDP member of the House of Councillors, winning the largest number of votes throughout the country; in December 1972 he became a member of the House of Representatives, again winning the largest number of votes in his Tokyo constituency.

18 *Asahi Shimbun* (11 January 1971), evening edn.

19 *Ibid.* (12 January 1971).

20 *Ibid.* (13 January 1971).

Select Bibliography

This bibliography is selective and is arranged under the following heads:

    I. GENERAL REFERENCES (in alphabetical order of the authors) in English and in Japanese

    II. ANTHOLOGIES (in alphabetical order of the editors)

    III. INDIVIDUAL AUTHORS (1 to 12), subdivided into

a Collections in English and in Japanese (in chronological order)

b Selected individual works (in chronological order), with asterisks indicating the availability of English translation, followed by the details.

c References in English and in Japanese (in chronological order of the works cited; if an author has written more than one book or article, he is listed according to the date of his earliest work cited)

Since this book is intended for the English-speaking reader and its purpose is not too specialist, reference works written in Japanese are not included except for those which are unanimously considered standard works, those which are mentioned in the notes to the text, and those which are up to date and supersede most of the preceding works.

I. GENERAL REFERENCES

Keene, Donald. *Landscapes and Portraits: An Appreciation of Japanese Culture.* Tokyo: Kōdansha 1971; London: Secker & Warburg, 1971

Kimball, Arthur G. *Crisis in Identity and Contemporary Japanese Novels.* Tokyo: Tuttle, 1973

Miyoshi, Masao. *Accomplices of Silence: The Modern Japanese Novel.* Berkeley, Los Angeles and London: University of California Press, 1974

Nakamura, Mitsuo. *Nihon no Kindai Shōsetsu* (Modern Japanese Fiction, 1868–1926).* Tokyo: Iwanami Shoten, 1954. [English version] Tokyo: Kokusai Bunka Shinkōkai, 1968

Nakamura, Mitsuo. *Nihon no Gendai Shōsetsu* (Contemporary Japanese
    Fiction, 1926–68).* Tokyo: Iwanami Shoten, 1968. [English
    version] Tokyo: Kokusai Bunka Shinkōkai, 1969
Nihon Kindai Bungakukan (ed.). *Nihon Kindai Bungaku Daijiten*
    (A Dictionary of Modern Japanese Literature), 6 vols. Tokyo:
    Kōdansha, 1977
Tsuruta, Kinya and Thomas E. Swann (eds.). *Approaches to the Modern
    Japanese Novel.* Tokyo: Sophia University Press, 1976
Ueda, Makoto. *Modern Japanese Writers and the Nature of Literature.*
    California: Stanford University Press, 1976

II. ANTHOLOGIES

Hibbett, Howard S. (ed.). *Contemporary Japanese Literature: An
    Anthology of Fiction, Film, and Other Writings since 1945.*
    New York: Knopf, 1977
Keene, Donald (ed.). *Modern Japanese Literature: An Anthology.* New
    York: Grove Press, 1956; Tokyo: Tuttle, 1957
Mishima, Yukio and Geoffrey Bownas (eds.). *New Writing in Japan.*
    Harmondsworth, Middlesex: Penguin, 1972
Morris, Ivan (ed.). *Modern Japanese Stories: An Anthology.* Tokyo: Tuttle,
    1962

III. INDIVIDUAL AUTHORS

1 Tsubouchi Shōyō (Yūzo, 1859–1935)
a *Shōyō Senshū* (The Collected Works of Tsubouchi Shōyō),
    12 vols. and 3 supplementary vols. Tokyo: Shunyōdō, July
    1926–December 1927
b *Tōsei Shosei Katagi* (The Temperament of Present-Day
    Students). Tokyo: Banseido, June 1885–January 1886
    Shōsetsu Shinzui (The Essence of the Novel). Tokyo: Shōgetsudō,
    September 1885–April 1886
    Translation of the complete works of Shakespeare. Tokyo:
    Chūō Kōronsha, September 1933–May 1935
c Yanagida, Izumi. *Wakaki Tsubouchi Shōyō* (The Young
    Tsubouchi Shōyō), in *Meiji Bungaku Kenkyū* (A Study of Meiji
    Literature), vol. 1. Tokyo: Shunjūsha, September 1960
    Ryan, Marleigh Grayer. *The Development of Realism in the
    Fiction of Tsubouchi Shōyō.* Seattle, Washington: University of
    Washington Press, 1975

2 Futabatei Shimei (Hasegawa Tatsunosuke, 1864–1909)
a *Futabatei Shimei Zenshū* (The Complete Works of Futabatei

Shimei), 9 vols. Tokyo: Iwanami Shoten, 1964–5
b 'Shōsetsu Sōron' (A Theory of the Novel), *Chūō Gakujutsu Zasshi*, April 1886
Ukigumo (The Drifting Clouds)* part I, Tokyo: Kinkōdō, June 1887; part II, Tokyo: Kinkōdō, February 1888; part III, *Miyako no Hana*, July–August 1889. Tokyo: Kinkōdō, September 1891. Translation by Ryan (2. *c*)
Sono Omokage (In his Image).* *Tokyo Asahi Shimbun*, October–December 1906. Tokyo: Shunyōdō, August 1907. Translation by Buhachirō Mitsui and Gregg M. Sinclair entitled *An Adopted Husband*. New York: Knopf, 1919; Greenwood Press, 1969
Heibon (Mediocrity).* *Tokyo Asahi Shimbun*, October–December 1907. Tokyo: Bun'endō and Jozandō, March 1908
Translation by Glenn W. Shaw, Tokyo: Hokuseidō, 1927
c Nakamura, Mitsuo. *Futabatei Shimei Den* (The Life of Futabatei Shimei). Tokyo: Kōdansha, 1958
Ryan, Marleigh Grayer. *Japan's First Modern Novel: Ukigumo of Futabatei Shimei.* New York: Columbia University Press, 1967

3 Kitamura Tōkoku (Montarō, 1868–94)
a *Tōkoku Zenshū* (The Complete Works of Tōkoku), ed. Seiichirō Katsumoto, 3 vols. Tokyo: Iwanami Shoten, 1950
Kitamura Tōkoku Shū (The Selected Writings of Kitamura Tōkoku), ed. Hideo Odagiri, in *Meiji Bungaku Zenshū* (The Collected Works of Meiji Literature), vol. XXIX. Tokyo: Chikuma Shobō, October 1976
b *Soshū no Shi* (A Prisoner). Tokyo: Shunshōsha, April 1889
Hōrai Kyoku (Mt Hōrai). Tokyo: Yōshindō, May 1891
'Naibu Seimei Ron' (On the Inner Life). *Bungakukai*, May 1893
c Mathy, Francis. 'Kitamura Tōkoku: The Early Years', *Monumenta Nipponica*, XVIII, 1–4 (1963) pp. 1–44; 'Kitamura Tōkoku: Essays on the Inner Life', *Monumenta Nipponica*, XIX, 1–2 (1964) pp. 66–110; 'Kitamura Tōkoku: Final Essays', *Monumenta Nipponica*, XX, 1–2 (1965) pp. 41–63
Kitagawa, Tōru. *Kitamura Tōkoku Shiron* (An Essay on Kitamura Tōkoku), 3 vols. Tokyo: Tōjusha, 1974, 1976, 1977

4 Shimazaki Tōson (Haruki, 1872–1943)
a *Tōson Zenshū* (The Complete Works of Shimazaki Tōson), 18 vols. Tokyo: Chikuma Shobō, 1966
b *Wakanashū* (A Collection of Young Greens). Tokyo: Shunyōdō, August 1897

Ichiyōshū (A Collection of Single Leaves). Tokyo: Shunyōdō, June 1898

Natsukusa (Summer Grass). Tokyo: Shunyōdō, December 1898

Rakubaishū (A Collection of Fallen Plum Blossoms). Tokyo: Shunyōdō, August 1901

Tōson Shishū (The Collected Poems of Tōson), Tokyo: Shunyōdō, 1904

Hakai (The Broken Commandment).* Written 1904. Privately published 1906. Translation by Kenneth Strong, Tokyo: University of Tokyo Press, 1974

Haru (Spring). *Tokyo Asahi Shimbun*, April–August 1908. Privately published, October 1908

Ie (The House).* Part I, *Yomiuri Shimbun*, January–May 1910; part II, *Chūō Kōron*, January and April 1911. Privately published, November 1911. Translation by Cecilia Segawa Seigle entitled *The Family*, Tokyo: University of Tokyo Press, 1976

Shinsei (A New Life). Part I, *Asahi Shimbun*, May–October 1918, Tokyo: Shunyōdō, January 1919; part II, *Asahi Shimbun*, August–October 1919, Tokyo: Shunyōdō, December 1919

Yoake Mae (Before the Dawn). *Chūō Kōron*, April 1929–October 1935. Tokyo: part I, January 1932: part II, November 1935

c Miyoshi, Yukio. *Shimazaki Tōson Ron* (A Study of Shimazaki Tōson), 1966

McClellan, Edwin. *Two Japanese Novelists: Sōseki and Tōson.* Chicago: University of Chicago Press, 1969

5 Natsume Sōseki (Kinnosuke, 1867–1916)

a *Sōseki Zenshū* (The Complete Works of Natsume Sōseki). Tokyo: Iwanami Shoten, 19 vols., 1935–7; 16 vols., 1965–7.

b *Wagahai wa Neko de Aru* (I am a Cat).* *Hototogisu*, January 1905–August 1906, 3 vols., Tokyo: Ōkura Shoten. Vol. I, October 1905; vol. II, November 1906; vol. III, May 1907. Translation by Aiko Itō and Graeme Wilson, Tokyo: Tuttle, 1972

Botchan (Little Master).* *Hototogisu*, April 1906. Collected in *Uzura Kago*, Tokyo: Shunyōdō, January 1907. Translation by Alan Turney, Tokyo: Kōdansha, 1972

Kusamakura (Pillow of Grass).* *Shinshōsetsu*, September 1906. Collected in *Uzura Kago*, Tokyo: Shunyōdō, January 1907. Translation by Alan Turney entitled *The Three-Cornered World*, London: Peter Owen, 1965; Tokyo: Tuttle, 1965

Nowaki (Autumn Wind). *Hototogisu*, January 1907. Collected in *Kusa-awase*, Tokyo: Shunyōdō, September 1908

Bungakuron (A Theory of Literature). Tokyo: Ōkura Shoten, May 1907

Gubijinsō (Wild Poppy). *Asahi Shimbun*, June–October 1907. Tokyo: Shunyōdō, January 1908

Yume Jūya (Ten Nights of Dream).* *Tokyo Asahi Shimbun*, July–August 1908. Tokyo: Shunyōdō, May 1910. Translation by Aiko Itō and Graeme Wilson, Tokyo: Tuttle, 1974

Sanshirō.* *Asahi Shimbun*, September–December 1908. Tokyo: Shūnyodō, May 1909. Translation by Jay Rubin, Tokyo: University of Tokyo Press, 1977

Bungaku Hyōron (Literary Criticism). Tokyo: Shunyōdō, March 1909

Sorekara (And Then. . .). *Tokyo Asahi Shimbun*, June–October 1909. Tokyo: Shunyōdō, January 1910

Mon (The Gate).* *Tokyo Asahi Shimbun*, March–June 1910. Tokyo: Shunyōdō, January 1911. Translation by Francis Mathy, London: Peter Owen; Tokyo: Tuttle, 1972

'Gendai Nihon no Kaika' (The Enlightenment of Modern Japan). Delivered, August 1911. Collected in *Asahi Kōen Shū*, Osaka: Asahi Shimbunsha, November 1911. Collected in *Shakai to Jibun*, Tokyo: Jitsugyō no Nihonsha, February 1913

Higan Suigimade (Until After the Equinox). *Asahi Shimbun*, January–April 1912. Tokyo: Shunyōdō, September 1912

Kōjin (The Wayfarer).* *Asahi Shimbun*, December 1912–February 1913. Tokyo: Ōkura Shoten, January 1914. Translation by Beongcheon Yu, Detroit: Wayne State University Press, 1967; Tokyo: Tuttle, 1969

Kokoro (Heart).* *Tokyo Asahi Shimbun*, April–August 1914. Tokyo: Iwanami Shoten, September 1914. Translation by Edwin McClellan entitled *Kokoro*, Chicago: Henry Regnery, 1957; London: Peter Owen, 1968; Tokyo: Tuttle, 1969

'Watakushi no Kojinshugi' (My Individualism). Delivered, November 1914; The Peers' School magazine, March 1915.

Michikusa (Grass on the Wayside).* *Tokyo Asahi Shimbun*, June–September 1915. Tokyo: Iwanami Shoten, October 1915. Translation by Edwin McClellan, Chicago and London: University of Chicago Press, 1969; Tokyo: Tuttle, 1971

Meian (Light and Darkness).* *Tokyo Asahi Shimbun*, May–December 1916. Tokyo: Iwanami Shoten, January 1917. Translation by Valdo H. Viglielmo, London: Peter Owen, 1971; Tokyo: 1972

c Natsume, Kyōko. *Sōseki no Omoide* (A Memoir of Sōseki). Tokyo: Kaizōsha, 1928

Komiya, Toyotaka, *Natsume Sōseki*, 3 vols. Tokyo: Iwanami Shoten, 1938

Etō, Jun. *Natsume Sōseki*. Tokyo: Keisō Shobō, 1965

– 'Natsume Sōseki: A Japanese Meiji Intellectual', *American Scholar*, XXXIV (1965) pp. 603–19

– *Sōseki to sono Jidai* (Sōseki and his Time), parts I and II. Tokyo: Shinchōsha, 1970

– *Sōseki to Āsāō Densetsu* (Sōseki and the Arthurian Legend). Tokyo: University of Tokyo Press, 1975

– (ed.). *Natsume Sōseki*. Tokyo: Asahi Shimbunsha, 1977

McClellan, Edwin. *Two Japanese Novelists: Sōseki and Tōson*. Chicago: University of Chicago Press, 1969

Yu, Beongcheon. *Natsume Sōseki*. New York: Twayne, 1969

Doi, Takeo. *Sōseki no Shinteki Sekai* (The Psychological World of Sōseki).* Tokyo: Shibundō, 1969. Translation by William Jefferson Tyler, Harvard East Asian Monographs, no. 68. Cambridge, Mass.: East Asian Research Center, Harvard University, 1976

Hibbett, Howard S. 'Natsume Sōseki and the Psychological Novel' in Donald S. Shively (ed.), *Tradition and Modernization in Japanese Culture*. Princeton: Princeton University Press, 1971, pp. 305–46.

Ochi, Haruo. *Sōseki Shiron* (A Personal View of Sōseki). Tokyo: Kadokawa Shoten, 1971

Yamoto, Sadayoshi. *Natsume Sōseki: Sono Eibungakuteki Sokumen* (Natsume Sōseki and English Literature). Tokyo: Kenkyūsha, 1971 Ara, Masahito. *Sōseki Kenyū Nenpyō* (The Chronology for Sōseki Studies). [Supplement to *Sōseki Bungaku Zenshū* (The Literary Works of Sōseki) 10 vols.] Tokyo: Shūeisha, 1974

Matsui, Sakuko. *Natsume Sōseki as a Critic of English Literature*. Tokyo: Higashi-Ajia Bunka Kenkyū Sentā, 1975

Hirakawa, Sukehiro. *Natsume Sōseki: Hiseiyō no Kutō* (Natsume Sōseki: The Struggle of a Non-European). Tokyo: Shinchōsha, 1976

Yamazaki, Masakazu, *Fukigen no Jidai* (An Age of Distemper). Tokyo: Shinchōsha, 1976

6 Shiga Naoya (1883–1971)
a *Shiga Naoya Zenshū* (The Complete Works of Shiga Naoya), 14 vols. Tokyo: Iwanami Shoten, 1973–4
b 'Kurōdiasu no Nikki' (The Diary of Claudius). *Shirakaba*, September 1912

'Ōtsu Junkichi'. *Shirakaba*, September 1912
'Kinosaki nite' (At Kinosaki).* *Shirakaba*, May 1917. Collected in *Yoru no Hikari*, Tokyo: Shinchōsha, January 1918. Translation by Edward G. Seidensticker in Keene (ed.), *Modern Japanese Literature* (11 above)
'Wakai' (Reconciliation). *Kuroshio*, October 1917. Collected in *Yoru no Hikari*, Tokyo: Shinchōsha, January 1918
Anya Kōro (A Dark Night's Passing).* *Kaizō*, January 1921–April 1937. Collected in *Shiga Naoya Zenshū*, Tokyo: Kaizōsha, September–October 1937. Translation by Edwin McClellan, Tokyo: Kōdansha, 1976
  c Mathy, Francis. *Shiga Naoya*. New York: Twayne, 1974
Yamazaki, Masakazu. *Fukigen no Jidai* (An Age of Distemper). Tokyo: Shinchōsha, 1976

  7 Akutagawa Ryūnosuke (1892–1927)
a.i *Akutagawa Ryūnosuke Zenshū* (The Complete Works of Akutagawa Ryūnosuke). Tokyo: Iwanami Shoten, 8 vols., November 1927–February 1929; 10 vols., October 1934–August 1935

Collections in English translation:
a.ii *Tales Grotesque and Curious* translated from the Japanese by Glenn W. Shaw. Tokyo: Hokuseidō, 1930. (Contains 'Tobacco and the Devil', 'The Nose', 'The Handkerchief', 'Rashōmon', 'Lice', 'The Spider's Thread', 'The Wine Worm', 'The Badger', 'The Ball', 'The Pipe' and 'Mōri Sensei')
a.iii *Hell Screen and Other Stories* translated by W. H. H. Norman. Tokyo: Hokuseidō, 1948. (Contains 'Jigokuhen', 'Jashūmon', 'The General' and 'Mensura Zoilii')
a.iv *Rashōmon and Other Stories* translated by Takashi Kojima with an introduction by Howard S. Hibbett. Tokyo: Tuttle, 1952. (Contains 'In a Grove', 'Rashōmon', 'Yam Gruel', 'The Martyr', 'Kesa and Morito' and 'The Dragon')
a.v *Japanese Short Stories by Ryūnosuke Akutagawa* translated by Takashi Kojima with an introduction by John McVittie. New York: Liveright, 1961. (Contains 'The Hell Screen', 'A Clod of Earth', 'Nezumikozō', 'Heichū', 'The Amorous Genius', 'Genkaku Sanbō', 'Otomi's Virginity', 'The Spider's Thread', 'The Nose', 'The Tangerines' and 'The Story of Yonosuke')
a.vi *Exotic Japanese Stories: The Beautiful and the Grotesque* translated by Takashi Kojima and John McVittie. New York: Liveright, 1964. (Contains 'The Robbers', 'The Dog, Shiro',

'The Handkerchief', 'The Dolls', 'Gratitude', 'The Faith of
Wei Sheng', 'The Lady Roku-no-miya', 'The Kappa', 'Saigō
Takamori', 'The Greeting', 'Withered Fields', 'Absorbed in
Letters', 'The Garden', 'The Badger', 'Heresy' and 'A Woman's
Body')

b 'Rashōmon'.* *Teikoku Bungaku*, November 1915. Collected in
Rashōmon, Tokyo: Oranda Shobō, May 1917. Translation by
Shaw (*a.ii*) and by Kojima (*a.iv*)

'Hana' (The Nose).* *Shinshichō*, February 1916. Collected in
Rashōmon, Tokyo: Oranda Shobō, May 1917. Translation by
Shaw (*a.ii*) and by Kojima (*a.v*)

'Imogayu' (Yam Gruel).* *Shinshōsetsu*, September 1916.
Collected in *Rashōmon*, Tokyo: Oranda Shobō, May 1917.
Translation by Kojima (*a.iv*)

'Hankachi' (The Handkerchief).* *Chūō Kōron*, October 1916.
Collected in *Rashōmon*, Tokyo: Oranda Shobō, May 1917.
Translation by Shaw (*a.ii*) and by Kojima (*a.vi*)

'Tabako to Akuma' (Tobacco and the Devil).* *Shinshichō*,
November 1916. Collected in *Tabako to Akuma*, Tokyo:
Shinchōsha, November 1917. Translation by Shaw (*a.ii*)

'Ogata Ryōsai Oboegaki' (Ogata Ryōsai's Memorandum).
Shinchō, January 1917. Collected in *Rashōmon*, Tokyo: Oranda
Shobō, May 1917

'Aruhi no Ōishi Kuranosuke' (One Day in the Life of
Ōishi Kuranosuke). *Chūō Kōron*, September 1917. Collected in
Tabako to Akuma, Tokyo: Shinchōsha, November 1917

'Gesaku Zanmai' (Absorbed in Letters).* *Ōsaka Mainichi
Shimbun*, October–November 1917. Tokyo: Shinchōsha, January
1919. Translation by Kojima (*a.vi*)

'Jigokuhen' (The Hell Screen).* *Ōsaka Mainichi Shimbun*,
May 1918. Collected in *Kairaishi*, Tokyo: Shinchōsha, January
1919. Translation by Norman (*a.iii*) and by Kojima (*a.v*)

'Hōkyōnin no Shi' (The Martyr).* *Mita Bungaku*, September
1918. Collected in *Kairaishi*, Tokyo: Shinchōsha, January 1919.
Translation by Kojima (*a.iv*)

'Kareno Shō' (Withered Fields).* *Shinshōsetsu*, October 1918.
Collected in *Kairaishi*, Tokyo: Shinchōsha, January 1919.
Translation by Kojima (*a.vi*)

'Anokoro no Jibun no Koto' (My Life in Those Days). *Chūō
Kōron*, January 1919. Collected in *Kagedōrō*, Tokyo: Shunyōdō,
January 1920

'Kirishitohoro-shōnin Den' (The Life of St Christopher).
Shinshōsetsu, March and May 1919. Collected in *Kagedōrō*,

Tokyo: Shunyōdō, January 1920.

'Mikan' (The Tangerines).* *Shinchō*, May 1919. Collected in *Kagedōrō*, Tokyo: Shunyōdō, January 1920. Translation by Kojima (*a.v*)

'Butōkai' (The Ball).* *Shinchō*, January 1920. Collected in *Yarai no Hana*, Tokyo: Shinchōsha, March 1921. Translation by Shaw (*a.ii*)

'Aki' (Autumn). *Chūō Kōron*, April 1920. Collected in *Yarai no Hana*, Tokyo: Shinchōsha, March 1921

'Shōgun' (The General).* *Kaizō*, January 1922. Collected in *Sara no Hana*, Tokyo: *Kaizōsha*, August 1922. Translation by Norman (*a.iii*)

'Yabu no Naka' (In a Grove).* *Shinchō*, January 1922. Collected in *Sara no Hana*, Tokyo: Kaizōsha, August 1922. Translation by Kojima (*a.iv*)

'Rokunomiya no Himegimi' (Princess Rokunomiya).* *Hyōgen*, August 1922. Collected in *Shunpuku*, Tokyo: Shunyōdō, May 1923. Translation by Kojima (*a.vi*)

'Shuju no Kotoba' (A Dwarf's Words). *Bungei Shunjū*, January 1923–September 1925. Tokyo: Bungei Shunjūsha, December 1927

'Yasukichi no Techō kara' (From Yasukichi's Notebooks). *Kaizō*, May 1923. Collected in *Kōjakufū*, Tokyo: Shinchōsha, July 1924

'Ikkai no Tsuchi' (A Clod of Earth).* *Shinchō*, January 1924. Collected in *Kōjakufū*, Tokyo: Shinchōsha, July 1924. Translation by Kojima (*a.v*)

'Daidōji Shinsuke no Hansei' (The Early Life of Daidōji Shinsuke). *Chūō Kōron*, January 1925. Collected in the *Complete Works*, vol. IV, Tokyo: Iwanami Shoten, November 1927

'Tenkibo' (In Memoriam). *Kaizō*, October 1926. Collected in the *Complete Works*, vol. IV, Tokyo: Iwanami Shoten, November 1927

'Shinkirō' (Mirage).* *Fujin Kōron*, January 1927. Collected in *Konan no Ōgi*, Tokyo: Bungei Shunjūsha, June 1927. Translation by Beongcheon Yu, *Chicago Review*, XVIII, 2 (1965)

'Genkaku Sanbō' (Genkaku's House).* *Chūō Kōron*, January–February 1927. Collected in the *Complete Works*, vol. IV, Tokyo: Iwanami Shoten, November 1927. Translation by Kojima (*a.v*)

'Kappa'.* *Kaizō*, March 1927. Collected in the *Complete Works*, vol. IV, Tokyo: Iwanami Shoten, November 1927. Translation by

Geoffrey Bownas with an introduction by G. H. Healey, London:
Peter Owen, 1970; Tokyo: Tuttle, 1971. Also by Kojima (*a.vi*)
'Bungeitekina Amarini Bungeitekina' (Artistic, too Artistic).
Kaizō, April–August 1927. Collected in *Shuju no Kotoba*,
Tokyo: Bungei Shunjūsha, December 1927
'Aru Kyūyū e Okuru Shuki' (A Note to an Old Friend).
Written July 1927. Collected in the *Complete Works*, vol. VI,
Tokyo: *Iwanami Shoten*, August 1928
'Seihō no Hito' (The Western Sage). *Kaizō*, August–September
1927. Collected in the *Complete Works*, vol. VI, Tokyo:
Iwanami Shoten, August 1928
'Anchū Mondō' (A Dialogue in Darkness).* *Bungei Shunjū*,
September 1927. Collected in the *Complete Works*, vol. IV,
Tokyo: Iwanami Shoten, November 1927. Translation by
Beongcheon Yu, *The East–West Review*, IV, 1 (Spring 1971)
'Aru Ahō no Isshō' (A Fool's Life).* *Kaizō*, October 1927.
Collected in the *Complete Works*, vol. IV, Tokyo: Iwanami
Shoten, November, 1927. Translation by Will Petersen, New
York: Grossman, 1970
'Haguruma' (Cogwheels).* *Bungei Shunjū*, October 1927.
Collected in the *Complete Works*, vol. IV, Tokyo: Iwanami
Shoten, November 1927. Translation by Beongcheon Yu,
Chicago Review, XVIII, 2 (1965)
c Yu, Beongcheon. *Akutagawa*. Detroit: Wayne State University
Press, 1972
Miyoshi, Yukio. *Akutagawa Ryūnosuke Ron* (On Akutagawa
Ryūnosuke). Tokyo: Chikuma Shobō, 1976

8 Tanizaki Jun'ichirō (1886–1965)
a.i *Ashikari and the Story of Shunkin* translated by Roy Humpherson
and Hajime Okita. Tokyo: Hokuseidō, 1936; Westport, Conn.:
Greenwood Press, 1970
a.ii *Seven Japanese Tales by Tanizaki Jun'ichirō* translated by
Howard S. Hibbett. New York: Knopf, 1963; London: Secker &
Warburg, 1964. Tokyo: Tuttle, 1967. (Contains 'A Portrait of
Shunkin', 'Terror', 'The Bridge of Dreams', 'The Tattooer',
'The Thief', 'Aguri' and 'A Blind Man's Tale')
a.iii *Tanizaki Jun'ichirō Zenshū* (The Complete Works of Tanizaki
Jun'ichirō), 28 vols. Tokyo: Chūō Kōronsha, 1966
b 'Shisei' (Tattoo).* *Shinshichō*, November 1910. Collected in
Shisei, Tokyo: Momiyama Shoten, December 1911. Translation
by Hibbett (*a.ii*) and by Morris in *Modern Japanese Stories*
(II, above)

'Haha o Kouru Ki' (Yearning for Mother). *Tokyo Nichinichi Shimbun*, January–August 1919

Chijin no Ai (A Fool's Love). Part I, *Ōsaka Asahi Shimbun*, March–June 1924; part II, *Josei*, November 1924–July 1925. Tokyo: Kaizōsha, July 1925

Manji (A Swastika). *Kaizō*, March 1928–April 1930. Tokyo: Kaizōsha, April 1931

Tadekuu Mushi (Some Prefer Nettles).* *Tokyo Nichinichi Shimbun* and *Ōsaka Mainichi Shimbun*, December 1928–June 1929. Tokyo: Kaizōsha, November 1929. Translation by Edward G. Seidensticker, New York: Knopf, 1955; Tokyo: Tuttle, 1955

Mōmoku Monogatari (A Blind Man's Tale).* *Chūō Kōron*, September 1931. Tokyo: Chūō Kōronsha, February 1932. Translation by Hibbett (*a.ii*)

Ashikari.* *Kaizō*, November–December 1932. Ōsaka and Tokyo: Sōgensha, April 1933. Translation by Humpherson (*a.i*)

Shunkinshō (A Portrait of Shunkin).* *Chūō Kōron*, June 1933. Ōsaka and Tokyo: Sōgensha, December 1933. Translation by Hibbett (*a.ii*) and by Humpherson (*a.i*)

'In'ei Raisan' (In Praise of Shadows).* *Keizai Ōrai*, December 1933–January 1934. Collected in *Setsuyō Zuihitsu*, Tokyo: Chūō Kōronsha, May 1935. Translation by Edward G. Seidensticker, *Japan Quarterly*, I (1955), pp. 46–52

A Modern translation of *The Tale of Genji*, 26 vols. Tokyo: Chūō Kōronsha, January 1939–July 1941

Sasameyuki (A Fine Flake of Snow).* Part I, *Chūō Kōron*, January–March 1943: part II, *Fujin Kōron*, March 1947–October 1948. 3 vols., Tokyo: Chūō Kōronsha, March 1946–December 1948. Translation by Edward G. Seidensticker entitled *The Makioka Sisters*, New York: Knopf, 1957; London: Secker & Warburg, 1958; Tokyo: Tuttle, 1958

Shōshō Shigemoto no Haha (The Mother of Captain Shigemoto).* *Mainichi Shimbun*, November 1949–February 1950. Tokyo: Mainichi Shimbunsha, August 1950. Translation by Edward G. Seidensticker in Keene (ed.), *Modern Japanese Literature* (II above)

Kagi (The Key).* *Chūō Kōron*, January 1956, May–December 1956. Tokyo: Chūō Kōronsha, December 1956. Translation by Howard S. Hibbett, New York: Knopf, 1960; London: Secker & Warburg, 1961; Tokyo: Tuttle, 1971

Fūten Rōjin Nikki (Diary of a Mad Old Man).* *Chūō Kōron*, November 1961–May 1962. Tokyo: Chūō Kōronsha, May 1962. Translation by Howard S. Hibbett, New York: Knopf, 1965;

London: Secker & Warburg, 1966; Tokyo: Tuttle, 1967

c Itoh, Sei. *Tanizaki Jun'ichirō no Bungaku* (The Literature of
Tanizaki Jun'ichirō). Tokyo: Chūō Kōronsha, 1970
Noguchi, Takehiko. *Tanizaki Jun'ichirō Ron* (On Tanizaki
Jun'ichirō). Tokyo: Chūō Kōronsha, 1973
Kōno, Taeko. *Tanizaki Bungaku to Kōtei no Yokubō* (The
Tanizaki Literature and his Wish for Self-approbation). Tokyo:
Bungei Shunjūsha, 1976

9 Kawabata Yasunari (1899–1972)
a.i Kawabata Yasunari Zenshū (The Complete Works of Kawabata
Yasunari), 19 vols. Tokyo: Shinchōsha, 1969–74.
a.ii The House of Sleeping Beauties and Other Stories translated by
Edward G. Seidensticker with an introduction by Mishima
Yukio. Tokyo: Kōdansha, 1969; New York: Ballantine, 1970.
(Contains, apart from the title story, 'One Arm' and 'Of Birds
and Beasts')
b Izu no Odoriko (The Izu Dancer).* *Bungei Jidai*,
January–February 1926. Tokyo: Kinseidō, March 1927.
Translation by Edward G. Seidensticker, *Atlantic Monthly*,
January 1955, pp. 108–14
'Jojōka' (Lyric Poem).* *Chūō Kōron*, February 1932.
Translation by Francis Mathy, *Monumenta Nipponica*, xxvi
(1971) pp. 287–305
'Kinjū' (Of Birds and Beasts).* *Kaizō*, July 1933. Collected in
Kinjū, Tokyo: Noda Shobō, May 1935. Translation by
Seidensticker (*a.ii*)
Yukiguni (Snow Country).* *Bungei Shunjū* and other
magazines, January 1935–May 1937; *Shōsetsu Shinchō*, October
1947. Tokyo: Sōgensha, December 1948. Translation by
Edward G. Seidensticker, New York: Knopf, 1956; London:
Secker & Warburg, 1957; Tokyo: Tuttle, 1957
Meijin (The Master of Go).* *Yagumo* and other magazines,
August 1942–May 1954. Tokyo: Bungei Shunjūsha, July 1954.
Translation by Edward G. Seidensticker, New York: Knopf,
1972; Tokyo: Tuttle, 1973
Senba Zuru (Thousand Cranes).* *Yomiuri Jiji Bessatsu* and
other magazines, May 1949–October 1951. Tokyo: Chikuma
Shobō, February 1952. Translation by Edward G. Seidensticker,
New York: Knopf, 1958; London: Secker & Warburg, 1959;
Tokyo: Tuttle, 1960
Yama no Oto (The Sound of the Mountain).* *Kaizō Bungei* and
other magazines, September 1949–April 1954. Tokyo: Chikuma

Shobō, May 1954. Translation by Edward G. Seidensticker,
New York: Knopf, 1970; Tokyo: Tuttle, 1970; London:
Secker & Warburg, 1971; Harmondsworth, Middlesex: Penguin,
1974
Mizuumi (The Lake).* *Shinchō*, January–December 1954.
Tokyo: Shinchōsha, April 1955. Translation by Reiko
Tsukimura, Tokyo: Kōdansha, 1974
Nemureru Bijo (The House of Sleeping Beauties).* *Shinchō*,
January–June, 1960; January–February, 1961. Tokyo:
Shinchōsha, November 1961. Translation by Seidensticker (*a.ii*)
Utsukushisa to Kanashimi to (Beauty and Sadness).* *Fujin
Kōron*, January 1961–October 1963. Tokyo: Chūō Kōronsha,
February 1965. Translation by Howard S. Hibbett, New York:
Knopf, 1975; London: Secker & Warburg, 1975; Tokyo: Tuttle,
1975
Utsukushii Nihon no Watakushi: Sono Josetsu (Japan the
Beautiful and Myself).* Delivered in the Swedish Academy,
Stockholm, on the occasion of the award to Kawabata of the
Nobel Prize for Literature, December 1968. The *Asahi, Yomiuri,
Mainichi, Tokyo* and *Chūnichi* newspapers, 16 December 1968.
Tokyo: Kōdansha, March 1969. Translation by Edward G.
Seidensticker, Tokyo: Kōdansha, 1969
  c Hasegawa, Izumi. *Kawabata Yasunari Ronkō* (On Kawabata
Yasunari). Tokyo: Meiji Shoin, 1965

10 Mishima Yukio (Hiraoka Kimitake, 1925–70)
a.i Death in Midsummer and Other Stories translated by Edward
G. Seidensticker, Ivan Morris, Donald Keene and Geoffrey W.
Sargent. New York: New Directions, 1958; London: Secker &
Warburg, 1967; Harmondsworth, Middlesex: Penguin, 1971.
(Contains 'Death in Midsummer', 'Three Million Yen',
'Thermos Bottles', 'The Priest of Shiga Temple and his Love',
'The Seven Bridges', 'Patriotism', Dōjōji', 'Onnagata', 'The
Pearl' and 'Swaddling Clothes')
a.ii Mishima Yukio Zenshū (The Complete Works of Mishima
Yukio), 35 vols. and a supplementary volume. Tokyo:
Shinchōsha, April 1973–June 1976
  b Kamen no Kokuhaku (Confessions of a Mask).* Tokyo: Kawade
Shobō, July 1949. Translation by Meredith Weatherby, Norfolk,
Conn.: New Directions, 1958; London: Peter Owen, 1960;
Tokyo: Tuttle, 1970
Ai no Kawaki (Thirst for Love).* Tokyo: Shinchōsha, June 1950.
Translation by Alfred H. Monks, London: Secker & Warburg,

1969; New York: Knopf, 1969; Tokyo: Tuttle, 1969

Kinjiki (Forbidden Colours).* Part I, *Gunzō*, January–October
1951; part II, *Bungakukai*, August 1952–August 1953. Tokyo:
Shinchōsha, September 1953. Translation by Alfred H. Monks,
London: Secker & Warburg, 1968; New York: Knopf, 1968;
Tokyo: Tuttle, 1969

'Manatsu no Shi' (Death in Midsummer).* *Shinchō*, October
1952. Translation by Seidensticker (*a.i*)

Shiosai (The Sound of Waves).* Tokyo: Shinchōsha, June 1954.
Translation by Meredith Weatherby, New York: Knopf, 1956;
London: Secker & Warburg, 1957; Tokyo: Tuttle, 1956

Kinkakuji (The Temple of the Golden Pavilion).* *Shinchō*,
January–October 1956. Tokyo: Shinchōsha, October 1956.
Translation by Ivan Morris, London: Secker & Warburg, 1959;
New York: Knopf, 1959; Tokyo: Tuttle, 1959

Kindai Nōgaku Shū (Five Modern Noh Plays).* Tokyo:
Shinchōsha, April 1956. Translation by Donald Keene, New
York: Knopf, 1957. (Contains 'Sotoba Komachi', 'The Damask
Drum', 'Kantan', 'The Lady Aoi' and 'Hanjo)

Rokumeikan (The Hall of the Crying Deer). First performed
at the Bungakuza Theatre, November 1956. *Bungakukai*,
December 1956: Tokyo: Sōgensha, March 1957.

Utage no Ato (After the Banquet).* *Chūō Kōron*, January–
October 1960. Translation by Donald Keene, London: Secker
& Warburg, 1963; New York: Knopf, 1963

'Yūkoku' (Patriotism).* *Shōsetsu Chūō Kōron*, January 1961.
Collected in *Sutā*, Tokyo: Shinchōsha, January 1961. Translation
by Sargent (*a.i*)

Gogo no Eikō (The Sailor Who Fell from Grace with the Sea).*
Tokyo: Kōdansha, September 1963. Translation by John Nathan,
New York: Knopf, 1965; Tokyo: Tuttle, 1972; Harmondsworth,

Haru no Yuki (Spring Snow).* *Shinchō*, September 1965–January
1967. Tokyo: Shinchōsha, January 1969. Translation by Michael
Gallagher, New York: Knopf, 1972; Tokyo: Tuttle, 1972

Sado Kōshaku Fujin (Madame de Sade).* *Bungei*, November 1965.
Tokyo: Kawade Shobō, November 1965. Translation by Donald
Keene, New York: Grove Press, 1967; Tokyo: Tuttle, 1971

Taiyō to Tetsu (Sun and Steel).* *Hihyō*, November 1965–June
1968. Tokyo: Kōdansha, October 1968. Translation by
John Bester, Tokyo: Kōdansha, 1970; London: Secker &
Warburg, 1971

Honba (Runaway Horses).* *Shinchō*, February 1967–August
1968. Tokyo: Shinchōsha, February 1969. Translation by
Michael Gallagher, New York: Knopf, 1973: Tokyo: Tuttle,
1973
Akatsuki no Tera (The Temple of Dawn).* *Shinchō*, September
1968–April 1970. Tokyo: Shinchōsha, July 1970. Translation by
E. Dale Saunders and Cecilia Segawa Seigle, New York: Knopf,
1973; Tokyo: Tuttle, 1974
Tennin Gosui (The Decay of the Angel).* *Shinchō*, July
1970–January 1971. Tokyo: Shinchōsha, February 1971.
Translation by Edward G. Seidensticker, New York: Knopf,
1974; Tokyo: Tuttle, 1974.
  c Nathan, John. *Mishima: A Biography*. Boston: Little, Brown,
1974; London: Hamish Hamilton, 1975
Scott-Stokes, Henry. *The Life and Death of Mishima Yukio*.
London: Peter Owen, 1975; New York: Farrar, Straus &
Giroux, 1975; Tokyo: Tuttle, 1975
Saeki, Shōichi. *Hyōden Mishima Yukio* (Mishima Yukio: A
Critical Biography). Tokyo: Shinchōsha, 1978

11 Abé Kōbō (1924–)
 a *Abé Kōbō Zensakuhin* (The Collected Works of Abé Kōbō),
15 vols. Tokyo: Shinchōsha, May 1972–July 1973
 b *Owarishi Michi no Shirube ni* (The Road Sign at the End of the
Road). *Kosei*, January 1948. Tokyo: Shinzenbisha, September
1948
'Dendorokakariya' (Dendrocacalia). *Hyōgen*, August 1949
'Akai Mayu' (Red Cocoon).* *Ningen*, December 1950.
Translation by John Nathan in *New Writing in Japan* (II above)
'Kabe – S. Karuma shi no Hanzai' (The Wall: The Crime of
Mr S. Karuma). *Kindai Bungaku*, February 1951
'Baberu no Tō no Tanuki' (A Badger in the Tower of Babel).
Ningen, May 1951
Kiga Dōmei (The League of the Hungry). Tokyo: Kōdansha,
February 1954
'Bō' (Stick).* *Bungei*, July 1955. Translation by John Nathan in
New Writing in Japan (II above)
Kemonotachi wa Kokyō o Mezasu (The Beasts Go Homeward).
Gunzō, January–April 1957
Daiyon Kampyōki (Inter Ice Age 4).* *Sekai*, July 1958–March
1959. Tokyo: Kōdansha, July 1959. Translation by E. Dale
Saunders, New York: Knopf, 1970; Tokyo: Tuttle, 1971
Suna no Onna (The Woman in the Dunes).* Tokyo: Shinchōsha,

June 1962. Translation by E. Dale Saunders, New York:
Knopf, 1964; Tokyo: Tuttle, 1967
Tanin no Kao (The Face of Another).* Tokyo: Kōdansha,
September 1964. Translation by E. Dale Saunders, New York:
Knopf, 1966; Tokyo: Tuttle, 1967
Enomoto Buyō. Chūō Kōron, January 1964–March 1965. Tokyo:
Chūō Kōronsha, July 1965
Tomodachi (Friends).* *Bungei*, March 1967. Tokyo: Kawade
Shobō, November 1967. Translation by Donald Keene, New
York: Grove Press, 1969; Tokyo: Tuttle, 1971
Moetsukita Chizu (The Ruined Map).* Tokyo: Shinchōsha,
September 1967. Translation by E. Dale Saunders, New York:
Knopf, 1969; Tokyo: Tuttle, 1970; London: Jonathan Cape,
1971
Bō ni Natta Otoko (The Man Who Turned into a Stick).*
Bungakukai, August 1969. Tokyo: Shinchōsha, September 1969.
Translation by Donald Keene, Tokyo: University of Tokyo
Press, 1975

12 Ōe Kenzaburō (1935–)
a.i Ōe Kenzaburō Zen Sakuhin (The Collected Works of
   Ōe Kenzaburō), 6 vols. Tokyo: Shinchōsha, 1966–7. Second
   series: 6 vols. Tokyo: Shinchōsha, 1977–
*a.ii Teach Us to Outgrow our Madness: Four Short Novels by
   Kenzaburo Ōe* translated with an introduction by John Nathan.
   New York: Grove Press, 1977. (Contains 'The Day He Himself
   Shall Wipe my Tears Away', 'Prize Stock', 'Teach Us to
   Outgrow our Madness' and 'Aghwee the Sky Monster')
b 'Kimyōna Shigoto' (A Strange Job). *Tōdai Shimbun*, May 1957.
   Collected in *Shisha no Ogori*, Tokyo: Bungei Shunjū Shinsha,
   March 1958
   'Shisha no Ogori' (The Arrogance of the Dead). *Bungakukai*,
   August 1957. Collected in *Shisha no Ogori*, Tokyo: Bungei
   Shunjū Shinsha, March 1958
   'Shiiku' (The Catch).* *Bungakukai*, January 1958. Collected in
   Shisha no Ogori, Tokyo: Bungei Shunjū Shinsha, March 1958.
   Translation by John Bester in *New Writing in Japan* (II above)
   'Ningen no Hitsuji' (The Human Sheep). *Shinchō*, February
   1958. Collected in *Shisha no Ogori*, Tokyo: Bungei Shunjū
   Shinsha, March 1958
   Memushiri Kouchi (Plucking Buds and Shooting Lambs). *Gunzō*,
   June 1958. Tokyo: Kōdansha, June 1958
   'Miru maeni Tobe' (Leap Before You Look). *Bungakukai*,

June 1958. Collected in *Miru maeni Tobe*, Tokyo: Shinchōsha, October 1958

'Tatakai no Konnichi' (Today the Struggle). *Chūō Kōron*, September 1958. Collected in *Miru maeni Tobe*, Tokyo: Shinchōsha, October 1958

Warera no Jidai (Our Age). Tokyo: Chūō Kōronsha, July 1959

Okurete Kita Seinen (The Youth Who Arrived Late). *Shinchō*, September 1960–February 1962. Tokyo: Shinchōsha, January 1962

Sevuntiin (Seventeen). *Bungakukai*, January 1961. Collected in *Seiteki Ningen*, Tokyo: Shinchōsha, June 1963

Seiji Shōnen Shisu (The Death of a Political Boy). *Bungakukai*, February 1961. (Not collected later as a result of the right-wing threat to Ōe's life)

Sakebigoe (Outcries). *Gunzō*, November 1962. Tokyo: Kōdansha, January 1963

Seiteki Ningen (The Sexual Man). *Shinchō*, May 1963. Tokyo: Shinchōsha, June 1963

'Sora no Kaibutsu Aguī' (Aghwee the Sky Monster).* *Shinchō*, January 1964. Translation by Nathan (*a.ii*)

Kojintekina Taiken (A Personal Matter).* Tokyo: Shinchōsha, August 1964. Translation by John Nathan, New York: Grove Press, 1968; Tokyo: Tuttle, 1969

Hiroshima Nōto (Hiroshima Notebook). Tokyo: Iwanami Shoten, June 1965

Man'en Gannen no Futtobōru (The Football Match in the First Year of the Man'en Era).* Tokyo: Kōdansha, September 1967. Translation by John Bester entitled *The Silent Cry*, Tokyo: Kōdansha, 1974

Okinawa Nōto (Okinawa Notebook). Tokyo: Iwanami Shoten, September 1970

Mizukara Waga Namida o Nuguitamau Hi (The Day He Himself Shall Wipe my Tears Away).* Tokyo: Kōdansha, October 1972. Translation by Nathan (*a.ii*)

Kōzui wa Waga Tamashii ni Oyobi (The Flood Has Reached My Soul), 2 vols. Tokyo: Shinchōsha, September 1973

Pinchi Rannā Chōsho (A Report on a Pinch-runner). Tokyo: Shinchōsha, October 1976

Index